THE OPEN HAND

D1536369

THE OPEN HAND

Arguing as an Art of Peace

BARRY M. KROLL

UTAH STATE UNIVERSITY PRESS
Logan

KH

Published by Utah State University Press
An imprint of University Press of Colorado
5589 Arapahoe Avenue, Suite 206C
Boulder, Colorado 80303

 The University Press of Colorado is a proud member of
The Association of American University Presses.

The University Press of Colorado is a cooperative publishing enterprise supported,
in part, by Adams State University, Colorado State University, Fort Lewis College,
Metropolitan State University of Denver, Regis University, University of Colorado,
University of Northern Colorado, Utah State University, and Western State Colorado
University.

Cover design by Dan Miller

Library of Congress Cataloging-in-Publication Data
Kroll, Barry M., 1946–
  The open hand : arguing as an art of peace / Barry M. Kroll.
    pages cm
  Includes bibliographical references and index.
  ISBN 978-0-87421-926-5 (pbk.) — ISBN 978-0-87421-927-2 (e-book)
1. Persuasion (Rhetoric)—Study and teaching. 2. English language—Rhetoric—Study
and teaching. 3. Reasoning—Study and teaching. 4. Persuasion (Psychology) I. Title.
  P301.5.P47K76 2013
  303.3'42—dc23
                                    2013019568

9/8/15

CONTENTS

ACKNOWLEDGMENTS

I wrote *The Open Hand* with the help and support of many individuals. I'm especially grateful to my wife, Kathleen Hutnik, and my sons, Patrick and David, for their inspiration and encouragement. Friends and colleagues have also encouraged my work over the years, particularly my close friends since graduate school, Irvin Hashimoto and John Schafer. I've worked in supportive departments at each of the universities where I've taught throughout my career—Iowa State University, Indiana University, and Lehigh University. The project I describe in *The Open Hand* took its current shape at Lehigh, where several colleagues fostered or contributed to my work: Michael Raposa (who introduced me to aikido), Greg Skutches (who encouraged my work on mindfulness), Scott Gordon and Vivien Steele (who allowed me to teach a first-year seminar repeatedly), and Edward Lotto (who assumed administrative duties that freed me to teach and write).

I would not have been able to develop a course on arguing as an art of peace without some training in both aikido and contemplative pedagogy. I'm grateful to the members of Lehigh Valley Aikikai for accepting me into their dojo; in particular, I want to thank Minh Nguyen, Sensei, as well as Scott Toonder and Andrew and Richard Grochowski, for their instruction and encouragement. For my introduction to contemplative pedagogy, I'm grateful to the Center for Contemplative Mind in Society for its programs for college teachers, including the summer training program at Smith College as well as annual meetings and retreats for academics sponsored by the Association for Contemplative Mind in Higher Education. Mirabai Bush and Arthur Zajonc have been especially important influences. I also benefited from participating in a summer workshop on contemplative pedagogy at Naropa University: special thanks to Susan Burggraf for her continuing interest in my work.

Of course I'm especially grateful to the first-year students who enrolled in my courses on arguing as an art of peace and gave me permission to quote from their notebooks and papers. Without their wholehearted participation and willing cooperation, there would have been no project and no book.

Four individuals reviewed part or all of *The Open Hand* when it was being considered for publication, and I benefited greatly from their substantive and constructive responses to the draft. Comments from Kristin Arola and Asao Inoue, who reviewed a prospectus and sample chapter, proved quite useful as I moved into a phase of intensive revising. Later, Debra Hawhee and Donna Strickland reviewed a complete manuscript for Utah State University Press: their insightful comments and thoughtful suggestions improved the final version in numerous respects.

Finally, I want to say how enjoyable it has been to work with the University Press of Colorado, especially Laura Furney. And a special bow of gratitude goes to Michael Spooner, acquisitions editor at Utah State University Press, whose responsiveness and encouragement have meant so much throughout the process of revising, editing, and publishing *The Open Hand*. From our first discussion of the project, Michael understood what I was trying to say and believed that it mattered.

THE OPEN HAND

There is no one in the world that does not know
That the soft prevails over the hard,
And the weak prevails over the strong.
And yet none are able to act accordingly.

Dao de jing, ch. 78

The art of peace is the principle of nonresistance.
Because it is nonresistant, it is victorious from the beginning.

Morihei Ueshiba (1883–1969), founder of Aikido

1

CLAPPING IN

What is the sound of one hand?
Hakuin Ekaku (1686–1768)

"Let's begin," I'd say, and all of us would clap our hands three times, in unison, twice softly followed by a louder third clap. In my course Arguing as an Art of Peace, I opened class sessions by "clapping in" with students, a ritual that signaled the beginning of our work for the day. I introduced this practice on the first day of the semester, evoking a few looks of confusion and concern. Arguing as an Art of Peace fulfilled the first-year seminar requirement in the College of Arts and Sciences, so the students were all freshmen, taking one of their first college courses, and clapping in wasn't quite what they were expecting. But I had their attention and seized the opportunity to introduce some features of the course.

Quite a few things about this course would, I said, be different from most of their other college classes. I explained that I had learned about the clapping-in ritual from my exposure to Japanese martial arts, where sessions often begin with two or three claps. The practice probably has roots in Shinto, the indigenous religion of Japan, in which clapping the hands at a shrine alerts the deities to one's presence.[1] The gesture also awakens the clapper to the present moment. In our case, clapping would serve as a call to attention and an announcement that our work was about to begin (no invoking of deities, for better or worse). It was an unusual ritual for my students, drawn from an unfamiliar context, and the fact that we were clapping to start each class suggested, I hoped, my interest in new and different approaches. It also indicated the degree to which I would be drawing on Asian arts, ideas, and practices to defamiliarize our work on arguing and provide fresh perspectives from a non-Western tradition. The martial connection was suggestive too because we would be learning some movement sequences drawn from Chinese and Japanese martial arts, focusing on arts of the "open hand." And the notion that a clap provides a wake-up call resonated with the emphasis on mindful awareness that would permeate the course. When they

DOI: 10.7330_9780874219203.c001

clapped in that first day, students were performing a ritual that antici-pated many aspects of their seminar, Arguing as an Art of Peace.

First-year seminars at Lehigh are small classes, usually offered in the fall semester when students are making the transition from high school to college. Each seminar focuses on a topic of inquiry in the arts and sciences and, in most cases, includes intensive writing.[2] The project for students in my seminar was to explore how arguing could be conducted with an open hand, as an art of peace. I used the images of an open hand and closed fist to represent, metonymically, different approaches to the arguments that occur when people disagree with one another.[3] In this course, I explained, we would be exploring the kinds of intense disagreements that arise when people have differing views, values, or goals, and when they have a stake in how those differences get resolved. Hence, our focus would be on argumentative conflict, situations in which one could form a combative fist or offer an open palm.

CLOSED FIST, OPEN HAND

The semiotics of fist and palm are complex and multivalent: a closed fist can be used to defend oneself or to protect good causes in peril, whereas an open palm can signal resignation or suggest appeasement. Because our work in Arguing as an Art of Peace would focus on the open hand, it was important to explore that symbol's function as a signifier of peaceful intentions . . . but *not* a sign of passive submission. Figured against the fist of power and victory, the open hand can all too readily be construed as weak or acquiescent. I wanted to present another option, based on a different conception of the open hand.

I encouraged students, therefore, to think about an open hand not simply as a gesture of peaceful intent but also as an instrument of con-tact, a way to connect with an opposing force and, ultimately, control it. In a conflict, this open hand provides a way to establish a connection with an adversary in order to receive aggressive energy and redirect it. This hand is neither belligerent nor passive, neither confrontational nor submissive, yet it has within its reach elements of both assertiveness and receptivity.[4] The hand that connects and controls lies at the heart of a number of Asian martial arts; the one I know best is the Japanese art of aikido.[5] In aikido, one responds to an opposing force by blend-ing, repositioning, redirecting, or spinning around it—all the while stay-ing in contact, using an open hand. While there are no kicks, punches, or hard blocks in aikido, its movements involve, nonetheless, a cer-tain amount of forcefulness combined with yielding or acquiescence, creating a dynamic response to an unfolding encounter. The goal is to resolve conflicts nonviolently, protecting everyone (even one's opponent) from harm. That is why aikido is called an *art of peace*, a phrase I have appropriated and applied to a mode of argument based on similar goals and tactics.[6]

THE AIM AND SCOPE OF THE BOOK

Over the course of six semesters, from 2007 through 2012, I taught a version of my first-year seminar on the topic of arguing as an art of peace. Although I will regularly refer to *the course* in what follows, that course is in fact a composite of six seminars. While the class was substantially the same in terms of structure and projects, the activities changed to some extent each time I taught it. In a sense, *the course* is a fictional construct, yet it is, nevertheless, an accurate and responsible representation of what Arguing as an Art of Peace became as it developed over several years.

I decided to write about the experience of teaching the course because I believe that my curriculum, class activities, and pedagogical approach are sufficiently different from traditional ways of teaching argument to merit consideration. The course I will be presenting differs from most others I've encountered in the following respects:

- It includes rhetorical tactics and modes of arguing that differ from traditional approaches, offering alternatives to the familiar thesis-support patterns of arguing that many college students know from prior experience.
- It encourages students to analyze interpersonal conflicts along with arguments about controversial public issues, grounding the study of rhetoric in the experiences of real people in real conflicts in the situations they encounter in their lives.
- It emphasizes Asian practices and modes of analysis that expand the usual Western approach to composition pedagogy.
- It employs a kinesthetic modality of learning, encouraging students to explore the art of arguing by practicing martial movements.
- It incorporates contemplative practices and meditative arts as ways to cultivate awareness and equanimity in the midst of conflict.

This account is based on my classroom experience, primarily, so the focus is on projects, activities, assignments, informal responses, and final papers—a focus that will appeal, I hope, to college teachers, especially those who have an experimental attitude and are willing, perhaps even eager, to try something different. Although I touch on some theoretical issues and refer to the work of scholars who have influenced my thinking, I have avoided a comprehensive review of the literature as well as extensive citations, believing that they would detract from my purpose. That goal is to present readers with enough details about my course, Arguing as an Art of Peace, to pique their interest and expand their options for teaching argumentation to college students.

SOME KEY INFLUENCES

When I reflect on the origins of my interest in an open-hand approach to arguing, I go back to the 1970s, when I was a new doctoral student at the University of Michigan. I recall that when I arrived in Ann Arbor in 1973, students in my graduate program were talking about a book, *Rhetoric: Discovery and Change*, which had been published a few years before, in 1970, by three Michigan professors: Richard Young, Alton Becker, and Kenneth Pike. I read their work with interest and excitement, particularly the chapter on Rogerian argument, in which the authors posit the need for a "new rhetoric." The vision for the Rogerian project was to "develop a rhetoric that has as its goal not skillful verbal coercion but discussion and exchange of ideas" (Young, Becker, and Pike 1970, 8). Young, Becker, and Pike claimed that the times (the late 1960s and early 1970s) required a new approach to argument: "Perhaps never before in our history," they say, "has there been such a need for effective communication, but the old formulations of rhetoric seem inadequate to the times" (8–9). This call for a new rhetoric resonated with my observations and experiences: American society was indeed divided, with a great deal of intense argumentation but little hope, it seemed, of bridging those divisions or fostering cooperation. But nearly four decades later, has the situation changed appreciably? Deborah Tannen's analysis of contemporary conditions suggests that it has not.

In *The Argument Culture*, Tannen describes the prevalence of a "pervasive warlike atmosphere that makes us approach public dialogue, and just about anything we need to accomplish, as if it were a fight," portraying a culture in which people approach issues with "an adversarial frame of mind" (Tannen 1998, 3). This approach assumes that "opposition is the best way to get anything done":

> The best way to discuss an idea is to set up a debate; the best way to cover news is to find spokespeople who express the most extreme, polarized views and present them as "both sides"; the best way to settle disputes is litigation that pits one party against the other; the best way to begin an essay is to attack someone; and the best way to show you're really thinking is to criticize. (Tannen 1998, 3–4)

Although Tannen calls attention to the excesses of the argument culture, she refrains from rejecting tactics of the closed fist completely. As she recognizes, assertive approaches are sometimes warranted: "There are times when we need to disagree, criticize, oppose, and attack—to hold debates and view issues as polarized battles" (Tannen 1998, 26). The problem, in Tannen's view, is "the ubiquity, the knee-jerk nature, of approaching almost any issue, problem, or public person in an adversarial way." "What I question," she says, "is using opposition to accomplish *every* goal, even those that do not require fighting" (8).

My project, like Tannen's, is an attempt to moderate, not invalidate, the emphasis on tactics of arguing with a closed fist; whereas she points to the excesses of adversarial argument, I want to focus on some promising alternatives to it: tactics of reframing, attentive listening, and mediating. My approach—like that of Young, Becker, and Pike—assumes that a writer can enter a dispute with intentions that differ from those that prevail in an argument culture, where goals are usually conceived in terms of winning and losing, defending and defeating, supporting and critiquing, and so forth. Instead, I want to explore what it means to argue for common concerns, shared values, mutual benefits, respectful listening, and joint problem solving. My project is not about rejecting the closed fist but rather about recognizing the possibilities of the open hand that connects and controls.

When I first began to experiment with courses that emphasized alternative modes of arguing, starting in the late 1990s, I structured my syllabi around three projects, each representing a way to expand traditional argument: I called them the *deliberative, conciliatory,* and *integrative* approaches.[7] These three approaches continued to play a key role as I developed the writing projects for Arguing as an Art of Peace. Thus, the first project in the course—the subject for chapter 2—involves making a *deliberative argument*. The concept of *deliberative argumentation* is as venerable as Aristotle's *Rhetoric* and as current as contemporary writing courses, often appearing in the guise of proposal arguments or problem-solution essays. Although my approach has some distinctive elements, it is nonetheless consistent with certain aspects of both conventional and more experimental conceptions of deliberation, with links to work on the rhetoric of inquiry as well as the rhetoric of cooperation. Thus my approach is broadly compatible with a conception of deliberative argument as a process of inquiry or a rhetoric of reason, a search for the best answers to pressing questions. In *The Shape of Reason*, one of the most thoughtful textbooks in this tradition, John Gage says that in the "context of argumentative writing in college," the word *argument* "does not mean a verbal battle between opponents, each of whom desires to silence the other. It means, instead, the search for reasons that will bring about cooperation among people who differ in how they view ideas but who nevertheless need to discover grounds for agreement" (Gage 2006, 43). In Gage's view, as in my conception of deliberative rhetoric, argumentative writing "may be seen as a process of *reasonable inquiry into the best grounds for agreement between a writer and an audience who have a mutual concern to answer a question*" (43; italics in original). In the unit on deliberative argument, students in Arguing as an Art of Peace would learn how to reframe disputes so that the focus was on problems or questions that drew writers and readers away from contentious argumentation and into mutual inquiry, a search for what Gage calls "grounds for agreement."

In his more theoretical account of a rhetoric of reason, James Crosswhite describes argumentation as "the practice of a very tenuous hope that people can settle their conflicts nonviolently, that they can act differently from the way they otherwise would because they can open themselves to the dialogues that arguments are" (Crosswhite 1996, 47). While I share this hope, I worry that Crosswhite defines deliberative argument too narrowly, so that it becomes an idealized form of argumentative rationality. In his view, argument is not simply conflictual disagreement but rather a process in which interlocutors are already willing to be part of a cooperative rational discussion, one designed to resolve the disagreement through a series of claims, challenges, and supporting reasons. Crosswhite says that argumentation requires "a respect for one's interlocutor, a modesty or willingness to change on the part of the initiator of the argument, and the renunciation of violence by all parties." If these conditions do not obtain, "it could be argued that argumentation does not take place" (174). Crosswhite believes that unless argumentation is separated from the everyday understanding of "having an argument," which is usually understood as "something like having a fight" (43), there's a chance that students will view "'rational' argumentation or 'scholarly' argument as continuous with the attempts at discursive domination that are so familiar in everyday life" (43).[8] While I understand this concern, my strategy has been to focus on the continuities between everyday disputes and argumentation about social issues; rather than urging students to avoid deeply conflictual arguments, I have tried to teach them how to respond to high-intensity conflicts in ways that maximize opportunities for communication and cooperation.

At the same time my project shares certain features with a rhetoric of inquiry, it also aligns itself with more experimental work on deliberative argument, such as the innovative conception developed in Dennis Lynch, Diana George, and Marilyn Cooper's article "Moments of Argument: Agonistic Inquiry and Confrontational Cooperation." Not only do I share their concern that students have learned "to argue vigorously and even angrily, but not think about alternatives, or listen to each other, or determine how their position may affect others" (Lynch, George, and Cooper 1997, 61), but I also embrace their goal of teaching argument in a way "that prepares students to participate in serious deliberations on *issues that face all of us everyday*" (62; italics added). As my discussion of the complexities of the open hand—marked by the dynamic interplay of yin and yang, as I explain later—suggests, I am, like Lynch, George, and Cooper, working out a way of "reconceiving argument that includes both confrontational and cooperative perspectives, a multifaceted process that includes moments of conflict and agonistic positioning as well as moments of understanding and communication" (63). At the same time, I am particularly interested in cooperative perspectives on argument because of my focus on disputes and intensive conflicts. For that reason, my work stretches in the direction of the approach that Josina Makau and Debian Marty develop in *Cooperative Argumentation*, in which they aim to teach students "not to avoid disagreement, but rather to develop tools for confronting disagreement peacefully, ethically, and effectively" (Makau and Marty 2001, 8). For Makau and Marty, "Cooperative argumentative practice" involves a "process of reasoned interaction intended to help participants and audiences make the best assessments or the best decisions in any given situation" (87). I draw on a number of Makau and Marty's ideas in the chapters that follow.

In Arguing as an Art of Peace, I wanted to give students a clear, straightforward definition of *deliberation*, so I used a succinct dictionary entry that describes it as a process of "careful consideration before decision,"[9] a four-word phrase I asked students to commit to memory. In addition, I linked deliberation to a tactic called *reframing*, a method that entails shifting the focus of an argument away from points of intense conflict so that "careful consideration" can, in fact, take place. Reframing is useful in situations in which adversarial arguing (about positions) is likely to occur unless a controlling hand can guide the conversation toward deliberation about issues and options. This emphasis on reframing is a distinctive component of my approach to deliberative argument as an art of the open hand.

The second project in my course asked students to adopt a *conciliatory* approach to arguing, and I linked the approach with the tactic of attentive listening. The verb *conciliate* means to "overcome distrust or hostility"[10] so that conciliatory argument suggests an approach that opens the hand in a gesture of receptivity, trust, and peaceful intentions. In *The Rhetoric of Rhetoric*, Wayne Booth uses the term *listening rhetoric* in a way that intersects with my understanding of listening as the basis for conciliatory argument. Booth foregrounds a kind of argument in which "opponents in any controversy listen to each other not only to persuade better but also to find the common ground behind the conflict." Thus rhetoric becomes an attempt "to lead both sides in any dispute to discover the ground they share—thus reducing pointless dispute" (Booth 2004, 10). But perhaps the most important influence on my thinking about conciliatory argument has been Rogerian rhetoric. In *Rhetoric: Discovery and Change*, Young, Becker, and Pike explain that the Rogerian approach (derived from Carl Rogers's ideas about communication) employs tactics that differ from those used in traditional argument: "Instead of stating your own case and refuting your opponent's," the authors say, you should strive to "state the opponent's case with as much care as your own, and you analyze the sound points of his argument" (Young, Becker, and Pike 1970, 282). My indebtedness to Rogerian rhetoric will be clear in chapter 3, where I discuss the features of conciliatory argument.[11]

For the third project in Arguing as an Art of Peace, students learned about *integrative argument*, drawing on tactics that have proven successful for mediating conflicts. The basic meaning of *integrate* is to "bring together,"[12] suggesting that the goal of integrative argument is to bring opponents or adversaries together to consider where their interests overlap and how their goals might be mutually achievable. The major influence on this strand of the course was *Getting to Yes: Negotiating Agreement without Giving In*, the popular book by Roger Fisher, William Ury, and Bruce Patton (2011), first published in 1981. In *Getting to Yes*, I found a useful account of the key tactics of focusing on interests and inventing options for mutual gain, tactics that were central to my presentation of integrative argument, as I explain in chapter 4.

In writing this book, I have tried to present Arguing as an Art of Peace in a way that is practical, engaging, and accessible. I've kept the focus on projects and activities, and I've included multiple examples of students' responses as well as excerpts from their essays. To enhance readability, I've avoided strings of in-text references and citations, mentioning some key books and articles but using notes for most references. Many of my in-text references are to essays or examples we discussed in class, often selections drawn from the fields of mediation, conflict resolution, and consensus building—fields in which the tactics of reframing, attentive listening, and mediating figure prominently. Because these tactics originate in work on interpersonal disputes, they invite analysis of everyday disagreements and difficult conversations, and I encouraged students to explore the conflicts they encountered in their lived experience. But as a final project for each unit, students were expected to adapt the tactics, using them to write deliberative, conciliatory, and integrative arguments about controversial issues.

CONCEPTUAL-PROCEDURAL MODE OF LEARNING

As I developed Arguing as an Art of Peace, one of my goals was to incorporate three different modalities of learning into the course: conceptual-procedural, kinesthetic, and contemplative. This multiple-modality approach is, I believe, a distinctive and important feature of my course. The mode that provided the backbone was the conceptual-procedural so that rhetorical issues (both conceptual and tactical) were prominent. The pedagogy associated with this rhetorical component was, in many respects, traditional since it included reading assignments and quizzes, short lectures, and guided discussions. Because Arguing as an Art of Peace was a hybrid course—part inquiry-driven seminar, part class in composition and communication—there was a substantial writing component as well, so students worked with samples of professional and student writing, paid careful attention to structures and strategies, participated in workshops and conferences, and submitted three papers for evaluation. But there were also some less traditional aspects to the students' work on rhetoric and writing. From the beginning, students were expected to set aside the structures and strategies that had worked well for them in high school in order to try some new and unfamiliar approaches. I remember the look on their faces when, early in the semester, I said they would *not* be using a traditional thesis statement in their first essays. There was a sense of near panic, as though masks had just dropped from the ceiling because the oxygen had been sucked from the cabin. While many of the day-to-day activities (reading, discussing, writing, etc.) seemed familiar from previous schooling, the writing projects and modes of arguing puzzled some students. I tried to alleviate anxiety, of course, but I nurtured the edge that came with a bit of disorientation.

There were other elements that made Arguing as an Art of Peace different from the classes students had taken previously. For example, I asked each of them to choose a controversial issue that would serve as a topic for their writing *throughout the semester*. To expedite the process of choosing a topic, I sent a message to students before the semester began, telling them they'd be writing a series of papers on the same topic and offering the following rationale for this unusual practice:

> By keeping your topic constant, you'll be able to focus on new strategies for arguing (rather than on researching a number of different topics). It may sound as though you'll be writing the same paper repeatedly, but you'll find you can shift focus a bit in each paper as you employ a new approach. (You can switch topics if you want to, but it's more work and can shift the emphasis to research and away from strategies for writing arguments.) The advantages of writing about a topic you choose, rather than one I assign, should be obvious. But the system depends on your willingness to commit yourself to an interesting and generative topic early in the course. Therefore, I'm going to ask you to start immediately to think about an issue or topic you'd be interested in working on for a few months.[13]

I met with each student, usually during the first week, to confer about topics. Asking students to write all three papers on the same controversial issue meant that each new project was an occasion to think about a different rhetorical situation, focusing on the structures and strategies associated with a mode of arguing with an open hand.

Another way in which I tried to defamiliarize our work on argument was to use non-Western terms and concepts, drawn from Asian arts and modes of analysis. In a later section, I will explain how movement sequences derived from Chinese and Japanese martial arts created opportunities for a kinesthetic mode of inquiry; I'll also discuss the influence of Eastern practices on the contemplative strand of the course.[14] But there was a non-Western element in the rhetorical strand as well because I introduced the terms *yin* and *yang* to provide a fresh vocabulary for talking about the interplay of receptivity and assertiveness in arguing with an open hand. These are ancient terms, infused with many layers of meaning, and I realize I have used them in a loose way. My aim was to capture students' attention, providing a novel—yet sophisticated—framework for exploring the interplay of forces in arguments. While yin is associated with a soft and open hand, and yang with a hard, closed fist, I also encouraged students to see them as dynamic elements at play in most arguments. As LuMing Mao points out, yin and yang are related not through opposition but rather "mutual interdependence and interpenetration. What is yin in one context can be yang in another, and neither can exist independently of the other" (Mao 2009, W46). The terms *yin* and *yang* became part of our vocabulary for talking about the relationships between receptivity and assertiveness.[15] As I will note in the chapters that follow, those relationships were clearest when students worked on them through body movement activities.

KINESTHETIC MODE OF LEARNING

One of my aims in Arguing as an Art of Peace was to offer opportunities for inquiry and learning that extended beyond the conceptual-proce-dural modality that prevails in college teaching. To employ a kinesthetic modality, I devised some exercises that offered embodied expressions of argument strategies so that students had opportunities to "feel" the movements associated with tactics of reframing, attentive listening, and mediating.[16] I attached a lab section to my regularly scheduled class meetings, creating additional time for movement activities. I focused on aikido because it is the martial art I know best, even though I am not an advanced practitioner.

Aikido is a Japanese martial art developed in the first half of the twentieth century by Morihei Ueshiba, a martial arts prodigy who, in 1925, had an experience of awakening that led him to revise his approach so that it emphasized harmony and peace. Following World War II, he named this art *aikido*, a word consisting of three characters that literally mean "way [*do*] for the Coordination or Harmony [*ai*] of Mental Energy or Spirit [*ki*]" (Westbrook and Ratti 1970, 17; brackets in original). The new name reflected a deepened spirituality and com-mitment to an art of peace,[17] or what I also call *an art of the open hand*— an apt description of aikido since it almost never deploys a closed fist, relying on the open hand for contact, connection, and control. As Gaku Homma says in *Aikido for Life*, "The open hand is emphasized in Aikido; making fists is not" (Homma 1990, 33). Or as C. M. Shifflett notes, the practitioner of aikido "does not punch or kick to injure or harm unnecessarily, does not block or resist attacks but blends with, redirects and transforms the attacker's energy, maintaining the flow. The result is devastating softness, invisible technique and an art that makes no sense to most observers accustomed to force against force" (Shifflett 2009, 1). Thus, aikido is, not surprisingly, designed as a defen-sive system, based on the principle that soft conquers hard, that the flexible can control the rigid—a Daoist principle basic to jujutsu and many of the "soft" martial arts. But aikido is distinctive. As Morihei's son and successor, Kisshomaru Ueshiba, explains, "In ancient jujutsu they taught that 'when pushed, pull back; when pulled, push forward.' In the spherical movements of aikido, this becomes, 'when pushed, pivot and go around; when pulled, enter while circling'" (Ueshiba

1984, 40–41). Pivoting around, circling in: these movements are fundamental to aikido.

I learned about aikido, initially, from books and articles: when I read
about its theory of conflict and way of responding to aggressive attacks,
I recognized that this martial art—with its open-hand approach to conflict—was relevant for my search for less adversarial ways to argue. Here
was a self-described art of peace that accepted conflict as an opportunity
to protect people from harm and create more harmony in the world.
It was not an aggressive art; instead, aikido used principles of yielding,
blending, entering, and turning to disarm and defeat an aggressor.
Aikido exemplified the philosophy of nonresistance, the idea that the
most effective response to aggression is often to use the attacker's energy
against him or her.[18] I was intrigued and began to investigate not only
the philosophical and technical literature but also work that applied
aikido's principles to leadership, conflict management, mediation, and
dispute resolution.[19]

I soon realized, however, that to get an insider's understanding of
aikido I needed to practice it. Although I had studied tai chi for several
years in the mid-1990s, I didn't continue after I moved to a new job in a
different state. When I began to train in aikido in the fall of 2003, I felt
as though I were starting from scratch, although I began to sense connections between the principles and body mechanics of the two arts.[20]
I was fifty-seven years old when I began to practice aikido: too old to
acquire much proficiency, but young enough at heart to be an enthusiastic learner. As I trained each week—learning to take the falls, to endure
the painful joint locks, and to apply a series of defensive techniques—I
sensed that I was using an underdeveloped modality to learn about conflict and argument. I was discovering the power of kinesthetic inquiry,
and I wanted to share the experience with students.

So I began, slowly at first, to introduce students to movement exercises derived from aikido, using those movements as a physical analogy for tactics of arguing.[21] I found an especially receptive audience
among student athletes, who were eager to use their bodily intelligence
in an academic course although all of my first-year students seemed to
appreciate the opportunity to learn by moving. Aikido is practiced in
pairs: one person plays the role of the attacker, the other the receiver;
the receiver performs a defensive technique, and the attacker takes the
fall. Then the roles reverse. I wanted to retain the partner element of
traditional training but didn't have access to a space that would accom-
modate throws and falls. I also worried about the possibility of injury,
the complications of "risk management." But I discovered, during my

first efforts to introduce aikido movements, that students were able to grasp the core principles—the ones that mattered for my purposes, at least—by doing movement activities that did not involve throws or falls or advanced proficiency. This meant that I could ask students to practice movement sequences in a classroom. And by developing a low-impact version of aikido, I didn't have to worry about injuries.[22] In the three central chapters of this book, I explain in more detail how I have been using movement sequences from aikido (as well as related exercises from tai chi push hands) in my classes. This deployment of kinesthetic learning is one of the most interesting and important features of my project, I believe.[23]

CONTEMPLATIVE MODE OF LEARNING

The weekly lab session I used for martial movement exercises also provided time and space for a contemplative mode of learning. Students practiced sitting quietly, concentrating on their breathing and clearing their minds; they learned to recenter rapidly by bringing attention to their breath for a few cycles of inhalation and exhalation; and they explored mindfulness, both within the lab and without, recording their observations in a notebook they submitted each week. I presented meditation and mindfulness as practical arts that enhanced one's effectiveness in the world, especially in difficult conversations, interpersonal disputes, and arguments about divisive issues. We also explored connections between mindfulness practices and our martial arts activities, noting that mindfulness is a quality prized within many Asian martial traditions because it fosters presence, focused attention, and clarity of mind when confronting an adversary. As Jeffrey Mann notes in his book about the "curious relationship between Zen and the martial arts," many practitioners of these arts have been drawn to meditation because it develops a capacity for "conscious lucidity" or "the freedom to act as the situation unfolds," a response that's superior to habituated reaction. As Mann says, "Falling back on one's training in a moment of panic is good; the freedom of mind and action which *zazen* can inculcate is better" (Mann 2012, 73). I suggested that this capacity for "conscious lucidity" promised to be as helpful in difficult conversations and argumentative conflicts as it has proven to be in physical confrontations. Thus, I tried to highlight connections between the kinesthetic, contemplative, and rhetorical strands of our work.

My attraction to contemplative experience was driven, in part, by a long-standing interest in Asian ideas, arts, and practices, but I finally started meditating, around 2000, for more pragmatic reasons: I was seeking a way to cope with increasingly demanding professional obligations.[24] What started as stress relief expanded, over the course of several years, into a determination to live, as far as possible, in a manner that is mindfully aware, fully present, and wide awake—a goal that is, perhaps needless to say, still a work in progress. But my experience led me to a movement in higher education that focused on the benefits of fostering contemplative mind in college teaching.

The term *contemplative* has emerged as a useful way to refer to meditative practices because it is broad enough to be nonsectarian and inclusive. It has become the term of art in academic circles (contemplative studies, contemplative pedagogy, contemplative education) as meditation and mindfulness have made their way into college teaching through the efforts of such organizations as the Association for Contemplative Mind in Higher Education, which runs summer workshops for college teachers, retreats for academics, and an annual conference. I have benefited from participating in a number of these programs.[25] There are now a growing number of courses that include a contemplative component in a wide range of academic disciplines and types of institutions.[26] In her essay "Contemplative Higher Education in Contemporary Life," Mirabai Bush (2011) sketches the history of the movement, providing a survey of notable events and programs.

When I introduce meditation and mindfulness to my students, I draw on insights from the Buddhist tradition—in keeping with my emphasis on Asian arts and ways—but my orientation is eclectic, secular, and pragmatic: contemplative practices deserve a place in my seminar because these first-year students are learning new ways to argue, using tactics of the open hand. Just as the figure of the open hand represents a connection with an opponent, so the gesture suggests the openness of mind and expansiveness of heart associated with meditation and mindfulness. In *Opening the Hand of Thought*, Kosho Uchiyama, a Zen teacher, uses the image of the open hand to capture the difference between conceptual and nonconceptual modes of understanding. Uchiyama writes: "Thinking means to be grasping or holding on to something with our brain's conceptual 'fist.' But if we open this fist, if we don't conceive the thought, what is in our mental hand falls away" (Uchiyama 2004, 28).

The phrase *opening the hand of thought* provides an apt description of mindfulness (nonanalytical awareness) as well as of sitting meditation, or *zazen*, where one recognizes thoughts as they arise but then lets go of them, returning to the act of just sitting—or, in some traditions, just observing the breath. Uchiyama explains: "When we are doing zazen, does this mean that thoughts no longer arise and that our heads become empty? No, of course not. As long as we are alive it is only natural that various thoughts arise, even when we are doing zazen. What is crucial is to let them come and go of themselves without pursuing them or driving them out" (Uchiyama 2004, 105). The open hand provides an image of releasing thoughts rather than grasping onto them, but it also suggests a nonaggressive approach to dealing with mental distractions—thoughts are let go rather than being driven out (closed fist). This act of letting go is congruent with the open palm of argument as well as the open hand of aikido so that meditating can be considered an internal art of peace. Perhaps most importantly, meditation-like equanimity and concentration are relevant for arguing, especially in high-conflict disagreements, in which it is easy to react emotionally, respond impulsively, and fail to listen to others' views. As I will discuss in later chapters, while it's essential to know *what to do* to resolve disagreements peacefully, another consideration is *how to be at peace* when intervening in high-intensity arguments.

Finally, students considered how a clear mind—relatively free of distractions, preconceptions, and judgments—might provide a receptive space for insights, hunches, intuitive connections, and imaginative leaps. As Uchiyama suggests, thinking about how to solve a problem, while important, can encourage one to grasp onto conventional solutions, clinging to what we know with our mind's "conceptual fist." I wanted students to recognize that inventive, lateral, out-of-the-box thinking might also be important, especially when arguments get stale and disputes become stuck in well-worn ruts (a topic I discuss at greater length in chapter 4).

Mindfulness is the other form of contemplative practice I introduced in Arguing as an Art of Peace, a practice related to meditation (sitting meditation is often called *mindfulness meditation* or *mindful breathing*). In his oft-quoted definition, Jon Kabat-Zinn defines mindfulness succinctly as "paying attention in a particular way: on purpose, in the present moment, and nonjudgmentally" (Kabat-Zinn 1994, 4). Andrea Miller notes that mindfulness is "being purposefully aware. It is noticing what we are experiencing and our response to those experiences. It isn't simply *knowing* we are eating an apple. It is paying precise yet relaxed attention to the sweet smell and to the crunch between our teeth; it is paying attention to the glossy red skin and the bruise near the stem" (Miller 2008, 56). This capacity to be purposefully attentive serves many purposes in a conflict, especially when one is trying to use arguing as an art of peace. It allows one to notice that an argument is arising, that certain emotions are being generated, and that various intentions and strategies can be mobilized, depending on the situation. Mindfulness also helps one to listen well by developing a capacity to focus on what is occurring in the present. In each of the three chapters about tactics and modes of argument, I discuss how I included contemplative practices and connected them with both movement exercises and principles of arguing with an open hand. My first-year students were drawn to mindfulness, and in subsequent chapters I will try to capture the enthusiasm with which they took the practices of meditation and mindful awareness into their everyday lives.

THREE SCENARIOS

But on the first day of the semester, when they were clapping in for the first time, students were intent on getting their bearings in a course that, they were being told, would be different, engaging, and challenging. After the clapping in, I tried to connect names with faces, presented an overview of projects and assignments, distributed a syllabus, and reminded students that they needed to settle on a controversial issue that they'd be writing about all semester, in a series of projects. In the three chapters that follow, I will examine their work in detail, focusing on each of the projects in the course. When I was developing the units, I had in mind three scenarios in which disputes and disagreements often arise, along with strategies for engaging the conflicts in those situations—open-hand strategies that provide alternatives to the most familiar responses, such as assertion, refutation, critique, and counterargument.

In the first situation (the subject of chapter 2), I assumed that the "heat index" of a dispute was not quite at the combustion point, so that some or all of those involved would be able to think broadly about the issues under discussion if a conducive framework were available. Under these circumstances, I suggested that one might be able to enter into an argument by reframing it. Controversial issues tend to generate pro/con arguments, but it is possible for a speaker or writer to "facilitate" the encounter differently, presenting it as an opportunity for a deliberative discussion by shifting the focus from positions in conflict to problematic situations that need to be addressed for the common good. Thus, in this first scenario, an encounter that might easily have become a two-sided debate is instead reframed as a careful analysis of the situation, with an assessment of options for addressing a significant problem.

In the second scenario (examined in chapter 3), I presented a situation in which the speaker or writer has strongly held views about a controversial issue, views that are in tension with a position held by others who are also solidly committed to their point of view. In this case, members of the audience are one's adversaries in what has already become a two-sided dispute. Reframing might work. But I assumed that the argument was polarized around commitments that were so deeply held that participants' attention could not easily be shifted to a larger problematic situation or to options that ought to be considered before making a decision. In addition, the speaker or writer might have difficulty playing the role of facilitator in this discussion, given his or her strong point of view. In such cases of deep division, the best you could hope to achieve would be to induce the opposition to lend your views a respectful ear, attending to your reasoning about the issue. And an effective way to move opponents to listen to your views is to hear out theirs first, demonstrating that you have paid attention, achieved a measure of understanding, and sympathized with their concerns and perhaps some of their ideas. Even if one's opponents refuse to cooperate and reciprocate, a conciliatory approach enables one to achieve some important goals, such as defusing hostility, demonstrating respect and good will, creating a climate for ongoing conversations, and learning about the opposition's perspective—all without conceding any of one's views.

The third scenario (chapter 4) involves a different situation, one in which the speaker or writer stands outside of a disagreement that is occurring between others. I imaged a scenario in which two parties who hold divergent views on an issue are positioned to engage in an argument that seems destined to become a fight—an argument based on a win-lose dynamic likely to distract participants from seeking opportunities for cooperative action on important issues. The goal for the speaker or writer, therefore, is to find a way to induce cooperation between adversaries, mediating a dispute so that it becomes (so far as possible) a productive encounter.

Although I presented students with three different scenarios, I also explained that the deliberative, conciliatory, and integrative approaches were like siblings, so students should expect to find family resemblances as well as individual differences. Moreover, the tactics they would be learning—reframing, attentive listening, and mediating—could be adapted and combined in various ways in specific rhetorical situations. For purposes of learning, however, students would be practicing each separately, in three different projects. These projects were on the horizon, however, that first day of the semester, as the students gathered their books, zipped up their backpacks, and headed out the door.

DIFFICULT CONVERSATIONS

For the rest of the week, the orientation to Arguing as an Art of Peace continued. In our second meeting, I introduced the idea of *difficult conversations*, an important topic because the kinds of arguments we would be considering throughout the course involved strong differences of view. To prepare for the class, students consulted excerpts from two books with the title *Difficult Conversations*. From this assignment, they learned that when a conversation (or any exchange of views) is "difficult," people tend to draw on a couple of deeply engrained responses: confrontation and avoidance—or fight and flight. Gretchen Hirsch says that any time we feel threatened (even when the threat is "only potentially uncomfortable"), the "body responds in the same way: it prepares us either to fight or to flee" (Hirsch 2007, 42). She notes that the "fight or flight response is a life-saving mechanism that has come down to us from prehistory" and that it is a "hardwired reaction" (42). Douglas Stone, Bruce Patton, and Sheila Heen, in their book *Difficult Conversations*, point out that because fight and flight are so deeply rooted in human behavior, it is not easy to change one's response, saying that it is like "changing your golf swing, adapting to drive on the other side of the road, or learning a new language" (Stone, Patton, and Heen 1999, xviii).

During this second meeting of the term, the topic of difficult conversations was at the center of class discussion, but I also spent some time on organizational matters. I introduced the course notebook, an electronic forum on which I expected students to post one entry each week, recording an observation or reflecting on significant themes connected with our work in the class. As a guideline, I asked for a substantial paragraph, about three hundred words, although students could write more if they wished. I wrote a response to every entry, and every four weeks I rewarded active participation with points. The notebook was an important feature of the course, not only because it gave students a forum for writing about their insights and experiences (especially outside class) but also because it gave me a window into their lives and thoughts. I will be quoting frequently from students' entries in the chapters that follow.

I tried not to spend too much time on course mechanics, however, because I wanted to keep the focus on difficult conversations. To promote discussion, I gave students a scenario that presented a situation some of them might encounter one day in college, a situation in which they had missed a deadline for an assignment and wanted to ask the professor to accept it despite his policy of no late submissions. I made the scenario difficult in the following ways:

- The missed deadline was just an oversight since you are a conscientious student trying to manage too much. You'd finished the assignment but left it in your residence hall.
- The professor is aloof and does not seem easily approachable.
- There is a strict policy of no late submission of assignments, printed on the course syllabus and stated in class.
- The grade on this assignment will probably have an effect on your overall grade in the class.
- The course is in a field you are considering as a major, and the professor is a highly regarded faculty member in that field.

"What would you do?" I asked. "Let's assume you are not only disappointed in yourself but also annoyed and angry about the rigidity of the policy on late assignments, which seems not to recognize the difference between blowing it off and forgetting work you completed diligently." We discussed the following options:

- Perhaps you should just let it go. Since you're unquestionably at fault, asking for an exception to a clearly stated policy could make you look foolish. Better to hunker down and do your best on subsequent assignments. Besides, going to see the professor to ask for an exception might not be pleasant.
- Alternatively, you could go to the professor and ask that an exception be made. Even if missing the assignment will have a minor impact on your grade, it still matters—and that's not fair because you deserve to be graded on your effort and knowledge, not on the trivial fact that you forgot to bring your assignment to class. The professor is being unreasonable and punitive, and you're a victim of an unfair policy. You need to be assertive!
- Finally, you could seek a middle way between acquiescence and anger. If the first approach involves "flight" and the second a "fight" response, what other options do you have?

I told students: "Assume you decide to visit the professor during office hours that afternoon. You're apprehensive because your goal (to get the professor to accept your assignment) is in conflict with his policy (no late submissions). You can imagine ways that this confrontation could turn out badly. But you muster the courage to have this difficult conversation. We begin as you arrive at the professor's office, during scheduled office hours, to find the door closed. What happens next?"

We then did a role-playing exercise in which I was the grumpy professor, and a volunteer (who went outside the classroom to knock on the closed door) was the petitioner. Each time I used this exercise, it turned out a bit differently, but the student volunteer usually did a good job of approaching the professor with a combination of respect and confidence. During the debriefing and discussion, I tried to elicit comments that pointed to some of the tactics associated with an open hand: demonstrating that you understand the policy, viewed from the professor's perspective; framing the conversation not as a request for an exception but as an explanation, apology, expression of disappointment or concern, and so forth; exploring options (that don't entail making an exception) that might be available to make up the lost points; and expanding your goals so there is something to be gained from the conversation, even if the professor doesn't make an exception (you present yourself as a concerned, dedicated student, perhaps mentioning your interest in the field of study, creating the most positive impression you can). This last point was significant because I wanted students to consider the possibility that they might "win" something from this encounter even if they didn't achieve the immediate goal of having the late assignment accepted.

MEDITATORS AND MARTIAL ARTISTS

The role-playing activity got students thinking about situations in which they might need to apply some of the tactics of the open hand. With those skills in the foreground, I closed the session by discussing a passage from *Warriors of Stillness: Meditative Traditions in the Chinese Martial Arts*, where Jan Diepersloot addresses the fight-flight reaction, which he calls the "neurophysiology of emergency." This reaction is so deeply engrained in humans, Diepersloot believes, that "we have literally incorporated the fight-flight syndrome in our bodies and minds," becoming physically as well as culturally "conditioned to need and crave the intense stimuli of anxiety, fear and terror, anger and rage" (Diepersloot 1995, xvi), the result of which is a spiral of intensifying fear and aggression. While Diepersloot may overstate the consequences of the neurophysiology of emergency, he provides a suggestive alternative that he calls the "neurophysiology of harmony," a state that can be achieved through "training in the meditative and martial arts" since these practices nurture the ability to "operate with calm equanimity in the face of extreme danger" (xv). I tried to emphasize the point that the "neurophysiology of harmony" provides an alternative to both fight and flight—a third way to respond to conflict, the way of the open hand. And in Diepersloot's view, to respond in that way we must "acquire the skills and knowledge of meditators and martial artists" (xvi).

It would not, of course, be possible for my students to acquire such skills and knowledge in a semester, in one lab session a week. Serious skill in either domain takes years of determined practice, and I am, myself, a beginner in both of these arts. But this fact did not deter me from encouraging my students to begin the process of kinesthetic and contemplative learning because the martial and meditative arts promised to change the way they conceived of argument and practiced it in their interactions with others. As they moved to the lab class on Friday, students needed to be ready for some new kinds of learning.

For that final class of the first week, I devoted most of the double session to mindfulness, meditation, and movement activities. I brought meditation cushions to class and began by pushing back the chairs to create space in the middle of the room, arranging the cushions in a circle. I wanted students to move quickly into the experience of mindfully observing the breath, so I asked them to focus on breathing in and out, letting all other thoughts go—if only for a couple of minutes. I gave them minimal instructions: a few suggestions about how to sit on a cushion, if they were willing to give it a try (a few stayed in chairs), and some words about concentrating on the breath, noticing thoughts when they arose but letting them go and returning to the flow of the breath, in and out of the belly. As preparation for this class, students had read a couple of brief articles about the practice of mindfulness meditation, so they weren't clueless about what was happening.[27] But in only a few cases had students had any prior experience with meditation (usually as part of a yoga class). I typically began with a two- or three-minute session, ringing a bell to begin and end but otherwise just sitting along with the students. At the conclusion we piled up the cushions and pulled the desks back into a circle.

I posed several questions for students. *Is mindfulness a religious practice?* No, they said—not necessarily. From their reading, they understood that mindfulness has been making its way into the mainstream in such areas as health (stress reduction and pain management), social services, leadership studies, conflict resolution, athletic performance, and education. In "The Mindful Society," Andrea Miller notes that "most spiritual traditions, including Christianity, Hinduism, Judaism, and Islam, have profound contemplative practices. The Buddhist approach to mindfulness, however, is often seen as a valuable tool for people of all faiths (or no faith) because it doesn't require a belief system" (Miller 2008, 56). Students had also read an excerpt from a book by Andrew Weiss, *Beginning Mindfulness*, in which he claims that mindfulness could coexist with his Jewish identity. "You do not have to be a Buddhist," Weiss says, "to practice mindfulness in a nonsectarian context."

You can be a Christian, a Jew, a Hindu, or an agnostic and still practice the Buddha's teachings on mindfulness without any conflict. I refer to the Buddha's teachings throughout this book; in fact, this book would not be possible without them. But I have absorbed those teachings in my experience living as a North American in the late twentieth century from a middle-class family with deep roots in Judaism. . . . Even so, the Buddha's teachings speak directly to me. I find that I can practice them without having to abandon my ancestral spiritual roots, without giving up one iota of who I am. (Weiss 2004, xvi)

What is mindfulness? Students offered definitions, usually variations on paying attention or focusing on the present moment. I summarized their ideas by saying that mindfulness can be described in several ways, with slightly different emphases: being purposefully aware, or becoming fully present, or being wide awake to what's happening in each moment. The focus of attention can be outward, to what's there to be apprehended in a moment of experience; or it can be inward, directed to one's inner space and conscious attention; or it can be on the sensation of being in the world, moving one's body with awareness.

What can mindfulness contribute when we engage in conflicts and arguments? This was a question that students were not quite ready to answer at the beginning of the course, although they could say some things about being relaxed and attentive when faced with stressful encounters. At this point, I sometimes asked them to replay the situation in which a student talks with a professor about a late assignment. One of them left the room, knocked on the door, and was invited to enter. This time, I let the student get only a few sentences into an opening pitch when I halted the exercise, asking about the first step in handling this difficult conversation. Some students wanted to talk about the first words, but I asked what came before that step to set up the conversation. Others pointed to the student's body language, including how he or she knocked on the door. Before that? I wanted students to see that in the moments just before the knock on the door, there was an opportunity to pause to be fully present, taking several conscious breaths to induce calmness and readiness. This isn't just "taking a deep breath," the common wisdom we've all heard before, but an attentive kind of breathing from the center of one's body. It involves a kind of rapid recentering we would be exploring in later sessions.

In the next segment of the lab session, I focused on mindfulness of movement, asking students to take two steps, slowly and with full awareness. My purpose was to illustrate how easy it is to take the familiar for granted. We arrive at the professor's door, for example, and knock without pausing because that's what one does spontaneously. So I asked students to concentrate on the process of taking these steps, defamiliarizing the habitual process of walking so they would experience it from a fresh perspective. What did they notice? Students were often struck by the pivoting motion at the ankle, or the way one foot is rising as the other falls, or the shifting of weight from the trailing to leading foot. When the exercise worked well, students realized how little attention they'd paid to the mechanics and felt experience of an activity that most of them engage in throughout their waking hours. The exercise suggested how many things we do routinely and unconsciously, how much opportunity there is to pay attention.

When students paid attention to the simple act of walking, they were learning to be aware of body movements, a kind of mindfulness that would be relevant later when they learned some patterns derived from Asian martial arts. And when they brought their attention to the flow of the breath or the movement of their feet, students were learning to be mindful of experiences they took for granted, with an attention they would also bring to disputes and everyday arguments. The first step was to encourage them to make the familiar strange, to see the ordinary with fresh eyes.

In the Buddhist tradition, one approach to defamiliarizing the ordinary is the practice of contemplating a paradoxical or puzzling story, called a *koan*. As we will see in chapter 4, where I discuss a Zen story about an argument, a koan is tricky, presenting situations that defy logical analysis. As an epigram for this chapter, I used a line from the famous koan that Hakuin devised about the sound of one hand, and I followed that quotation by introducing the clapping-in activity that signaled the beginning of just about every class session. The full version of the koan goes something like this: "In clapping both hands a sound is heard; what is the sound of the one hand?" (Minnema 2002, 21). In a letter written in 1753, Hakuin elaborated: "Now if you bring your two hands together like this, you will produce a clapping sound, but thrust out a single hand and what sound does it make?" (Hakuin 2006, 215). Perhaps the most prudent response to a puzzling question is to pose others. Is the hand thrust out as a closed fist? Or is it extended as an open palm? The difference between these gestures was at the heart of Arguing as an Art of Peace. What is that hand signifying?

Notes

1   For a concise explanation of the etiquette observed at Shinto shrines, see Nakano (2004). For an engaging account of Shinto, see Kasulis (2004).

2   The first-year seminar program in the College of Arts and Sciences was launched in fall 1991, following the model of an academic seminar with variable content. The goal was to provide a gateway to college learning, exposing students to the attractions of intellectual inquiry and preparing them for college-level analysis. The guidelines for first-year seminars state that courses should be small (no larger than twenty students), interactive and discussion based, and focused on a specific topic of inquiry, ideally one of personal as well as intellectual interest to the professor. Although there is no formal stipulation about the amount of writing in these seminars, many, if not most, are writing intensive, as mine was. First-year students are provided with descriptions of the seminars before coming to campus and can indicate their preferences. In one case, my seminar was designated for students in an honors program, but the other five were open to any first-year students in the College of Arts and Sciences. Of the eighty-five students who enrolled in my seminars, sixty (about 70%) were women.

3   Edward P. J. Corbett's article "The Rhetoric of the Open Hand and the Rhetoric of the Closed Fist" influenced subsequent understanding of these figures. Corbett attributes the metaphors to Zeno and notes that during the Renaissance they were used to refer to logic (closed fist) and rhetoric (open hand). After logic became a theory of inquiry, the two figures came to represent "two varieties of communicative discourse": the open hand representing persuasive discourse that relies on "reasoned, sustained, conciliatory discussion of the issues," the closed fist suggesting a kind of persuasion that uses "non-rational, non-sequential, often non-verbal, frequently provocative means" (Corbett 1969, 288). In his response to Corbett's article, Robert Browne defends the closed fist and questions the open hand: "A fist may be closed in order to strike, but it may as well be closed to protect its members from danger, or to keep a grip on something precious. Maybe it's holding a seed. As for the open hand, it looks friendly, but isn't it empty?" (Browne 1970, 190). In a later response, Richard Marback is even more critical of the open hand, noting that "the open hand that invites discursive participation in democratic processes can be far from benevolent and not wholly inclusionary" (Marback 1996, 182) and arguing for the necessity of "closed fisted coerciveness" and "contestatory rhetorics" when confronting "race, class, and gender inequities" (196). I have offered a view of the open hand from within the context of the Asian martial arts, where it provides a means of contact, connection, and control that is neither aggressive nor submissive.

4   The concepts of *assertiveness* and *receptivity* figure prominently in my discussion of arguing with an open hand. I am indebted to the discussion of the "tension between empathy and assertiveness" in Mnookin, Peppet, and Tulumello (2000).

5   There are some distinctions to make about different schools of Asian martial arts to clarify what's meant by the open hand and closed fist styles. According to Mortensen, the "martial arts can be broadly divided into two groups, predominantly *empty hand* styles and predominantly *weapon* styles. Among empty hand styles, there are predominantly *grappling* styles and predominantly *kick-punch* styles. *Judo* and *Aikido* are examples of grappling styles, while *Karatedo, Taekwondo,* and *Kungfu* are kick-punch. These distinctions are somewhat loose: just about all martial arts have elements of all of the above, it is just a matter of the predominant emphasis" (Mortensen 2010, 160). It's the "grappling style" that I've described as open hand, whereas the "kick-punch" style is associated with a closed fist. It's important not to confuse open and empty hand as categories; karate, for example, is classified as an empty-hand style (the literal definition of the term) because it is mainly concerned with blocking, punching, and kicking, rather than using weapons; yet karate is considered a closed-fist style because it prioritizes kick-punch techniques. Aikido, however, is both an empty-hand and open-fist (grappling) form, primarily.

All categories need to be treated cautiously, however, especially tight distinctions between hard and soft techniques, as well as presumptions that open-hand arts are ineluctably more ethical or spiritual than closed-fist ones. A great deal depends on the attitude and orientation of the practitioner. In my view, a martial art that is truly a *do* (a path or way, not just a set of techniques for fighting) has the potential to provide, as Krein notes, "a framework for living a meaningful life in a world that lacks objective meaning" (Krein 2010, 82).

6   See Morihei Ueshiba and John Stevens, *The Art of Peace*, for a collection of short writings by the founder of aikido. "What we need," said Ueshiba, "are techniques of harmony, not contention. The Art of Peace is required, not the Art of War" (Ueshiba 2002, 33).

7   I've discussed this earlier work in "Broadening the Repertoire: Alternatives to the Argumentative Edge" (Kroll 2000) and "Arguing Differently" (Kroll 2005).

8   In fact, students might have good reason to view scholarly arguments as exercises in "discursive domination" if they knew how academics argued with one another in professional venues, such as graduate seminars or academic conferences. Jane Tompkins has written about her realization, while listening to a paper at a prestigious academic conference, that she was witnessing "a ritual execution of some sort, something halfway between a bullfight, where the crowd admires the skill of the matador and enjoys his triumph over the bull, and a public burning, where the crowd witnesses the just punishment of a criminal" (Tompkins 1988, 588). Tompkins concludes: "Violence takes place in the conference rooms at scholarly meetings and in the pages of professional journals; and although it's not the same thing to savage a person's book as it is to kill them with a machine gun, I suspect that the nature of the feelings that motivate both acts is qualitatively the same" (589). Others concur. Olivia Frey finds the "adversary method in our pedagogy and classroom structures, in our faculty meetings, in the formats of our conferences, in informal encounters in the hall, in every corner of our public lives. The adversary method is only a symptom of a pervading ethos that stresses competition and individualistic achievement at the expense of connectedness to others" (Frey 1990, 522). Linda Hutcheon remarks that the "classroom and the academic conference can equally be sites of combat and one-upmanship. The clever and articulate win the battle of words that has become the defining characteristic of education" (Hutcheon 2003, 43). And a professor of philosophy responded to a colleague's skepticism about his commitment to boxing by saying that "if violence is defined as purposefully hurting another person, then I had seen enough of that in the philosophical arena to last a lifetime. At the university where I did my graduate studies, colloquia were nothing less than academic gunfights in which the goal was to fire off a question that would sink the lecturer low" (Marino 2010, 189–90). Crosswhite would surely say that these examples violate the normative ideals of rational argumentation, but the point is that adversarial argument is prevalent in the academy.

9   *Random House College Dictionary*, Rev, ed., s.v "deliberation."

10   *Random House College Dictionary*, Rev. ed., s.v "conciliate."

11   Rogerian rhetoric is often mentioned in composition textbooks, but my sense is that professional interest peaked in the late 1980s and early 1990s, indexed by the publication of Nathaniel Teich's important collection of essays, *Rogerian Perspectives*, in 1992, and the review essay by Doug Brent, which provided a "twenty-year reassessment" of *Rhetoric: Discovery and Change* in 1991. Brent concludes that "we still do not have anywhere else such a well-articulated combination of dialogic principles combined with a practical set of techniques for implementing them" (Brent 1991, 462) and that, all things considered, "Rogerian rhetoric genuinely has something to offer us" (463). Now, more than forty years after the publication of Young, Becker,

and Pike's influential book, that conclusion is still warranted, in my view, although there would be much more to discuss in a forty-year reassessment. In an informative study, A. Abby Knoblauch examined popular argument-based composition textbooks, considering the extent to which they included an "expansive" notion of argument—that is, the degree to which they supplemented traditional persuasion-based goals with alternatives such as listening for understanding, finding common ground, or negotiating differences. She found that while more space was being devoted to "potentially radical" alternatives such as Rogerian rhetoric, these apparently "expansive" definitions were often "retooled" in ways that emphasized "more traditional notions of argument, those that privilege winning and persuading one's opponent(s)" (Knoblauch 2011, 248). Even Rogerian argument, she notes, "tends to be turned toward persuasive purposes within these texts" (248). While a textbook might include a section on Rogerian argument, presenting it as an option for special situations, the approach is ignored when the focus shifts to academic argument, making it "easy for students to leave behind less common forms such as Rogerian and invitational rhetorics, seeing them as less important or less useful than these more traditional forms" (253). Paradoxically, while Rogerian argument is "fast becoming a staple in argument-based composition textbooks," there is, Knoblauch discovered, a "clear shift away from Roger's notions of empathetic listening and toward persuasive goals" (253–54).

12   *Random House College Dictionary*, Rev. ed., s.v "integrate."

13   I also included several guidelines, urging students to choose a topic that was broad and interesting enough to sustain their attention, important to a significant number of Americans, complex enough to demand sustained investigation, controversial enough to warrant argument, not (for them) a one-sided issue, and substantial enough to have generated sufficient information for research and writing. The only topic I excluded was abortion because we would be working with it as a class during the unit on conciliatory argument (see chapter 4).

14   Whenever I've taught Arguing as an Art of Peace, I've tried to be cognizant of my "outsider" status in relation to Asian arts and ways, aware that because I am a Westerner with no Asian cultural roots, I run the risk of appropriating Eastern practices merely because they serve my purposes—in the way that so many Westerners have mined the Orient for its treasures and resources. But I can say that the most important Asian elements I incorporate in my classes—movement sequences derived from aikido and contemplative arts that have a Buddhist association—are ones I practice myself, though clearly within the parameters of my position (white, male, middle class), cultural background (Judeo-Christian), context (contemporary Western), and idiosyncrasies and personal limitations. I attempt to respectfully adapt, rather than unreflectively appropriate, Asian arts and ways. Thus I am careful to tell students that I am not, for example, teaching them "real" aikido or "authentic" practices of *zazen*; on the contrary, I describe the movement exercises as aikido-based and the meditation exercises as contemplative practices that foster mindfulness. I position myself as a practitioner, a student, a person who has, over a period of years, found that an Asian-inspired conceptual framework and set of martial and contemplative arts offer an illuminating approach to conflict and its resolution. I try to cultivate and communicate an attitude of humility and respect toward the Asian practices (Japanese, Chinese, Vietnamese) that have been of benefit to me as a person and teacher, aware that I will always remain an outsider, yet grateful for whatever proximity I have been able to achieve.

15   Peter Elbow has been a prominent advocate of the idea of including contraries in the teaching of writing. In an essay appended to *Writing Without Teachers* (first published in 1973), Elbow argued that "believing" was as important to the intellectual

enterprise as the more ubiquitous act of "doubting." The skills of the "doubting game" are, Elbow says, "necessary and valuable as long as they are balanced by their complements" (Elbow 1998, 179). The two games are "interdependent," since they are "halves of a full circle of thinking" (191). In this essay and others, Elbow appears to be using something like the yin-yang framework since he is arguing for the inclusion of contradictory tendencies—the necessity of both belief (yin) and doubt (yang). Nevertheless, Elbow's strategy is not quite the same as the one I'm describing here because he pushes students toward the poles, urging them to doubt with all their power and then to reverse and believe as wholeheartedly as possible. In "Bringing the Rhetoric of Assent and the Believing Game Together," Elbow describes his approach quite clearly, as a "counsel *not* of the golden mean but of extremes. Extreme belief: go over-board and believe everything . . . . Then extreme doubt—go over-board and doubt everything. . . . I'm arguing for a dialectical alter- nation over time" (Elbow 2005, 391). My approach is closer to the one that Tannen describes when she uses the terms *yin* and *yang* to refer to principles that are "con- ceived *not as irreconcilable polar opposites* but as elements that coexist and should be brought into balance as much as possible" (Tannen 1998, 284; italics added).

16   A number of terms are available for referring to the mode I am calling *kinesthetic*, including *somatic, embodied, sensorimotor, tactile,* and *gestural.* I settled on *kinesthetic* because it suggests the sensation of bodily position and movement experienced in a person's muscles, tendons, and joints. In *Frames of Mind*, Howard Gardner identifies "Bodily-Kinesthetic" as one of the multiple intelligences humans possess, dividing the category into "control of one's bodily motions and capacity to handle objects skillfully" (Gardner 2011, 218). My use of the term *kinesthetic* is not, however, based on Gardner's theory, nor is it derived from the popular idea that individuals have a preferred style of learning. I assumed that if my students participated in the activities I had devised, they would bring a kinesthetic (bodily movement) mode of understanding to bear on conflict and its resolution. As I note later, those activities were gentle, low-impact versions of martial movements, similar to ones devised for the injured, elderly, or people with limitations on their capacity for physical move- ment. I use the terms *mode* or *modality* to suggest a method, manner, avenue, or simply way of understanding that could be identified as distinctive.

17   Why is aikido called an *art of peace*? In *Aikido and the Dynamic Sphere*, Westbrook and Ratti explain that a martial art can be designed to respond either to the aggressor (fighting back) or to the act of aggression (neutralizing without harm). In many arts, they say, there is "really very little choice, since the techniques themselves and the methods by which they are employed all work toward and are intended to injure if not actually destroy an attacker." In aikido, however, one has a choice because even though the art includes techniques that could be used in ways that can injure or kill, the techniques can also be applied as "means of neutralizing aggressions, not aggressors." According to Westbrook and Ratti, Ueshiba believed that only through "neutralization of an aggressive action, rather than the aggressor himself, can harmony of existence be restored and improved upon through that reconcili- ation which is impossible if one or the other of the individuals involved is seriously injured or actually destroyed." By choosing to act on this imperative to neutralize aggression without seriously harming another person, one "achieves simultaneously the dual purpose of self-defense and restoration of that tenuous, living balance threatened by another man's temporary moral unbalance. And, in so doing, he will not create the conditions for another or different type of disorder" (Westbrook and Ratti 1970, 362).

18   A number of writers have called attention to the uses of nonresistance when resolv- ing disputes or engaging in mediation. For example, in *Getting to Yes*, Fisher, Ury,

and Patton discuss the concept of "negotiation jujitsu" as a way to break the cycle of attack and defense: "When they assert their positions, do not reject them. When they attack your ideas, don't defend them. When they attack you, don't counterattack. Break the vicious cycle by refusing to react." Instead, the authors recommend an aikido-like turning movement, advising negotiators to "sidestep their attack and deflect it against the problem. As in the Oriental martial arts of judo and jujitsu, avoiding pitting your strength against theirs directly; instead, use your skill to step aside and turn their strength to your ends" (Fisher, Ury, and Patton 2011, 110).

19   Among the books that have most influenced my thinking are the following: Thomas Crum's (1987) *The Magic of Conflict*, Terry Dobson and Victor Miller's (1978) *Aikido in Everyday Life*, and Richard Strozzi Heckler's (1993) *The Anatomy of Change*. There's a much larger literature—much of it on the web—that applies aikido principles to professional life in fields such as mediation, law enforcement, and business. "Aiki Extensions" is an organization at the forefront of extending aikido into these areas as well as applying its principles to deep conflicts in Africa and the Middle East (see http://www.aiki-extensions.org/).

20   Perhaps one reason I sensed connections between my earlier training in tai chi and my later experience with aikido is that I was learning a style of aikido that made its way to America through Vietnam, acquiring some elements of Chinese martial arts along the way. In my dojo, there is, at the front of the room, a large photograph of O Sensei (great teacher) Morihei Ueshiba, the founder, and a smaller one of Tri Thong Dang, the head of a lineage that extends from the founder, through Tri Sensei and his student, Ninh Le, to my own sensei, Dr. Minh Nguyen. Tri Sensei, who passed away in 1995, was the "father" of aikido in Vietnam. O Sensei, with whom Tri studied directly, charged him with bringing aikido to Vietnam, giving the Vietnamese branch the name *Tenshinkai*, meaning "association of heavenly hearts." Tri began teaching aikido in Vietnam in 1958; when he left for the United States in 1964, his brother Phong Thong Dang, another skilled martial artist, assumed leadership of the Tenshinkai Aikido Federation until the fall of South Vietnam, escaping from the country by boat in 1986 after years of imprisonment, and then establishing a Tenshinkai association on the West Coast (Dang and Seiser 2006, 178–92). Phong Sensei, with his coauthor Lynn Seiser, has written several manuals on aikido, including *Aikido Basics* (Dang and Seiser 2003) and *Advanced Aikido* (Dang and Seiser 2006). The lineage of my dojo, however, flows from Tri Sensei, a gifted student of Chinese martial arts (having studied the Chinese Tai-Mantis system with Grand Master Chiu Chuk-Kai), author of *Beginning T'ai Chi* (Dang 1994), and a teacher with a philosophical and spiritual bent, as reflected in his two philosophical novels, *Beyond the Known* (Dang 2001) and *Toward the Unknown* (Dang 1997). Although Vietnamese aikido follows the *aikikai* tradition of its Japanese roots, Tri's version alters some of the traditional movements, emphasizing graceful and flowing body mechanics and adding elements that practitioners of *tai chi chuan* or *bagua zhang* would recognize as Chinese inflections. Thus, the Vietnamese style of aikido I have studied is, to at least some extent, syncretistic in its incorporation of Chinese and Japanese martial elements. I make this point to say that when I use movement sequences drawn from tai chi (a Chinese art) and aikido (a Japanese one), I am not mindlessly borrowing from distinct traditions, unaware of cultural differences, but rather drawing on continuities in the Vietnamese style I have learned.

21   I've written about the relevance of aikido and some early classroom experiments in "Arguing with Adversaries: Aikido, Rhetoric, and the Art of Peace" (Kroll 2008), in which I discuss the rise of aikido as a modern martial discipline and suggest the reasons its principles are relevant to the work of teaching argument.

22   Paul Rest has proposed the idea of "low impact aikido," especially for the injured, elderly, or others who cannot safely take falls. See "A Low-Impact Aikido Program—Aikido for Everyone," *Aikido Journal* (blog), last modified 9 September 2009, http://blog.aikidojournal.com/2008/09/02/a-low-impact-aikido-program-%E2%80%94-aikido-for-everyone-by-paul-rest/.

23   Other scholars and teachers have also emphasized the kinesthetic elements in writing and arguing. For example, as Debra Hawhee (2004) notes in *Bodily Arts: Rhetoric and Athletics in Ancient Greece*, "The body's centrality in learning and performing is something the ancients knew so well as to almost take for granted" (195). I hope to make a contemporary contribution to what Hawhee calls "rhetoric's status as a bodily art" (196) by exploring the relationship between martial movements and argumentative tactics. In another important monograph, *Minding the Body*, Julie Cheville (2001) draws on her work with women college basketball players to show how bodily schemata are inseparable from cognition, concluding that the "human body can enhance the connection between activity and thought" (107). For additional work related to a kinesthetic or somatic approach to composition see Fleckenstein (1999), Kazan (2005), Mancuso (2006–2007), and Wenger (2012–2013). Outside the field of rhetoric, work on body-mind connections has become quite extensive; see, for example, Blakeslee and Blakeslee (2007), Gallagher (2005), Johnson (1987), and Shusterman (2008).

24   The first book I read about mindfulness meditation had the captivating title *Full Catastrophe Living* (Kabat-Zinn 1990). I picked it up because I felt I was living a kind of "catastrophe," trying to balance many personal and professional responsibilities. I moved on to other books by Jon Kabat-Zinn and quickly expanded my exploration of mindfulness and meditation.

25   My first sustained experience with the Center for Contemplative Mind in Higher Education came during the 2007 summer session on contemplative pedagogy for college teachers at Smith College, and I have participated in a number of subsequent workshops and conferences. Many of the lessons and principles from these sessions are available in Arthur Zajonc's (2009) book, *Meditation as Contemplative Inquiry*. In summer 2008, I participated in a week-long Contemplative Pedagogy Seminar at Naropa University, a program that also provided crucial support as I was developing Arguing as an Art of Peace.

26   See, for example, Keith Kroll's (2010) collection of essays, *Contemplative Teaching and Learning*, in the series New Directions for Community Colleges. Deborah Schoeberlein's (2009) *Mindful Teaching and Teaching Mindfulness* focuses on secondary education.

27   Students read excerpts from Weiss (2004) and Arpaia and Rapgay (2008). Other books that would work well as introductions to meditation for college students include Smalley and Winston (2010), Stahl and Goldstein (2010), and Williams and Penman (2011).

2
REFRAMING AND DELIBERATIVE ARGUMENT

Tell all the truth, but tell it slant —
Success in circuit lies
Emily Dickinson (1830–1886)

When we imagine a fight, most of us think about a face-to-face confrontation, an encounter in which combatants engage one another along a linear axis; it's a structure we recognize from fistfights, duels, and showdowns in old western towns. To demonstrate the linear nature of a fight, I often used large cardboard arrows, holding them up so students could see that they pointed directly at one another, representing a clash of forces in which the stronger will presumably overpower the weaker and emerge victorious. I illustrated the opposite situation, flight, by turning one arrow around 180 degrees and moving it away from the aggressor. In the unit Reframing and Deliberative Argument, I wanted to contrast the familiar fight-flight reaction (along a horizontal axis) with a response in which the angle of engagement is oblique. Instead of moving directly against an opposing force, as in a conventional fight, or fleeing from a confrontation, one could, I suggested, yield and blend with the attack, followed by moving off the horizontal axis and entering on an angle, redirecting the oppositional force. To illustrate, I began with the two arrows pointing toward one another, positioned for a fight. But rather than clashing, one of the arrows moved back and to one side, off the axis of confrontation—rotating about forty-five degrees so it pointed at the other arrow on an angle. When I pushed the arrows forward, the combined force moved them in a new direction, at something like ninety degrees to the original axis. This demonstration provided a visual depiction of reframing, a tactic that creates the necessary conditions for deliberative arguments. To borrow a line from Emily Dickinson's well-known poem, we would consider how to "tell all the truth, but tell it slant": how, that is, to change the angle of confrontation from direct to oblique—and how to do so with intention and integrity.[1]

DOI: 10.7330_9780874219203.c002

But before we began our work on reframing, I wanted students to become observers of the dynamics of everyday arguments, so I asked them to start paying attention to the conflicts taking place around them—with parents, with friends and romantic partners, and with roommates and new acquaintances in their residence halls. I encouraged them to record their observations in the weekly notebook entries, along with other reflections. Conflicts with roommates were common subjects, often over matters that seem unimportant from a distance—the temperature of the room, how to arrange the furniture in a small space—but clearly mattered to first-year students who were settling into a new life.

> My roommate and I got in a fight over the temperature of our room. I get hot easily and she is always cold, which poses problems. I always open the windows and when I return I see they are always shut. We began to fight, me talking about how hot I am and her saying she was cold and it's not fair to open *her* window.

As they began to pay attention to the arguments taking place around them, students were struck by the ubiquity of disagreements and disputes.

> The more I look around, the more arguments I see and hear. On my hall specifically, there has recently been constant arguing. A kid on my hall has been having a lot of problems with his girlfriend at home and is constantly arguing with her on the phone. I hear yelling and sad tones all the time, and it is rather depressing. A girl down the hall and her roommate have not gotten along since day one and often argue about various things. Instead of talking about what each of them should do to make their living environment better, they just yell and get angry about the things that are not going right.

And in the process of observing disagreements among others, students began to pay attention to their own habits of arguing. As one student noted, "From a young age, I have definitely been inclined to confrontation. In fact, my mom always jokes that my first word was *no.*" Another recognized the pattern of argument that prevailed in her family.

> I have always been a girl with a loud voice. I acquired my loud voice and high confidence from my family. For better or for worse, my house is one of the loudest houses anyone walks into. I am definitely someone who confronts people if there is an issue of importance to me.

Yet others reflected on the approaches to arguing they had used in high school or with their friends.

> In high school, I was opinionated and held little respect towards opposing viewpoints. My essays gave the illusion of understanding of the opposing

side's view, when in reality I was trying to destroy it. I used to love debating controversial issues, particularly those that reflected on how scientific progress impacts human society. It was actually fun to deliver the final point in a debate that would cripple the opposing view's entire argument.

Or as another wrote:

I have always been considered one to be up for any argument or controversial discussion, sometimes even trying to prove my point against an entire room of peers yelling opposing thoughts. If I feel that I am right, I am known to stick with my side until the point is across and proven in my favor.

There were also individuals who avoided conflicts and controversies. One student described herself as a "Division I avoider of confrontation," saying she "avoids conflict like it's my job." "In my life," said another, "conflict is something that I usually try to avoid. I almost never fight with my parents or friends." But nearly all of the students agreed that their prior experiences—personal interactions, observations of debates in the media, and training in high school—had encouraged arguing with a closed fist. What they needed, to expand their repertoire, was a sense of the alternatives, an appreciation of the options afforded by arguing with an open hand.

We began with reframing, the key tactic for deliberative argument. To start our investigation, we returned to the topic of difficult conversations, drawing, once again, on Stone, Patton, and Heen's discussion in *Difficult Conversations*, where they present reframing as a way to "translate" or recast a dispute so that a confrontation becomes a problem-solving discussion; this can be accomplished, they say, by shifting one's responses from "certainty to curiosity, from debate to exploration, from simplicity to complexity, from 'either/or' to 'and'" (Stone, Patton, and Heen 1999, 146). Although these were helpful guidelines, I formulated the tactics a bit differently for the purposes of deliberative argument, identifying several ways to reframe a potentially adversarial argument. I began with difficult conversations, however, to situate reframing in the context of everyday arguments, noting the similarities between interpersonal conflicts and arguments about controversial issues.

During the next couple of weeks, we would explore the tactic of reframing as a response to argumentative conflicts, a tactic that involves entering a confrontation on an angle, with an open hand, changing the dynamic from dispute to deliberation. We considered three versions of reframing. In the first, the goal is to *shift attention* from points of contention to larger issues, perhaps to the questions that generated the argument in the first place or to the problematic situation that various proposals are trying to address. In a second version of reframing, the aim is to *expand the options* being considered, slowing down the rush to decide on a course of action by arguing that a good decision must be based on careful consideration of alternatives. In the third version, the writer strives to *introduce new perspectives* that encourage participants to step back and reconsider their ideas; these new perspectives could be creative solutions, or they might offer fresh ways to understand the problem. And a writer might decide to use a combination of these tactics in a deliberative argument.

FOCUSING ON A QUESTION OR PROBLEMATIC SITUATION

To illustrate how an assertion can be reframed as a question, I began with a situation close to the hearts of many Lehigh students because of the strong Greek system on campus (and perennial efforts to reform it). I asked the class to consider the differences between the following sentences:

> The Greek system at Lehigh should be abolished because it has become irresponsible and unaccountable.

> How can we ensure that the Greek system at Lehigh remains as responsible and accountable as it was intended to be?

The first sentence is a closed fist, or—to use the yin-yang framework—it lies at the yang end of the continuum because of its assertiveness. This statement is likely to move a collegiate audience (students, faculty, administrators) into well-dug trenches, igniting the familiar pro-Greek/anti-Greek debate. As in trench warfare, there's not likely to be much movement no matter how many assaults are launched. The second statement seems less likely to polarize the audience. It may contain a whiff of criticism (an element of yang) with its suggestion that the Greek system is not being fully responsible, but it affirms the idea that responsibility and accountability are embedded in that system's stated values. There are a number of contrasts between these two statements. The agent in the first sentence is unstated or implied, whereas in the second the *we* subject is inclusive. The predicate in the first statement ("should be abolished") is aggressive, whereas in the second the action is less threatening ("ensure"). The keywords in the first statement are expressed as negatives ("irresponsible") whereas in the second they are rephrased in the positive ("responsible"). But perhaps the key shift is from assertion to question, from claim to query, from declarative to interrogative mode. A question invites answers rather than counterarguments.

I suggested that this tactic—shifting from assertion to question—was one way to reframe a dispute as a process of deliberation, a process we defined as "careful consideration before decision."[2] I offered examples of how even some of the hot-button topics of our day could be reframed by asking a question that drew people into dialogue and discussion. Instead of stating a position on assisted suicide, for example, one might inquire, "What should we do if many old people don't want to live and so look for ways to die?" Or instead of making an assertion about gun control, one could ask, "What should we do about situations in which children are being harmed by firearms?" These kinds of questions reframe the issue, moving the argument out of the well-worn tracks of an old debate. It's a tactic that seems promising when the argument is likely to become stuck, providing an alternative to proclaiming one's views more vigorously. Rather than arguing "harder," I wanted to explore the benefits of arguing "softer"—arguing with an open hand, rather than a closed fist.

One way to guide a conversation away from contentious proposals and toward broader issues is to use a well-framed question, but a related tactic is to call attention to the problematic situation that generated the dispute in the first place. In the heat of a debate about solutions, the larger context can get lost and the problem can become distorted. How could a speaker or writer use problem posing to foster deliberation? Students were intrigued by an idea that William Isaacs (1999) presents in *Dialogue and the Art of Thinking Together* in a chapter titled "A Conversation with a Center, Not Sides." The phrase "center, not sides" captures the ideal of deliberation, linking it to the image of a round table where people with different views can convene. But what would draw people to the table to think together? We considered the way a crisis, burning issue, or compelling problem can unite people who otherwise disagree, and we brainstormed some ways a writer could intensify— without sensationalizing—the problem: by describing its seriousness, by using an anecdote or example to illustrate it, by citing attention-getting statistics. These tactics offered a way to reframe a debate as a deliberative discussion, especially in the opening moments of an argument. In a paper on euthanasia, for example, a student cited statistics to emphasize the fact that the old and sick in our society are asking for help.

> The most recent study shows that there are 34,700 patients yearly who request euthanasia. That means 34,700 individuals asking for help to die, craving relief.

In a paper about school shootings, the writer used an example to call attention to the problem.

On April 20, 1999, in Littleton, Colorado, Eric Harris and Dylan Klebold set off homemade pipe bombs and fired their weapons on the unsuspecting student body of Columbine High School. The two succeeded in killing 13 people and wounding 23 before they turned their weapons and ended their own lives.

By asking questions and/or focusing attention on a significant problem, a writer can create a context for deliberation: careful consideration of issues and alternatives before making a decision.

KINESTHETIC AND CONTEMPLATIVE LEARNING

From our early discussions of reframing, students understood the rationale for shifting participants' attention to a question or problem. But because I wanted their understanding to go deeper, I introduced some movement activities during the lab session at the end of the week, exercises that fostered kinesthetic learning. Because this was our first lab session in the unit on reframing, I proceeded slowly, starting with an exercise in which students simply received a push by blending with it rather than resisting or collapsing. This exercise was a simplified form of tai chi push hands, a practice in which partners alternate the roles of pusher and receiver. In the lab exercise, students worked in pairs, exploring the experience of pushing and receiving in a flowing rhythm.[3] The aim was to learn something about yielding and blending as initial responses to conflict, as well as how to guide aggressive energy away from its target, the center of one's body, by using an open hand to control and direct it (for an illustration of the movement, see appendix 1).

The exercise also afforded a felt sense of yin and yang, concepts we would be using to discuss receptivity and assertiveness in arguments. In the role of receiver, a student felt what it means to yield to an incoming force while remaining in contact and control. I encouraged students to experiment with various levels of resistance to a push: too much resistance (yang) and the encounter becomes a struggle; too little (yin) and the receiver is exposed and vulnerable. In between, there are points of balance between reception and resistance as the receiver learns to blend with a push and lead it away from the target to a point at which the pusher is extended and the roles are then reversed. In the next lab session, students would develop this basic exercise, turning it into an aikido-like movement that provides a kinesthetic analogue for reframing. But the simple push-hands exercise laid the foundation. "It was fairly easy" one student wrote in her notebook "to connect the tai chi to arguments."

Most of the lab session was devoted to movement exercises—receiving, blending, guiding—interspersed with discussions of how these kinesthetic activities reflected the dynamics of yin and yang and how they could be applied to reframing and deliberative argument. In the final part of the lab, however, we did our second period of sitting meditation to engage students in the contemplative component of the course. Each week, I increased the duration of our sessions, moving toward the goal of fifteen to twenty minutes of sitting by the end of the semester. After the silence, we remained on the floor, reflecting on this session or talking about experiences of mindfulness from the preceding week. Students were typically relaxed and eager to talk. I didn't record their comments, but some of the notebook entries sound quite similar to what I heard in these sessions. In an early entry, for example, one student wrote:

> I am a very Type A person, and relaxing for me is sometimes even seen as a stressful thing. I am always thinking about what else needs to be done. The only thing I have been able to come up with regarding why I was able to clear my mind this time is the fact that this session was led by someone else. There was someone there basically telling me it was ok to let go and ok to clear my mind of everything.

Another student wrote the following entry about her second experience of sitting meditation:

> Last week, when we first did meditation, I had difficulty getting myself to relax, clear my mind, and actually meditate. In the short time we had I could not stop thinking about the day ahead and what the people around me were doing. I felt the situation awkward and I found myself counting the seconds, waiting for the three minutes to come to an end. When we meditated again this Friday in class, I found it much easier. Again, the first few moments were hard as I found myself trying too hard to clear my mind, only causing me to think more about the day ahead. But I was shortly able to zone out the fact that I was in a circle with a dozen other kids, and focus on only my breathing. I found the meditation this week much more relaxing and enjoyable because of this change. The three minutes seemed like only a minute to me as I lost complete track of time and when you finally announced time was up, I struggled opening my eyes right away.

When students talked about the benefits of meditation, they usually said it improved their concentration, provided a respite from stress, and helped them cope with anxieties and personal difficulties. And in some cases they noticed these effects within a few weeks of learning to meditate, as reflected in this notebook entry in which a student talked about how anxious she was because of how much work she needed to get done.

I immediately recalled the articles relating to meditation, saying to acknowledge concerns and then let them go. I knew no better way to calm my nerves than to simply meditate. I gave myself three minutes, for I did not have much time to spare, to sit down on my bed with my legs crossed and eyes shut. For reasons unknown, it was easy for me to keep out my thoughts for those three minutes. I concentrated on my breathing, gently thinking "in and out." I felt my body loosening all the knots in my shoulders, and I sensed the tension slowly dissipating. When the three minutes were over, I walked to my desk and started organizing the tasks. It became less confusing the more I wrote. I worked on my homework for the rest of the night and ended up sleeping better than I had in days.

Perhaps these benefits are reason enough to include contemplative practice in a required course for first-semester students, eighteen-year-olds who are adjusting to new—and often challenging—living and learning environments at a residential university. One of the points of emphasis for first-year seminars is, in fact, to support a successful transition to college, and I believe my course contributed to that goal for many students. But I had other goals as well, one of which was to teach students that such qualities as equanimity, sustained attention, and clear-mindedness could serve arguers well, especially in adversarial conflicts. Those kinds of conflicts are usually emotionally intense, and in the heat of an argument a person is likely to act impulsively rather than mindfully, responding with the tactics that come quickly to the tongue, pen, or fingers. Just as a meditator learns to notice thoughts arising in order to let them go, returning to clear-minded attention, so I wanted students to learn to recognize their first responses to arguments, opening the hand, figuratively, to release those initial impulses, after which they could consider the situation with a clearer mind.

CONSIDERING MULTIPLE OPTIONS

At the beginning of the next week, we focused on a second tactic for reframing: foregrounding multiple proposals in order to expand the number of options under consideration. The rationale for considering multiple proposals was based on Tannen's advice "not to think in twos" (Tannen 1998, 284). When there are only two options, people are "inclined to polarize them, to think of the two as opposite to each other." Rather than talking about "'both sides' of an issue," Tannen says, we should "talk instead about 'all sides'" (285). The lesson for our work on deliberative argument was clear: if possible, a writer should examine multiple approaches to a problem rather than two competing proposals, thereby reframing a two-sided debate as a discussion of several options. But once those options are identified, what happens next? This was a crucial point in the deliberative process because once the options were on the table, some students thought that the moment had arrived for "real" argumentation: now the writer could make a case for the proposal he or she supported, eliminating others from consideration. But in Arguing as an Art of Peace, I wanted students to think about a different role that the writer could play at this point in an argument. Instead of becoming a *participant* in a debate, supporting a specific proposal, a writer could be a *facilitator* of a discussion, guiding participants through the process of deliberation.[4] This shift, from arguer to facilitator, was consistent with the turn from a closed fist to an open hand—the hand that connects with proposals while controlling the process of careful consideration before decision.

The idea of the writer as facilitator was new to students, so we spent some time discussing it. The reading assignment for this topic, which proved helpful, was an excerpt from *The Facilitator's Guide to Participatory Decision-Making*. The author, Sam Kaner, says that the facilitator's job "is to support everyone to do their best thinking" so that participants are able "to search for inclusive solutions and build sustainable agreements" (Kaner 2007, 32). In other words, the writer must occupy a position slightly outside the conflict—still interested in the outcome, of course, but committed to a decision based on careful consideration of options. Thus, the writer's task is to draw the opponent(s) away from debate and into discussion, investigating alternatives in order to ensure that a good decision is reached. Our discussion of the facilitator's role helped students when they were writing their deliberative arguments, as suggested in the following notebook entry:

> What surprised me most was how our lessons on facilitators related so closely to the writing process. While writing my reframing essay, I thought of myself as a facilitator. I structured my essay so that if it were a true discussion, everyone would be able to participate. I aimed to build my essay so that every side of the issue can have some level of mutual understanding. The strategy of writing from a "facilitator" point of view hinders [avoids] the potential problems that naturally come with debates; it brings people away from being caught up in their own perspectives and allows room for conversations.

I pointed out that while a facilitator is not an assertive arguer, neither is he or she a passive moderator. The open hand of facilitation is energized with yang (actively leading) at the same time that it expresses the gentleness of yin (receptivity), a concept I hoped students were beginning to understand, kinesthetically, from their work in the lab. The reason a facilitator must be active, rather than passive, is that the discussion needs to be steered away from adversarial argument and toward thoughtful consideration of options. The facilitator is a leader. Kaner observes that without facilitation, "most problem-solving discussions degenerate into critiques, rationalizations, and sales jobs, as participants remain attached to their fixed positions and work to defend their own interests" (Kaner 2007, 35). Another reading assignment, an excerpt from Lawrence Susskind and Jeffrey Cruikshank's *Breaking Robert's Rules*, developed the idea of "facilitative leadership" as a necessary element in a problem-solving framework. The goal of this kind of leadership is to "bring people to an informed understanding of what their choices are, helping them evaluate the merits of each possible option, and encouraging them to search for a package that will be mutually advantageous" (Susskind and Cruikshank 2006, 80–81).

Throughout the unit, I encouraged students to pay attention to the arguments occurring around them, especially situations in which people used principles of deliberation to make decisions or resolve differences. Students found examples (good and bad) in the decision-making discussions that took place in their residence halls and student groups. One student, who was living in a special-interest residential unit, told the story of a meeting during which residents debated the idea of adopting a rescue dog for the house. At an earlier meeting, when the idea was first broached, only a couple of students had spoken against adopting a dog, so "it was assumed that, according to the usual rules of democracy, the majority would rule and we would adopt a dog." What's interesting to the student, however, is that rather than simply calling for a vote, the residence directors initiated a deliberative discussion in which multiple views were aired. The role of the facilitators seemed particularly important to the student.

> The facilitators listened to each comment and criticism from an unbiased standpoint and diffused some of the tension while offering opinions of their own. They were all dog-lovers and owners but realized the realities of the situation. After identifying the root problem, that the unity of the house might be threatened, they suggested that adopting a dog might not be the best idea for now. They acknowledged the house's hard work and altruism, but overall knew that the house's priority was to unify the members, not separate them.

This opened up further discussion, which the student describes as a "productive conversation" that included some "creative solutions." Because it was getting late, the facilitators tabled the proposal rather than forcing a vote before discussion was over. The student summarized:

It was a very productive evening, there being a peaceful discussion with all members present, all concerns addressed, and solutions proposed. I have seen and taken part in many other facilitated discussions in the past, although I have never experienced a discussion of this size. It was an interesting experience, and I look forward to the next house meeting.

Our readings and class discussions had, to this point, focused on the kind of interactive, face-to-face encounters that took place in interpersonal or small-group settings or facilitated meetings like the one in the residential unit. How did the concept of a deliberator-facilitator apply to written arguments? It was time to look at some examples.

REFRAMING: SERIOUS PROBLEM, MULTIPLE OPTIONS

I asked students to read several newspaper editorials in which the writers focus on a problem or question, assess multiple options, and frame the discussion as a search for the best course of action.[5] I want to focus on an editorial students found particularly instructive: a piece on the global energy crisis written by a professor of chemical engineering at Lehigh, John Chen (*Morning Call*, April 12, 2006). Here is how the editorial begins:

> In much of our nation's history, Americans have risen to great challenges, solving difficult problems that threaten our survival. Today, we face the challenge of energy—growing world demand, dependence on oil, uncertain sources, entangled alliances and concerns for environmental sustainability. This time, the problem cannot be solved by American ingenuity alone. It will take a long-term commitment from the United States working with the entire world, and will take decades, perhaps generations, to find the answers. And it will mean pursuing all of our energy options.

When we discussed this opening passage, students commented that Chen had certainly put a significant problem on the table, inviting readers to face a challenge rather than making an assertion about solutions. Chen casts himself as someone who is able to consider a larger framework—able to face up to the fact that we may not be able to rely on American ingenuity in this case—rather than presenting himself as an advocate for one solution or another. He will lead us as we consider our options in the face of a daunting problem.

The next two paragraphs provide more details about the problematic situation we face, citing examples and statistics. Then Chen solidifies his deliberative claim: "There is no quick fix. It will take a unified, long-term effort to find the best energy answers." The language is assertive, but not adversarial. Rather than pitting solutions against one another in a struggle to determine which is best, Chen will do something different: assess proposals in terms of what they might contribute to a comprehensive, long-term solution (what Susskind and Cruikshank call a "package"). As he examines each proposed solution, Chen recognizes, in a way that seems fair-minded and thoughtful, what each might contribute and the degree to which each offers only a partial solution to the difficult problem of global energy shortages.

Chen recognizes that "for now, the world will continue to depend heavily on oil, gas and coal, even with increased difficulty extracting them and growing concern about the impact of their use." However, with reserves diminishing, the issue becomes "how much effort in capital, manpower and energy the world is willing to expend to obtain these energy sources—and at what environmental cost." Given those costs, Chen says, "conservation and alternate energy sources must be part of the solution." But each of the alternate sources has limitations. He notes that the "role of renewable energy sources . . . is likely to remain minor." Then he examines a series of alternatives. "What about solar energy?" The problem is that "technology limits our ability to tap this resource." Hydrogen? Its production "requires a conversion that demands a substantial energy input." Nuclear energy? "It is one of the few energy sources that does not emit global warming pollutants, and its fuel supply is projected to last for centuries"; nevertheless, "we are all aware of concerns with plant safety, the issue of waste disposal, and a potential connection to arms proliferation." Some of the problems associated with nuclear energy are "solvable," Chen believes, but the potential contribution is "small relative to projected global need."

Where does this leave the argument? Chen concludes in a way that will not seem conclusive to those who want a definitive solution because he doesn't endorse one approach over another or even map out a comprehensive plan of action. His aim is to dissuade people from thinking that the search for a solution to this urgent problem is going to be easy or quick. He concludes that the "energy challenge is humanity's race against a diminishing quality of life and an economic crisis. This race will not be a sprint, but a marathon." Chen's editorial provided an example of how a writer could use tactics of reframing to facilitate a deliberative discussion, one that entails "careful consideration" of a problem and possible ways to address it. I pointed out that while deliberative argument is not adversarial, it is also not passive: the open hand of the facilitator acknowledges stakeholders and their positions, directs readers' understanding of the problem, leads them to consider multiple options, and guides their decision making. An assertive element

emerges when the writer must reject certain proposals after considering them carefully. Although a facilitator strives to be inclusive and fair
minded, some proposals on the table may make only a limited contribution to solving the problem. This is a difficult moment in a deliberative argument. If the writer ignores the flaws in certain proposals, the
argument can lose its credibility and integrity; however, if the writer's
critique of those proposals is too aggressive, the argument might lose its
deliberative ethos and become an adversarial dispute. How can a writer
identify flaws in proposals and yet maintain the role of a facilitator in a
problem-solving discussion?

In his editorial on the global energy crisis, Chen is able to keep
the focus on the larger problem while also claiming that some of the
proposed solutions will make a minor contribution in the foreseeable
future. Chen walks a fine line, pointing to the limitations of options that
others may find more promising than he does while maintaining that
there is no one quick fix, so multiple approaches should be pursued
simultaneously. This ability to be both critical and supportive—to blend
yang with yin—was an approach I encouraged students to consider
when they needed to reject elements in a proposal or even to eliminate
an option from serious consideration. The way to avoid generating an
adversarial argument is to focus on the goals of a problem-solving discussion, one that examines each proposal for what it might contribute to an
effective and lasting solution. If certain proposals have little to offer, it's
in everyone's best interest to eliminate them from serious consideration,
moving on to other options. In a deliberative framework, the contest is
not among competing proposals but rather among all those who have a
stake in finding a good solution to a recalcitrant problem.

In *Cooperative Argumentation,* Josina Makau and Debian Marty explore
alternatives to "aggressive and defensive refutation strategies," focusing on critique as a "critical and compassionate act of reflection rather
than an effort to be exclusively right and to exercise power over others" (Makau and Marty 2001, 228–29). I encouraged students to reject
proposals in this spirit of compassionate reflection, perhaps by showing that an idea addressed only part of the larger problem. In a paper
on the problem posed by patients in a persistent vegetative state, for
example, a student explored how communication breakdowns—among
physicians as well as between doctors and family members—exacerbated
a difficult situation. One solution he considered is the proposal to create an agency that would coordinate physicians' sometimes competing
assessments and recommendations. But he concluded that while helpful, this proposal is too limited: "Unfortunately, the creation of such

medical councils would only really help solve one aspect of this issue: doctors' ability to communicate and come to consensus with their peers." Similarly, a student who was writing about global warming considered cap-and-trade proposals, an option she found promising but insufficient: "Unfortunately, signing on to a cap-and-trade program isn't a solution in itself. These strategies don't address precisely how industry will lower emissions, or the best way to spend the carbon credits inevitably collected from industries dependent upon burning fossil fuels. Additionally, merely reducing energy usage won't lower carbon emissions enough to prevent global warming."

There are times when hard-edged criticism may be warranted, just as there are occasions when advocacy and confrontational argument are necessary. But critical refutation often becomes a default option so that writers deploy adversarial tactics without considering either the consequences or the alternatives that may exist for the circumstances. As Makau and Marty point out, in the traditional model of argumentation, refutation is a process of defeating the views of an opponent by weakening, invalidating, or undermining them. As they say, "This type of adversarial approach is unlikely to foster constructive dialogue, attentive and nondefensive listening, self-awareness, heightened sensitivity, understanding, and other qualities key to effective and ethical deliberation" (Makau and Marty 2001, 228). In order for critique to be "a tool of reflection," one that can "contribute meaningfully to the deliberation process" (228), refutation must become a "cooperative endeavor where we rely on one another . . . in our efforts to make the best decision possible" (230). Even refutation can be an art of the open hand.

SEARCHING FOR CREATIVE SOLUTIONS AND BETTER PROBLEMS

In the next class meeting, we focused on two additional reframing tactics, both of which rely on inventive thinking and expansive vision. The first entails a search for creative, rather than familiar, solutions to the problematic situation that has drawn people to the table for a deliberative discussion. This kind of reframing is similar to lateral thinking or to looking for solutions "outside the box" of conventional approaches. As Kaner notes, one of the skills a good facilitator can bring to a discussion is to "help groups break free from restrictive business-as-usual discussions and engage in divergent thinking" (Kaner 2007, 35). Fresh options can be invented, of course, but they can also be discovered. And one way to discover alternatives is to investigate how a problem is being addressed in places other than the United States. As a way of enlarging the discussion of options for our own country, students read several editorials in which the writers focus on how other nations are trying to address current issues or problems. For example, in an editorial on Social Security reform (*Morning Call*, May 23, 2005), Kerry Pechter calls for a review of reform efforts in other nations—France, Sweden, Chile, Germany, and New Zealand. His point is "not that we should adopt any specific solution, but that we should be discussing many more solutions than we currently are." Pechter's proposal is consistent with the spirit of deliberative argument: "Instead of considering one isolated idea at a time, we should put a lot of ideas on the table and compare them all at once." In that way, it's possible to avoid the mistake of "accepting the lesser of two evils instead of achieving the greatest good." We need, Pechter says, to "know the full range of our options." In another editorial (*Morning Call*, December 5, 2007), Julia Ross draws some lessons from Taiwan's recycling efforts. In yet another (*Morning Call*, July 10, 2007), Richard Reeves examines how Parisians are addressing traffic problems and pollution by making it easier to use bikes. But I usually focused on an editorial by Jonathan Gifford on the topic of highway congestion (*Morning Call*, November 24, 1995).

Gifford presents the problem of overcrowded freeways and asks the question, "What to do?" While he acknowledges the value of some conventional solutions (smart cars, better public transit systems, ride sharing), he believes that "the private automobile is likely to continue its dominance," so it makes sense to consider a new approach: the idea of building different kinds of highways. And to develop what this might mean, he examines highways in England and Italy, concluding that American engineers could look for opportunities to design "lower-speed, lower-scale highways that are safe and efficient for moving local traffic." A key feature of this editorial is the conclusion, where Gifford manages to make a subtle point about the value of considering alternatives. He is not, in fact, arguing that other countries have the answer to America's problem of highway congestion; rather, he is calling attention to the need for a more expansive approach to finding solutions: "While the English or Italian systems may not be right for us, they do show that there are alternative ways to design highway systems." In this way, Gifford illustrates that a discussion can be reframed by introducing options that have not typically been part of the debate.

Students appreciated the value of searching for fresh options and new perspectives. In their papers, some of them reviewed how other countries were addressing issues that divided Americans, such as gun control or euthanasia. In a paper on physician-assisted suicide, for example, a student compared existing regulations in Oregon, Holland, and South Africa to broaden her review of alternatives. Students could invent new options to put on the table for deliberation, but for first-year students who were writing papers about controversial public issues, it was often more feasible to search for fresh perspectives than to create them.

Another way to expand discussion beyond the familiar options is to focus on the problem that generated debate in the first place, looking for ways to reframe the issues. I called this process *searching for better problems*, adopting the term from Anthony Weston's book, *Toward Better Problems*. Like many others, Weston is concerned about situations in which arguments get stuck in ruts, often because of lack of imagination: participants simply follow the well-worn path. Not only are they blind to new, more imaginative solutions, but also, Weston says, to alternative ways to view the problem. Sometimes we are encouraged to reduce problematic situations to a simpler form, turning them into what Weston calls "puzzles." But Weston proposes that we reverse the common wisdom: he suggests that instead of narrowing focus and reducing complexity, we broaden the context and make the problem more complicated. When we do so, it's possible we will see approaches that don't so much attack the problem as address the conditions that led to the problematic situation in the first place. Weston cites the example of a lifeguard who is "so busy pulling drowning people out of the water that she can never ask why so many people are drowning in the first place" (Weston 1992, 26). Although it's important to save lives, it is also crucial to "refocus upstream," to see what is causing the situation. In Weston's view, "Lateral thinkers would do better to leave the lifeguard to her last-ditch labors and march upstream to check the guardrails" (26).

Weston summarizes his approach to "better problems" as an effort "to recast 'the' problems we are currently given, to rethink their causes and conditions, and to ask whether there are not other kinds of resolutions to the larger problematic situation such that 'the' immediate question, now seemingly so pressing, may not even arise at all. This is the essence of reconstruction's lateral thinking or end run" (Weston 1992, 27). Once they understood this tactic, students found ways to use it to reframe controversial issues as larger issues. For example, one student reframed the controversy over stem-cell research within the urgent problem of finding a cure for Alzheimer's disease. And in a paper about the controversy about whether same-sex couples should adopt children, the writer reframed the issue as a crisis over finding good homes for children with special needs.

American adoption agencies continue to overflow with "unadoptable" children. The term "unadoptable" was used in America until the late 1970's to describe any child over the age of ten, or any orphan with serious physical or emotional handicaps. Today, we refer to these orphans as children with "special needs." It is left up to each state to define what specific conditions dictate a special needs child. Most commonly, factors such as age, race or ethnicity, psychological or physical disabilities, emotional problems, and parental background contribute to a child's classification. The problem is not that there are not enough homes to place these children in, but that aspiring adoptive parents typically are not interested in adopting children with special needs; however, there are people out there willing to adopt special needs children if that is what it takes to start a family. In order to both place special needs children in safe and stable homes and find parents who truly *want* to adopt special needs children, we must strive to find a solution that will be most beneficial for adopter and adoptee.

By the middle of the third week of the unit, students had learned about three ways to reframe a dispute as a deliberative discussion: by focusing attention on a question or serious problem, by reviewing multiple options, and by generating creative solutions or posing better problems.

PRACTICING MINDFULNESS

The final class in the third week—an extended lab session—was devoted to meditation, mindful awareness, and movement activities. As I explained earlier in the chapter, I began with sitting meditation during our practice sessions because it cultivates equanimity and clear-minded attention, qualities that support arguing as an art of peace. However, I believed that putting too much emphasis on formal meditation was a mistake. For one thing, college students lead lives so full of activity and devoid of privacy that it isn't easy for them to engage in sitting meditation outside the classroom space; they need alternative modes of practice, especially models for how to move into a contemplative space internally while being in a variety of places doing various activities. Hence, the focus for this lab session was on everyday mindfulness, involving such activities as eating and walking.

At the beginning of class, students participated in a guided exercise that involved eating one raisin, very slowly, while focusing on aspects of the fruit that go unnoticed as well as the experience of tasting, chewing, and swallowing the raisin.[6] Students had been assigned a short essay on mindful eating, and we talked about how difficult it is to be fully present when we eat our food on the run or while we are multitasking or when we are enjoying an intensely social meal.[7] The idea of mindful eating and drinking made an impression on students, and quite a few wrote about it in their notebooks, often at some length. One wrote about an experiment he conducted during a weekend at home.

> This Saturday, I decided to experiment with mindfulness. Much like the eating a raising activity we had in class, only on a larger scale, I decided to eat each one of my meals slowly and mindfully. I wanted to actually notice the littlest of things, such as taking a bite out of a sandwich.

Another student wrote about becoming aware of the many qualities of the food on her plate and the flavors in her mouth.

> Lately I've been trying to focus more on eating. It is usually an activity that goes without much notice, so today I made an effort to be more aware of the experience of consumption. Similar to what we did with the raisin in class, I tried to clear my mind before I ate and appreciate the experience. I took a few breaths so that I could appreciate the aroma of my pasta before I actually tasted it. I noticed the colors, textures and smells of it and all the other foods around me. I stabbed two noodles with my fork and put them in my mouth. I made an effort to notice the texture and taste of it, while I chewed slowly. I repeated this process with each bite and felt a lot better about eating. Usually I eat so fast that I barely notice how much I am eating, and don't take the time to appreciate each bite. I think that mindful eating will probably result in eating less, which will help me ward off the dreaded freshman 15! It is too often that I am a few bites away from finishing my food and it hits me that I don't even remember eating it at all.

One final example (among many) captured the excitement with which students were discovering the pleasures of mindful eating.

> Last night I was sitting in my dorm room waiting to meet my friends, and I was hungry so I went for some ice cream. It was frozen, unfortunately, so I had to meticulously scrape off layers from the top, which slowed me down and made me enjoy each spoonful. It tasted really good—there was a mix of strawberries, graham crackers, and cheesecake. I thought to myself, "Wow, I really love this ice cream flavor." Then it was as if the articles hit me in the head. I was being mindful of eating the ice cream and noticing all of the tastes because I had to be; because the ice cream was frozen, I literally slowed down eating it, and because of that I noticed more and enjoyed it more. That was the best ice cream I've tasted, and I'm pretty sure it's because I slowed down eating it.

Students continued to reflect on mindful eating throughout the semester. The point was not to become a more appreciative eater (although that was beneficial) but to learn to pay attention in a situation in which most of us space out and consume our food mindlessly, on automatic pilot. One minute our plate is full and the next it is empty.

Were we awake when we ate our meal? The same thing can occur in disagreements and difficult conversations, when we activate a script for fight or flight before we know what is happening.

Another mindfulness practice we had explored in a previous lab was slow, meditative walking. We returned to the practice of walking but changed it so it involved an extended walk with an attentive mind. Because Lehigh students spend a good deal of time walking around a hilly residential campus, they had many opportunities to practice mindful walking outside of class, and quite a few of them wrote about the experience in their notebooks.

> For the first time, I have walked mindfully. On Thursday, I walked out of math tutoring and looked around. Lehigh's campus was deserted, but there was a sense of tranquility. As I walked back to the dorm, I took the time to absorb my surroundings. I watched the squirrels as they collected nuts. I recognized the familiar smell of rain still lingering from the previous night. I studied the trees, noticing that the leaves were beginning to turn colors.

As with eating, students were struck by the extent to which mindfulness changed their relationship to an everyday activity.

> Usually, I speed walk to class. Most of the time I'm running late, so I'm always in a rush to get to class. On Friday, though, I left early for my Philosophy class so that I could take my time walking there and not have to be so rushed. With my phone in my bag and no pressure to speed walk, it was an entirely different world. I looked around at the people who passed me; they all looked like they were in a rush like I usually am. I focused on my walking and realized how weird it was that it's just a process that we do so often without thinking. Mindfully putting one foot in front of the other felt better than usual. It was nice to slow down for a change and appreciate my surroundings; it helped to take some of the stress away that I was feeling.

And the following entry is an especially rich example:

> One specific area in which I am becoming more mindful is walking. I think we all take walking for granted. We do so much of it every day that we do not appreciate each individual step we take and all of the things walking accomplishes for us. I started to notice that whenever I walk somewhere I immediately enter "cruise control," never stopping to consider where I am going, where I have been, and the journey in between each destination. The readings on mindfulness practice have helped me discover how to be more mindful while walking from one location to the next. As I walked back to my dorm last week I felt as though I had walked that route for the first time—mindfully. I reached the middle of one of the staircases I had to climb when suddenly I asked myself how I got there. At that point, I turned around to look at all the steps I had climbed and

could not believe that I "zoned out" while I was walking. I continued to climb the stairs, trying to feel each step and appreciate each time my legs fluidly lifted my body up to the next step. When I climbed the stairs that night I tried to actually feel myself moving from one step to the next. The defining moment came when I reached the top. Instead of taking my usual not-so-mindful pause to regain my breath, I took a different kind of pause. I turned around to look back at all of the steps I just climbed. I had walked from the gym and could still see the doors off in the distance below. I followed the route I'd just walked with my eyes, from the gym's entrance all the way up to my current location. Then I gazed out into the distance where I could see the cities below lit up in every direction. I was being mindful of my body, my thoughts, and my surroundings. As I turned back around and took a long, deep breath, I shook my head, smiled, and thought to myself, "wow, what a moment!"

When I read the students' notebook entries each week, I saw evidence that the practice of mindful awareness had, for many of them, ceased to be a classroom exercise: it was becoming an experiment in living. As one put it, "Mindfulness has crept into my life without my realizing it." I was impressed by the enthusiasm with which many of them embraced mindfulness, bringing it to bear on many aspects of their lives—while working out or engaging in sports, when taking a study break, while driving a car, and even while performing such ordinary activities as painting their nails.

This morning, I mindfully painted my nails. I let myself take in each and every action. I opened the polish, feeling how the cap slowly became unstuck from the dried polish inside, and smelling its strong scent. I then focused on the dripping of the polish off the brush and back into the bottle. I began to paint my left hand. Because I was so concentrated on painting my nails, focusing on only what I was doing, there was an absence of scattered thoughts in my mind. I only realized this after the fact, because I was so calm throughout the process.

Or an activity as routine as brushing one's teeth:

This morning, as I was brushing my teeth, getting ready to go out for breakfast, I realized that my actions were very mechanical. I had not thought once about the entire process. As I was putting my toothbrush back into the cubby, I realized that I had no idea how I felt while I was running the toothbrush over my teeth. When I went back to brush my teeth after breakfast, I decided to look at this everyday process from a different angle. I decided to pay attention to it. To take note of how I felt, what the toothpaste tasted like, what mood I was in. What was I thinking about as I brushed my teeth? I felt as if I had finally woken up to a process I had been performing for years.

The experience of becoming more mindful—more purposefully aware, fully present, wide awake—was so meaningful for students that the connections to arguing sometimes seemed secondary to them. But I hoped that comments like the following indicate that those connections were nonetheless apparent:

> I'd be lying if I didn't admit that I find the mindfulness aspects of this class more interesting than the argument aspects. I feel like they add to one another, though. In order to argue more peacefully, you need to be mindful—mindful of the other person's view, feelings, biases, etc. If you can't do that, the argument probably won't be nearly as successful.

I also saw evidence that students were becoming mindful of their own propensities for aggressive arguing, and that this awareness led them to use alternative tactics. For example, a student wrote a detailed account of a potential argument with her roommate over locking the door to their room. Reaching the boiling point of frustration with her irresponsible roommate, the student decided to have a showdown conversation about shared responsibilities. As she anticipated this conversation, the student began to imagine the worst scenarios—that the roommate would bring in others to intimidate her, for example. As she ruminated about the encounter, the student prepared some "very offensive points to make if my first points didn't work." But then the student realized what she was doing.

> I realized that I was over reacting to a conversation that hadn't happened and might not happen. I closed my eyes and stopped thinking and just breathed for a bit. When I opened my eyes I felt calmer and not as angry or defensive. I realized that what I had just done was meditation. When she came back into our room I didn't attack her about locking the door, instead I said "hi." We didn't end up discussing locking the door that night, but she put a sticky note on the door that says, "Remember key."

REDIRECTING OPPOSITIONAL FORCE

In the initial lab sessions for the unit on reframing, I had focused on a basic version of push hands because it gave students an opportunity—in the role of the receiver—to feel what it means to blend with the energy of a push: yielding while offering just enough resistance to stay in contact with the incoming energy, controlling and guiding it—a yin response, overall, but one in which yang plays a crucial role, both in receiving the push and in the transition into pushing back, as the roles reverse. But a limitation of this exercise, at least in the version I used, is that the push occurs along a linear axis, primarily. To make a clearer connection to reframing, which involves moving into an argument on a "slant," I introduced some modifications, showing the receiver how to step into the push on an angle, moving both participants off the line of attack. At this point, the exercise became more like an aikido movement called *entering* (or *irimi*).[8] The exercise begins when the attacker grabs the receiver's wrist. Next, the receiver yields and blends (as in push hands), controls the attacker's wrist and arm, and turns both of them on a slant. The receiver steps forward and keeps walking after this first step, leading both participants away from the line of attack, in a new direction (see appendix 1 for an illustration of this movement).

I got out my cardboard arrows to illustrate what was happening: as the aggressive arrow pushed ahead, the receptive one yielded a bit then moved off line, turned on an angle, and moved ahead on a slant so that both arrows turned from the original line of confrontation. Students seemed to appreciate this visual depiction of reframing as well as the movement exercise that allowed them to get a kinesthetic feel for moving an argument in a new direction, off the line of direct confrontation. The following comment (from a course evaluation) captures a sentiment I found in a number of students' responses:

> I feel like sometimes, no matter how much I read about something, it's always the visual illustrations that will make the connections in my mind and stick with me. The movement exercises were even better because we had to physically act out what we were learning about in class. It just seemed to fit perfectly for me. Especially the deliberative exercise of yielding and redirecting. That first paper was difficult for me to grasp the concepts but when we talked about the physical movements and performed them I was able to really understand what the goal and strategy was.

Because the movement exercise involved moving forward and leading the other person in a new direction, I saw an opportunity to pose the following questions for consideration: When does redirection feel soft and when does it become aggressive? When, that is, does a redirective push become an adversarial shove? The point is subtle but would prove instructive for our work on reframing and deliberative argument. We looked back at some of the editorials we'd read to see how the writers had employed forceful elements as well as compliant ones in their efforts to reframe an argument as deliberation.

The editorial by John Chen (*Morning Call*, April 12, 2006) provides an instructive example because even though he focuses attention on several options and thus avoids a debate structure, at the same time he uses assertions to make his points in phrases such as "the problem cannot be solved by American ingenuity alone," "it will take a long-term commitment," "there is no quick fix," "conservation and alternate energy sources must be part of the solution," and so forth. In addition, as noted previously, Chen considers the limitations of certain options, such as solar energy, pointing out that "were the entire land and water area of Pennsylvania covered by solar cells, the electricity produced wouldn't meet our country's daily demand." Yet he doesn't argue that solar is a waste of time; rather, he concludes more charitably: "We still need breakthroughs." Where is the boundary between deliberative assertion and adversarial argument? Students agreed that Chen's editorial was an example of redirection—of moving decisively to reframe a potential debate so that it became a deliberative consideration of options—rather than an adversarial argument. A determining point was that Chen concludes not by endorsing one solution but by calling for commitment to use every means at our disposal to prevent "a diminishing quality of life and an economic crisis."

There's some force (yang) involved in redirecting or reframing movements because the facilitator takes control of the situation and moves the encounter in a direction other participants don't expect—and may not want to pursue. The lesson from tai chi and aikido, as I've explained, is that redirection can be forceful without being aggressive. Instead of strong-arming one's opponent onto a new path, one learns to yield, blend, and rearrange the forces in a confrontation so that the encounter moves along a vector that is oblique or slant to the dispute.[9] Much of the energy that drives this rearrangement comes from participants' engagement in the issue, from a commitment to address a problematic situation or find the answer to a perplexing question of policy. The goal is to guide the ensuing discussion away from divisive disputation and toward cooperative deliberation. This process of deliberation could involve a thoughtful analysis of the problem and its context; it might entail a fair-minded analysis of existing options to determine which are most (and least) promising; it might lead to a broadened search for new options or even a revised view of the initial situation itself, putting it in a framework that opens the issue up for innovative problem solving. But whichever direction(s) the argument takes, after this process of deliberating about the problem and its solutions, the writer must bring the discussion to a conclusion. The process of careful consideration must result in some kind of decision.

CONCLUDING A DELIBERATIVE ARGUMENT

The conclusion is a tricky point in a deliberative argument. A concluding paragraph that is too decisive runs the risk of undoing the work of reframing: the conclusion could appear to be the type of delayed thesis in which the arguer merely feigns a deliberative posture to draw a reader in, withholding advocacy until the end. On the other hand, a conclusion that is too indecisive might not be effective either, resulting in a paper that ends inconclusively, leading the argument nowhere. I encouraged students to conclude their papers with a recommendation but to express their proposal in terms that were consistent with the ethos of deliberation. As Makau and Marty say in *Cooperative Argumentation*, the goal for writers of deliberative arguments is to be advocates who "enact their commitments with the spirit of an ally, rather than an adversary" (Makau and Marty 2001, 201).

Although some students shifted into the voice of an advocate or adversary at the end of their papers, most found a way to make recommendations less assertively. One approach is to endorse a synthesis of ideas from several proposals, especially when no one of them alone is promising in every respect. This approach enables the writer to conclude with a recommendation, but one that embraces good ideas drawn from several alternatives, rather than endorsing one solution and rejecting all others. Here's how a student used this tactic to conclude a paper about global warming:

> Because there is no simple solution to solving the global warming crisis, many mitigation strategies must be utilized, at the international, state, and even corporate level. One alternative source of energy or conservation strategy won't do the trick; it will take a substantial number of initiatives and innovations. Some adaptation strategies are necessary to ensure safety, but cannot be the primary focus. A term has even been invented to describe this multifaceted approach to reducing carbon emissions: "Stabilization Wedge." Different conservation strategies combined with using alternate sources of energy form "wedges" which form the whole solution to substantially reduction the amount of carbon dioxide released into the earth's atmosphere. Rather than emissions increasing exponentially, each wedge lowers the total rate of greenhouse gasses emitted. Cap-and-trade legislation, biofuel technology, corporate initiatives and eco-friendly buildings all form wedges that, together, can work to avert this crisis. Let us work with the international community, not against it, to protect the planet that everyone shares. It is time America took responsibility for its actions.

Another student used this approach in a paper about alcohol abuse among teenagers, urging a multifaceted approach.

> The influence and abuse of alcohol is a growing prevalence in the lives of young Americans. Advertisements flaunt intrigue and attraction by inundating viewers with over 1000 commercials for beer and wine coolers on television each year. The appeal is everywhere. Alcohol is involved in more than half of all driving fatalities in the United States, subjecting

one person to an alcohol-related traffic accident every thirty minutes. Research shows that "over fifteen million Americans are dependent on alcohol, 500,000 of which are between the ages of nine and twelve." This suggests that between twelve and the existing legal minimum drinking age the figures must be multiplied. These growing statistics should motivate us to rethink the issue of alcohol substance abuse in the nation and consider a new set of legal options under which safety could be enforced through incentives, education, limitations, and restrictions. Whether that be imposing a higher tax on alcohol sales, prohibiting alcohol sales on national holidays in which motor vehicle alcohol-related fatalities are at their peak, enlisting a Choose Responsibility alcohol education and licensing program, registering parties to be sanctioned, or installing breathalyzer equipment in motor vehicles to prevent drunk driving, plausible and potentially very beneficial options exist. It is in the best interest of our nation and future generations to address this issue in a reasonable and realistic system now, before conditions continue to worsen in the future.

Although this kind of conclusion may not seem decisive, one learns, through the process of deliberation, that sustainable solutions take time, cooperation, creativity, and long-range thinking. While indecision has its risks, to be sure, and while serious problems (such as teenage alcohol abuse) need solutions, it's sometimes wise to invite stakeholders to linger at the table, considering all their options carefully.[10]

In yet other cases, students introduced a fresh idea after having considered the most widely discussed proposals, a new idea that focused "upstream," deployed lateral thinking, used a creative metaphor or analogy, or examined solutions from other nations. In a paper about the debate over how to respond to illegal immigration from Mexico, for example, the writer shifted attention away from the most familiar proposals to focus instead on the advantages of strengthening the Mexican economy. As he noted,

> If we are able to help Mexican citizens obtain higher incomes, the overall economy of the country will benefit, and the infrastructure—health care, road systems, etc.—will follow suit. This, in turn, will give Mexican citizens a better standard of living, thereby reducing their motivation to risk their lives and leave everything behind to get into America.

And here is the conclusion from a paper (written in fall 2009) that reframed the pro/con debate over the ethics of digital music piracy by introducing what was a novel solution at the time.

> Why can't the recording industry adopt a free, ad-supported distribution system? Incorporating advertisements into audio content is admittedly more difficult to do non-intrusively. Viewers have had their television broadcasts interrupted by commercials since the beginning of time, and the format of television shows conforms to these pacing breaks. Surely

it is possible to incorporate ads around the music, though. Perhaps the RIAA [Recording Industry Association of America] could partner with concert promoters to run matching ticket ads next to a band's streaming music. Perhaps the RIAA could create a Web site that married the social features of Lala.com to the extensive library of the iTunes Music Store and the openness of Napster. However the industry chooses to approach this task, the only dangerous move would be inaction. Another year spent targeting music fans for lawsuits, rather than advertisements, will amount to millions lost in ad revenue. As [Jeff] Zucker [President and CEO of NBC] says, "Hulu has shown that if you make quality content available on the Web and combine it with an unbeatable user experience, viewers will come, and so will advertisers." Internet users have demonstrated that they can accept a legal, ad-supported alternative to piracy. Now the recording industry should demonstrate that it can, too.

These kinds of conclusions suggest that students were learning to use the open hand of argument to address issues often approached in an adversarial, either/or framework. By taking controversial topics and reframing them as opportunities for deliberative discussion, rather than defaulting to pro/con debate, these first-year students were expanding their options for arguing about disputed issues.

DRAFTING, REVISING, AND SUBMITTING THE PAPER

During the first weeks of the unit, students had participated in a variety of activities, all designed to teach them about reframing and deliberative argument: they had read about the theory and practice of reframing; examined examples of deliberative tactics in newspaper editorials; paid attention to arguments in their lives and relationships; cultivated the capacity to be focused, fully present, and mindful; and participated in some movement exercises that expressed the tactics of reframing kinesthetically. In the final week, we turned our full attention to writing-related activities as students completed essays in which they applied the tactics we had been considering, producing a paper about the controversial issue they had chosen as a focus for the semester. Students had, of course, been conceptualizing their arguments and approaches throughout the unit, but during the last week they committed their ideas to paper, revising and refining them.

For the first meeting of the final week, students brought drafts of the introductory section of their papers to class. I knew, from reading their notebook entries, that some of them were stuck, so I asked them to get something on paper. Although the idea of reframing made sense when we were discussing it in class, writing the paper was a different matter.

As the deliberative argument paper draws near, I find that I'm having a hard time imagining how my paper is going to work. My topic seems very black and white to me. I've been thinking a lot about the idea of presenting multiple options, but I am just very confused and worry that in the end my own view will show through too much. In the end I think it's going to take a lot of thinking and creatively to master this assignment.

Another student made this notebook entry:

I'm not going to lie. I am having a lot of difficulty coming up with an opening paragraph for the deliberative paper. I understand the concepts of the paper itself—direct everyone's attention to something that is solvable or would at least open up a non-hostile discussion on the issue at hand. But applying this to my specific subject is difficult. I fail to see a lot of common ground to bring everyone to the table.

I believed that a workshop would help. I divided students into groups of three or four, giving them about twenty minutes to read and discuss the introductions written by their classmates. While the focus was on successful tactics, I told students to feel free to make suggestions if an introduction seemed not to accomplish the goal. At the end of this discussion, each group chose one introduction to present to the entire class, selecting an example that illustrated an effective way to establish a deliberative framework for an argument.

Many students found these sessions helpful. Even though we had explored reframing tactics and examined how writers had used them in editorials, it was still a challenge for the students to adopt a deliberative approach when writing their own essays. Requiring students to draft an introduction alerted them to the difficulties they were going to face. The following notebook entry registered this wake-up call:

With as much training and discussion as we have had I still had a difficult time not reverting to a combative tone when writing the deliberative argument. After reading through my first draft for the paper I thought, "That sounds terrible, even I feel attacked as the reader."

But the workshop provided feedback from peers and showed students examples of the strategies others were using to meet the challenges of the assignment. Then at midweek, students met with me for half-hour conferences, in lieu of the Wednesday class. I encouraged them to bring whatever they'd written to that point, ideally a full, even if still rough, draft. Some students came with finished essays; others were stuck and had little more than the introduction they'd written for Monday's workshop. I was willing to work with students no matter where they were in the process.

The papers were due on Friday, at the beginning of class. Since the Friday lab sessions were usually devoted to participatory activities, I wanted to maintain that focus during the class even though the students were handing in their first essays, so I asked them to participate in an exercise I called *mindfully submitting a paper.* I started the class by asking students to get out their finished papers and then to clear their desks, leaving only the paper in front of them. I explained that I wasn't going to rush around collecting the papers: end of old business, beginning of new. In this class, I wanted to proceed more mindfully. I told them to sit quietly for a few moments, reflecting on what they'd written and what they'd achieved in their papers. After this short period of reflective silence, I walked around the room, taking the paper from each student, bowing politely as I put it in my stack. For the rest of this shortened class, we practiced some movement patterns that anticipated the tactics we'd be exploring in the next unit, followed by a period of sitting meditation.

When I read the initial papers, I looked for evidence that students had used the tactics of reframing we'd explored—foregrounding a problematic situation, analyzing and assessing options, and searching for better problems and creative solutions—in an effort to shift the rhetorical dynamic from an adversarial framework to a deliberative one. I had highlighted this goal in the instructions I gave when I made the assignment: "The most important criterion for an excellent essay is that it reframes the debate, using the tactics and achieving the purposes of deliberative argument." In a majority of cases, students did submit papers that used tactics of reframing consistently, creatively, and successfully, writing strong deliberative arguments. (I include an example of a complete paper in appendix 2.) But the first writing project was a challenge: even though many of the students were proficient writers, they experienced the destabilizing effects of the unfamiliar—in this case, an assignment to argue in a different way than they were accustomed to.

> After handing in my deliberative argument paper I have been doing a lot of questioning because writing the paper was a very difficult assignment for me. I had such a hard time looking beyond the standard two sides to the issue. Every time I tried to expand the discussion to include different sides, I kept coming back to just two. I have become so accustomed to writing argumentative papers with the objective of forcing people to opposite ends of the spectrum. I could not seem to get my mind away from the type of controversial writing I was used to. I have to admit that writing a deliberative argument paper to reframe the debate over immigration was one of the hardest pieces I have ever had to write. I have been questioning why it was so hard for me. While writing my paper, I was surprised to discover that I have fallen into the trap of always wanting to advocate a

position rather than discussing multiple viewpoints with others. How did this happen? And at what point in my academic career did I adopt this type of writing?

As an epigraph for this chapter, I used two lines from Emily Dickinson's well-known poem, the first of which reads, "Tell all the truth, but tell it slant." I connected this line with the action of entering a conflict obliquely rather than head on—the movement I associated with reframing. The next line of the poem, "Success in circuit lies," is equally suggestive: the phrase captures, at least to my mind, the action of circling around the point of direct confrontation. In my unconventional reading of these lines, Dickinson expresses the two core movements of aikido—entering on an angle and circling outside. By exploring reframing, students had learned how to approach a controversial issue on a slant. In the next unit, they would explore how to use "circuit" to change the dynamics of an adversarial encounter.

Notes

1   In *The Rhetoric of Reason,* James Crosswhite talks about "oblique inquiry," a term similar to what I have called *arguing on a slant* or *entering conflict on an angle.* Crosswhite says that this kind of argument "is different from any kind of writing in which the thesis is stated explicitly somewhere near the outset, supported by succeeding sections, and restated near the end." He calls this a form that "follows the order of discovery a little more slowly—one that tracks the emergence of new foci of conflict, slowly removing its attention from the ostensive focus to the newly emerging ones. Such writing would make different demands on readers and would offer somewhat different rewards" (Crosswhite 1996, 263).

2   *Random House College Dictionary,* Rev. ed., s.v. "deliberation."

3   The exercises I used were similar to the ones Richard Strozzi Heckler describes in *The Anatomy of Change* (Strozzi Heckler 1993, 99–102). Although I had some exposure to formal push-hands practice when I was learning tai chi, I based my exercises on the diagrams and explanations in several helpful texts, especially Crompton's *T'ai Chi for Two* (Crompton 1989) and Kauz's *Push-Hands* (Kauz 1997). Another way to describe this interactive form of tai chi is *sensing hands,* a term that captures the way an open hand contacts and interprets another's assertive gesture. See, for example, Olson's *T'ai Chi Sensing-Hands* (Olson 1999).

4   James Crosswhite notes that there are kinds of argumentation in which the purpose is inquiry and exploration rather than settling of disagreements. In this kind of argument, he says, "a more nonantagonistic questioner is present, one who asks questions that further a line of inquiry without constantly escalating the level of conflict and without trying to force closure on the claims being entertained" (Crosswhite 1996, 121). This role of the nonantagonistic questioner seems similar to that of the facilitator.

5   Many of the pieces I used were editorials from the local (Allentown) newspaper, *The Morning Call,* which until recently had an excellent opinion section that published a wide range of pieces by both syndicated and local columnists. Some of the editorials I used as examples of reframing tactics were Philip Howe, "Entrepreneurship, Not

Spending Caps, Will Help Budget" (*The Morning Call*, November 10, 2005); Jeremy Wells, "Downtowns Are the Key to Valley's Quality of Life" (*The Morning Call*, August 4, 2005); and Richard Wertheimer, "To Make Welfare Reform Permanent, Wages of Poor Must Rise" (*The Morning Call*, September 13, 2000).

6   The raisin-meditation exercise is described in numerous introductory books on mindfulness. One particularly clear presentation is in Williams and Penman (2011, 73-75).

7   "The Principles of Mindful Eating," a one-page handout distributed for educational purposes by the Center for Mindful Eating. See www.tcme.org.

8   The pattern I used is based, loosely, on an aikido sequence called *ai hamni katat-edori kotegaeshi irimi*, one of the beginning movements in the style of aikido that I practice. In the "real" version, when an attacker grabs or punches the defender, she responds by absorbing and controlling the attack, shifting the angle off line ("slant"), and moving into the attacker's space. This action turns the attacker and usually leads to a throw and often a pin. In the low-impact version I taught students, the defender simply walks forward, leading the partner in a new direction.

9   As Tamara Kohn notes, the moment "the energy of an attack moves towards you in Aikido, then movement (entering or turning) becomes possible—the energy of the throw or pin that a proficient aikidoka produces from that attack does not come out of his or her own strength—it's taken out of the momentum and power from the Other—it draws the attacker into contact, and redirects the Other's movement to a point where balance is lost" (Kohn 2010, 120).

10   I sometimes called attention to the differences between inviting and urging or persuading readers to come to a decision, noting that inviting was a yin gesture. In doing so, I had in mind the work on invitational rhetoric (in the seminal article by Foss and Griffin, 1995). In their textbook, *Inviting Transformation*, Foss and Foss identify an alternative form of argument in which the goal "is not to win or prove superiority but to clarify ideas—to achieve understanding for all participants involved in the interaction. In invitational rhetoric, the speaker and audience jointly consider and contribute to thinking about an issue so that everyone involved gains a greater understanding of the subtlety, richness, and complexity of that issue" (Foss and Foss 2012, 9). In my approach, I encouraged students to extend invitations that were likely to lead to acceptances—not striving to coerce or persuade people to accept, but rather offering the fruits of careful deliberation as a basis on which others would be likely to concur with the writer's recommendations about the best way to address a problematic situation—a yin gesture that includes an element of yang.

3

ATTENTIVE LISTENING AND
CONCILIATORY ARGUMENT

Don't listen with your ear; listen with your heart and mind.

Chuang Tzu (4th century BCE)

By the beginning of the second unit, a month or so into the semester, students recognized that the seminar on arguing as an art of peace was different in a number of respects from a conventional college class. Of course, they were learning about some new ways to engage in conflicts, using tactics associated with an open hand. But the approach to teaching and learning was also different because it included movement and mindfulness practices alongside relatively familiar activities such as examining arguments and writing papers about controversial issues. One student wrote this reflection after her first month in college:

> Unorthodox argument tactics and martial arts are skills unlike anything I have ever learned or known. It can be expected that it is not going to be a smooth transition. As I sit here, though, and think about what sticks out in my mind so far, it has really begun to hit me that this is what true learning is all about. Learning, as I would have defined it before this class, is sitting, reading a chapter of a book, answering questions on the reading material, memorizing some vocabulary and concepts, and taking a test related to the material. Nothing like this is going on in our class, however I'm still learning. My learning has taken place in my bed at night as I attempt to meditate, in the library as I've scratched line after line out of my paper because I have accidentally reverted to traditional argument, on the meditation cushions as I struggle to clear my mind, and out on the patio of Drown Hall as I have practiced tai chi with a partner.

For their first project, students had used reframing to move an argumentative conflict in the direction of deliberative discussion. In the second unit, I asked them to consider what they would do if reframing weren't feasible, appropriate, or effective. We had spent the first weeks learning how to enter a disagreement on a slant, guiding the discussion toward deliberation about options or consideration of a broader problematic situation, giving the argument a fresh start or an expanded

DOI: 10.7330_9780874219203.c003

focus. But some disputes are difficult to reframe as a discussion of alternatives. Sometimes the opposition is fixated on the point of deepest contention and remains steadfast. Sometimes differences need to be acknowledged, not redirected. In the second unit of the course, students considered how to respond when a person or group was committed to a view in deep and seemingly irresolvable conflict with their own. I asked them to imagine a situation in which the other party—the opponent—was as firmly convinced of the validity of his or her views as they were of theirs. How is it possible to use arguing as an art of peace when a clash of views appears to be inevitable?

The option we would be exploring is based on the simple tactic of listening attentively before expressing one's own point of view.[1] To help students visualize this approach, I got out the two cardboard arrows, holding them up so they confronted one another point to point, representing a clash of positions. In the preceding unit, one of the arrows yielded a bit in order to move off line and then entered on a slant, leading the encounter in a new direction. This time, one of them circled around the line of attack, reversing direction so both of the arrows were side by side, pointing in the same direction. This was the first step in a conciliatory argument, representing the act of listening to what one's opponent is saying rather than standing firm and arguing back.

In the chapter on deliberative argument, I presented a series of activities and assignments in chronological order to provide a sense of the rhythms of the course. In this and the following chapter, I want to do something different, departing from a day-by-day presentation. Instead, I'm going to focus on the culminating projects for the other two types of argument—conciliatory in this chapter, integrative in the next—looking closely at the difficulties the assignments posed for students and the strategies they used to manage them. I will, of course, continue to weave the kinesthetic and contemplative strands into the account of students' work on argument, highlighting the points at which the modalities intersected and reinforced one another.

MOUNTING PRESSURES

For many students, the conciliatory assignment posed one of the greatest challenges of the semester—and for understandable reasons. Although the first project had its challenges as well—since it was based on reframing, an unfamiliar approach—the conciliatory paper was quite different from the kind of argumentative writing students had learned about in high school. Even after careful explanations and several examples, students were perplexed when they sat down to draft their papers. One wrote in his notebook:

> The conciliatory style of writing has given me a lot more trouble than I expected it would. We talked so much about it and I feel I have a really good idea about the concepts and techniques, but it is just so different from regular writing. I feel like I have been programmed for years to write in a certain way and it has become second nature. I really have to focus to write in this style.

Another student put her finger on part of the difficulty.

> I think that writing a conciliatory argument is harder than it seems. Upon first reading about it and reading the various examples, I thought that I understood it. I think that everyone thought it would be no sweat. They would just present both sides of the argument. No problem. But then I sat down to actually write my introduction, and I was stuck. For years, all essays have followed a formula: introduction with thesis, supporting body paragraphs, and conclusion. This style has been ingrained in our heads; we used it on the SAT's, high school papers, English papers, and other standardized tests. I had no idea that writing an argument without presenting a clear side would be so difficult.

Even with a set of guidelines, the conciliatory assignment was stressful for students. And the level of stress was exacerbated by the fact that the assignment came at a point in the semester when pressures were increasing in students' other classes. The weekly notebook entries began to include more accounts of distraction and poor concentration—along with overload and panic—as students worked on multiple papers and took exams. It was at this point in the semester that many of them were drawn more deeply into the contemplative strand of the course because it offered a respite from anxiety. Quite a few wrote entries about using mindfulness and meditation as aids when struggling to manage their workload.

> I sit here in the library, staring at the clock. Three o'clock already? I look back down at my assignment pad. I've only completed one of my assignments that's due tomorrow—the wrath and punishment of procrastination. My mind begins to wander. "Did I call my mom today?" "I have so much laundry to do." "I wonder how my home friends like their school? Should I call them?" "Wow, I have a lot of work left." "I haven't even had lunch yet." I stop myself to sit back. I close my eyes and I count my breaths. "One . . . two . . . three . . . ." The library seems to fade from me, and I'm in a different world. I focus on my breathing and let my mind clear. I breathe as the thoughts of home and work escape my mind. I breathe in and breathe out. I slowly open my eyes and I'm sitting back in the library. My work is still on the table. I go back to work more relaxed and with a lot less on my mind—and a new appreciation for mindful meditation.

Others found that meditation helped them prepare to take exams.

> I had my calculus exam at 4 o'clock on Thursday, and as I sat in my seat wait-
> ing for the test to be handed out, my nerves were raging out of control. My
> hands were trembling. I looked up, saw that I had about 3 minutes to spare,
> and decided to close my eyes and meditate. I focused on my breathing.
> There was chaos about me—students shouting, desks creaking, backpacks
> being zippered open and shut—but for those 3 minutes the noise faded
> into the background and all I could hear was my breath. Although it was
> slightly embarrassing to have my professor tap me on my shoulder because
> he thought I was sleeping, I started the exam with a fresh, calm mind.

And yet others discovered that meditation helped them achieve focus
if they made time for it.

> For the past few weeks, I have been incredibly stressed: papers, tests,
> exams, the election, plus a myriad of social options. It was easy to say,
> "I don't have time to meditate or be mindful, I have to study instead."
> However, the more I put off meditating, the more stressed I became. It
> became increasingly difficult to focus in classes. This of course made me
> stress more, making me even less likely to meditate and the entire thing
> dissolved into a downward spiral. During class today I could feel my atten-
> tion was scattered. And when we sat to meditate, I could feel myself think-
> ing "Oh great, now I have to suffer through another 15 minutes where
> nothing gets accomplished." However, I turned to my inner negativity and
> said stop. Meditation has its purpose. So I really focused on slowing down
> my brain and focusing on my breath. There were moments where I was
> tempted to start daydreaming or worry about lists, but I tried to be very
> disciplined. And for the first time in a long time, I felt present and ready
> to take on each challenge as it comes.

I was gratified, of course, that students were making these connections, largely on their own initiative. And I believe that the benefits they
identify—increased focus, better concentration, reduced stress—make a
compelling case for including contemplative practices in a seminar for
first-year students, especially in a course designed to facilitate the transition to college-level work and responsibilities. However, the rationale
for including a contemplative strand in my seminar was not just that it
helped students handle the stresses of college; a more specific reason
was my conviction that meditation and mindfulness can be enabling
practices for arguing as an art of peace, fostering equanimity and attention in situations that involve argumentative conflicts.

AN AIKIDO SEQUENCE

In the lab component, students were participating in both kinesthetic and
contemplative activities, and although I viewed them as interconnected,

students often saw the movement exercises as more directly relevant for arguing than the meditation or mindfulness activities. Their perspective is understandable because the kinesthetic activities provided a physical model for the moves a writer would make in a particular project. And I made those connections explicit by linking each of the five stages in a conciliatory argument to a comparable step in an aikido sequence, one that involves a series of turning movements.[2] Because the full movement is a bit complex, involving three turns of 180 degrees each, we worked on it slowly, starting with just one turn. The exercise begins with two partners facing each other, one playing the attacker, the other the receiver (or defender). The aggressor reaches out, across the receiver's body, and grabs her wrist (for purposes of illustration, right hand grabbing right wrist). The receiver responds by relaxing, taking a step to the left and forward with her left foot, and turning her right wrist and simultaneously placing her left hand on the attacker's right arm as a point of contact. Next she pivots on the left foot, swinging her right leg around behind her while keeping her right arm and hand extended, lined up with the center of her body. As she makes the turn, the receiver engages her opponent's wrist (with her left hand), guiding all three hands in front of her center.[3] Receiver and attacker end up standing alongside one another, facing in the same direction and, for a moment at least, no longer in a position of confrontation.[4]

We practiced this movement sequence in the lab as well as occasionally during class to familiarize students with this turn—as well as others in the sequence—and to explore connections to the steps in a conciliatory argument (see appendix 1 for a photographic illustration). Of all the kinesthetic activities, this one stood out for students as especially helpful for writing their papers. As one said, "The connection between the conciliatory paper and the aikido move that corresponds to it was really clear to me and really helped me visualize the progression of my second paper." Another noted that when "thinking about the 'turns' in the paper, I would picture the turns in the movement." Yet another commented:

> As I was trying to write the introduction for this conciliatory paper, I turned to what we've done using the aikido tactics. I never thought that just reflecting on these techniques would really help me get a move on my paper. The physical aspect of turning and facing different directions really helped illustrate the purpose and effectiveness of the strategy. Usually, I would focus on persuading my opposition. However from the aikido tactics, I physically saw how two opposing parties can reach a mutual understanding that makes the solution process a lot easier.

I will describe the next turns in this aikido-based movement sequence later after considering some of the steps in a conciliatory argument.

STEPS IN A CONCILIATORY ARGUMENT

In the guidelines I developed for writing a conciliatory argument, there are five components or steps; each fulfills a function that can sometimes be accomplished in a sentence or two but may require a paragraph or more of elaboration:

- an opening that identifies the issue and establishes a conciliatory tone;
- a section in which the writer summarizes—in a way that demonstrates fair-minded "listening"—the opponent's interests, concerns, and position on the issue;
- a transition into a presentation of the writer's differing perspective;
- a section that explains the writer's position and the reasons for it;
- and a concluding section that brings a degree of closure to the argument, but without urging the opposition to change views.

There are a number of similarities between these steps and the structure of a Rogerian argument: one of the most important is the strategy of presenting the opposition's position before explaining one's own.[5] As I explained in chapter 1, I encountered Young, Becker, and Pike's *Rhetoric: Discovery and Change* nearly forty years ago at a formative stage in my career, and while it hasn't always been at the forefront of my teaching, the Rogerian approach has been an abiding influence, as will be clear in the discussion of the five steps in a conciliatory argument.

STEP 1: INTRODUCTION

The opening section of a conciliatory argument is, like the aikido ready stance, open—in the sense that it prepares for an encounter without construing it as a fight. Alexandria Windcaller, an aikido practitioner, describes her ready stance this way: "I stand with my hands down along my sides and my feet slightly offset so that one foot is forward. My knees stay flexed, and I usually have a smile on my face, not a grimace. This stance looks completely non-threatening" (Windcaller 2010, 21). By contrast, the initial posture in a combative martial art suggests that one is poised for a confrontation: arms raised, fists clenched, legs loaded for action. In *Arguing as an Art of Peace*, our project was to consider the verbal analogues of these different styles, one an art of the open hand, the other of a closed fist. To explore those differences, students read several excerpts from *Verbal Judo* by George Thompson and Jerry Jenkins, an account they found entertaining as well as instructive. Thompson's background includes both an academic career (a PhD in English with a stint in college teaching) and a fascination with law enforcement, leading him to full-time police work. He also earned, through years of training, black belts in two contrasting styles of martial art: tae kwon do karate and judo. It's his appreciation of the differences between these two styles—as both physical and verbal responses to conflict—that lies at the heart of his story. As he summarizes, "At the risk of oversimplifying, let me assert that there are really only two kinds of language: Verbal Judo and Verbal Karate" (Thompson and Jenkins 1993, 87).

Thompson explains that "karate is a fighting, striking, kicking, attacking offensive system. When that approach is transferred to oral communication, it's easy to do, but it doesn't work. After thirty-five years of using both physical karate and Verbal Karate professionally, I can tell you the latter never once helped me. And I was an expert at it" (Thompson and Jenkins 1993, 87–88). By contrast, *judo* means "the gentle way" (32) and its first principle is "to not resist your opponent. Instead, move with him and redirect his energy" (43). As Thompson explains, the "gentleness lies in the technique. You are not counteracting their approach and hammering back at them. Rather, you are moving with them, using their momentum to pull them off-balance and then propelling them to the ground. . . . Verbal Judo, then, should be non-hurtful. It should be redirective rather than confrontational" (89). Thompson relates a number of stories to illustrate how verbal judo enhanced his effectiveness when communicating, both in his police work and in his personal interactions.

We spent most of a class period discussing Thompson's account of verbal judo (and how it was different from verbal karate). The students' engagement with Thompson's approach is revealed in the following notebook entry:

> I'm writing this account right now because after reading the Verbal Judo articles earlier this evening my head has been swimming with ideas and thoughts on it. As I read the articles, I could not help but think that Thompson and Jenkins wrote this book for me personally. I was particularly intrigued by the Judo v. Karate section. As an admitted follower of Verbal Karate, I could totally relate to the idea of feeling great after verbally knocking someone down, then later regretting it. I think the idea of using the enemy's momentum to fire back at them rather than full-on attacking is an interesting one and something I will try to remember.

Thompson's account bolstered my claim that techniques from aikido, a close relative of judo, were relevant to our work on difficult conversations and argumentative conflicts.[6] In addition, Thompson called attention to some of the limitations of more combative (closed-fist) styles of verbal interaction. When I talked about the closed-fist and open-hand approaches to argument, I drew a softer boundary between the two styles, however, acknowledging that adversarial argument has a place in a writer's repertoire.[7] Moreover, as I suggested in the chapter on deliberative argument, there are elements of assertiveness (yang) as well as receptivity (yin) in arguing as an art of peace. Nevertheless, the readings about verbal judo and verbal karate gave students a framework they could use to analyze conflicts.

> A conversation I had with my mom this weekend made me think over the concept of verbal judo. We got into a petty debate on Friday night, which unnecessarily became a serious argument. After getting off the phone with her, I realized all the wrong moves I made. First of all, I recognized that I used verbal karate, instead of the better alternative of verbal judo. Our fight showed me how easy it is to turn to verbal karate, but it far from the best choice.

I encouraged students to pay attention to the conflicts in their everyday lives, watching for opportunities to apply the principles of Arguing as an Art of Peace. But the focus for most of our class discussions was the culminating assignment, which involved writing a conciliatory argument about a controversial public issue.

The first step in this kind of argument is to introduce the topic and use neutral, nonadversarial language to provide some background on the controversy—the verbal analogue of what Windcaller describes as a stance that "looks completely non-threatening" (Windcaller 2010, 21). Most of the students in my classes could write the opening section without difficulty. The challenge came with the transition from the introduction to the body of the paper. In a conventional argument—at least the version students had learned in high school—the final sentence or two of the introduction consists of a thesis statement in which the writer makes a claim. In an open-hand approach, however, it would be counterproductive to assert a position on a controversial issue, since doing so would frame the encounter as a dispute and undermine the conciliatory ethos. And yet, without a thesis statement, the argument might have no direction. What kind of transition is appropriate in a conciliatory argument?

THE VALUE OF AN ABBREVIATED DISCLOSURE

I used the concept of *controlling the argument*—drawing on the aikido exercise—to introduce a tactic for moving from the background statement to a review of the opposing position (which would follow in the next section). When they did the first aikido turning movement, students could feel the interplay of yin and yang: in the initial phase of the movement, the receiver yields (yin) and turns outside the aggressive grab; in the second phase, he or she connects with the aggressor's arm and controls it (yang). The forces of yin and yang work together in an effective turning maneuver. The same forces needed to be marshaled in a written argument. A traditional thesis statement often contains too much yang for a conciliatory argument; even if the writer follows up by summarizing the opposing viewpoint, readers will be waiting for the refutation to begin. On the other hand, if a writer conceals his or her views in an effort to be gentle (yin), there will be difficulties later, when readers discover the writer's true sympathies on the issue.

The tactic I recommended was for the writer to disclose, at the end of the introduction, his or her position in a brief statement—without asserting or arguing for it—while emphasizing the importance of considering the opposing perspective. The risks of making a disclosure, even an abbreviated one, are apparent: nothing seems more likely to suggest pro/con argumentation than a statement of the writer's position. Disclosure at the end of the introductory paragraph might easily be construed as a thesis statement, suggesting a traditional argument. Why jeopardize the open hand of a conciliatory approach with a disclosure of the writer's views?

The tactical reason is that a bit of risk at this point helps address an even more serious challenge later in the argument when the writer makes the difficult turn from summarizing the opposing view to presenting the one he or she advocates. The disclosure also gives the reader a sense of the argument to follow. But an additional reason to take the risk is that the disclosure is transparent and nonmanipulative—an ethical gesture. I learned to appreciate the importance of a brief disclosure from Tom Rusk's discussion in *The Power of Ethical Persuasion*. In one section of the chapter "Exploring the Other Person's Viewpoint" (an assigned reading for students), Rusk says that even when your goal is to listen to the other side, it's better to make an "abbreviated disclosure" than to try to conceal your view. Rusk states the goal clearly: "to maintain a respectful conversation that is weighted toward revelation of the other person's viewpoint. You want to strike a balance between withholding your position as if it were a secret, and getting into a rapid exchange of opinions that outraces your capacity to understand the other person's major concerns" (Rusk 1993, 80).

I encouraged students to make an abbreviated disclosure at the end of their introductory paragraphs, before the summary of the opposition's views. Here is how the writer of a paper on surrogate motherhood disclosed her position as part of a transitional sentence (with the disclosure italicized):

> *Although I feel that surrogacy is ethical under certain circumstances,* I can see why others believe it is not. People who stand against surrogacy bring up many important points that should not be dismissed or taken lightly.

This writer discloses her view in a subordinate clause, using the phrase "under certain circumstances" to suggest a qualified rather than absolute endorsement of surrogacy. The phrase also invites readers to wonder what those circumstances might be. And by calling the opposition's points "important," the writer indicates that she is not setting them up to be refuted since they should "not be dismissed or taken lightly." In another example, from a paper about legalizing prostitution, a student disclosed her position while emphasizing the arguments for the opposing viewpoint:

> *While I tend to believe that prostitution should remain illegal,* proponents of legalization call attention to important issues such as legitimizing prostitution as a career for women, protecting women against violence, and controlling the spread of diseases.

Although both writers have suggested that the opposition's views are worth considering, neither has agreed with those views or conceded that the points of support for the opposing position are convincing.

STEP 2: DEMONSTRATE ATTENTIVE LISTENING

With the topic introduced and the writer's position disclosed, the next step is to demonstrate that the writer has listened attentively to the opposition by presenting a summary of those opposing views and concerns. This phase of a conciliatory approach is based on the Rogerian method, which asks one party to hear the other out—attentively, without any arguing back—until he or she has understood the other's position well enough to articulate it. In his key article, "Communication: Its Blocking and Facilitation," written in 1951, Carl Rogers claimed that a common reason for failed communication, especially when strong emotions are involved, is that both parties are absorbed in their own frame of reference, focused on judging the views of the other rather than listening to them. The solution is for interlocutors to avoid evaluation, listening with understanding. This means, Rogers said, "to see the expressed idea and attitude from the other person's point of view, to sense how it feels to him, to achieve his frame of reference in regard to the thing he is talking about" (Rogers 1992, 29). To operationalize this shift of perspective, Rogers articulated this rule: "Each person can speak up for himself only *after* he has first restated the ideas and feelings of the previous speaker accurately, and to that speaker's satisfaction" (30). In short, the key is attentive listening.

As students began to explore the act of attentive listening, they discovered that it was not as easy or natural as it sounds. One of the themes in their notebook entries was the degree to which people—mostly their peers—simply do not listen carefully to one another, not in ordinary conversations and especially not when engaged in an argument. Living in residence halls with other undergraduates, the students witnessed many conflicts and interpersonal disputes.

> Earlier today, I was laying in bed doing reading for my English class when I was interrupted by the girl who lives in the room across from me. The walls are super thin in my building, so I could easily hear her raising her voice at someone. She seemed to be in an argument. I soon realized that she was on the phone with her mother. She wasn't yelling at first, but I could tell there was tension between the two. The tension escalated into a full screaming fight, and I couldn't help but take an interest and eavesdrop because of my new appreciation for arguments that has come from this class. Screaming went on for what seemed like hours. [The girl] at one point said, "No, Mom, I don't care about what you have to say about it." She was not giving her opponent any time to explain her side of the story. No wonder this argument led to a screaming fight. I couldn't help but think that all of this could have been avoided, if she had used some of the tactics we discussed in class.

Quite a few students mentioned unsuccessful arguments, assessing what had gone wrong. For example, one student overheard a phone conversation that turned into "one of the most unproductive arguments I have ever heard." She concluded:

> I know that it's bad and nosy of me to listen to a very personal argument, but the whole thing sounded so ridiculous. If he had paused and let her fully express herself, he may have understood her reasons for being so upset. Also, she would have allowed him to express himself afterwards, without the need to interrupt. If these two had paused to listen to the other's side, I think that this fight would have been easily quelled.

In addition to recognizing the difficulties others were having, students discovered they were not always the best listeners themselves.

> I really noticed myself not listening in conversations. When I was talking to someone in more than just small talk, the only thing going through my head was what I planned on saying next in response. If I were the other person talking to me, I wouldn't want to talk to me. It's important to me

that I am heard in conversations, but then I learned that I don't listen to the other person.

TURNING TO STAND ALONGSIDE

The aikido sequence we were practicing in class reinforced the idea that attentive listening is a key step in a conciliatory argument. As I explained earlier, the exercise began when one student (in the role of the opponent) reached across to grasp another student's wrist (e.g., right hand crossing to grasp right wrist). This opening movement signified an oppositional encounter between two people who saw an issue from different perspectives, suggested by the fact that they were facing one another and, as a result, looking in opposite directions—for example, if one faced east, the other looked to the west. I asked students to imagine that both of the participants could see a cue card on the wall behind their opponent so that as they looked ahead, they noticed their adversary but focused on a list of statements that outlined their own position on the controversial issue. Although the goal is to get the opponent to turn and consider your views, the way to do this, in a conciliatory approach, is to first turn and stand beside your adversary, side by side, looking together at his or her claims and reasons. In this position, the writer is prepared to demonstrate fair-minded, nonoppositional listening. The turning movement embodies this reconfiguration of an oppositional encounter: from a position where two people confronted one another as adversaries, one has turned outside the attack to a place alongside the opponent, shoulder to shoulder and facing in the same direction.

In an interpersonal exchange, the listener can show he or she is paying attention by using a say-back protocol, checking periodically to gauge the level of understanding. Students were eager to try this technique when engaging in conversations. One student wrote, "[The] techniques I have learned in this class have saved my relationship with my boyfriend," and she went on to tell this story:

> My boyfriend happens to be a very hardheaded person, and at times having a conversation with him is quite difficult. For months now we have been trying to figure out whether or not to break up, and finally, at the last straw we were hanging by, I decided to give these methods a try and hope that they worked. I told him that I had a lot on my mind, and that it was important for him to hear me out, but that first, I had never really delved into his feelings on the matter before, and I guess since I was finally willing to hear him out completely, he was willing to take that step. After hearing his side, I then went on to do the step that I thought was the silliest,

the repeating of their side. I never really understood this part, until now. Once I repeated to him what I thought he was trying to say, he corrected me and said, "Yea that's part of it, but it's more about ..." and it turns out that I really didn't understand his side like I thought I did. This was a really useful step because once he had finished and I had understood he said, "You really heard me out this time. I want to hear what you have to say now." And the conversation took a turn in a direction that it never had before.

For several students, the power of attentive listening became clearest when someone they knew wanted to talk about a problem and, instead of giving advice right away, the students paused to listen. One wrote about a conversation with a friend from high school who asked to talk with her about transferring. At first, the student responded with suggestions, but when she gave advice she felt her friend "pulling away from the conversation." So she took a "different approach."

> I asked her questions. I felt like a shrink using the say back method, and at one point I even said, "And how does that make you feel?" I paused after she finished speaking, so that if she had the slightest inclination to elaborate, she would. I began to understand her problem. To make sure, I said it back to her. Once she confirmed that I understood, I began giving her advice once more. This time, her responses were much more positive. Being able to use the techniques we are learning in class makes me happy.

In another case, a student said that when she tried "just listening" it made her feel like a failure, at first, because she hadn't offered useful advice to her friend. "When the conversation was over," she wrote, "I felt bad because I was being a lousy friend. I had no idea what I could do to make her feel better." But when she talked with her friend the following day she revised her view.

> The funny thing is, the next day she approached me, thanking me profusely for being there to listen to her. At the time, I had not even been thinking about these techniques of listening and understanding, but unknowingly utilized them, and I have now really experienced first-hand how powerful they are. Since this experience, I have been practicing listening to people when they speak.

The method worked with professors, too, as a student explained in the following entry about a conference with her French instructor:

> I knew I wanted to approach this conference differently than the one I had for my first essay, so during the conference today I used the say-back protocol a lot to clarify his critiques and get a better idea of how to improve my essay. Many times what I understood to be his critique was incorrect, and he would further elaborate. This helped tremendously.

But the most important discovery for students was that by holding their tongues and demonstrating attentive listening, much of the heat could be dissipated from interactions prone to contentiousness, such as difficult conversations with parents, siblings, or roommates. One student reported on a conflict with her mother during a weekend at home, generated by the student's desire to spend more time with her friends than her parents.

> My mom got upset and approached me about this, saying how it wasn't fair that I came all the way back home and was barely paying any attention to her and my dad. I felt that this was an unfair accusation, I had gone to both lunch and dinner with my parents that day, and felt like I was actually doing a good job balancing my time between parents and friends. When she approached me, however, I remembered our class discussions and kept quiet for a bit, letting her vent and release some anger. I then calmly said, "Ok, let me make sure I'm understanding you right . . ." and proceeded to repeat her argument to her. I then asked her what amount of time she expected me to spend with them, and if she thought it was fair for me to blow off my friends. After this, she was much more open to a rational discussion, and began to understand where I was coming from. It was definitely a success.

When the context shifts to written communication, the writer can't, of course, participate in the say-back or checking-in process. But the same effect can be produced if the writer begins with a fair-minded summary of the opposing viewpoint. As Young, Becker, and Pike note in *Rhetoric: Discovery and Change*, the writer must strive to report the reader's position as "accurately, completely, and sensitively as he can, taking care not to judge it" (Young, Becker, and Pike 1970, 275). Although writing this kind of summary of the opposing view was not technically difficult for my students, there were a few challenges. Some students had difficulty restraining their critical impulses when presenting arguments with which they did not agree. For some, it just "felt right" to use a debate-like method of advocacy and refutation: they wanted to set up the opposition in order to knock it down. Another issue was how much detail to include in the summary. One tendency was to move quickly through the summary of the opposing viewpoint in order to get to the next section of the paper in which the writer presented his or her position, a tactic that sometimes made the summary seem perfunctory. The goal was a balanced presentation in which the writer devoted approximately the same space to summarizing the opposing viewpoint as in presenting his or her own. Most of the difficulties students experienced when drafting their summaries were addressed in peer workshops, class discussions, and conferences before the final drafts were submitted.

BROADENING MINDFULNESS ACTIVITIES

By the middle of the second major unit, the students were familiar with the ebb and flow of the course—several classes devoted to understanding the rationale for a new pattern of arguing followed by discussions of examples with a focus on tactics, culminating in the work of drafting, revising, and submitting a written argument. But punctuating the three regular classes each week were lab sessions, where the mode of learning shifted to kinesthetic and contemplative activities. The lab was a distinctive feature of the course, one the students appreciated. It was, of course, a welcome break from the routines of school in which students sat in chairs and listened to a teacher. As one student commented on the lab experience, "Every activity was fun and different. No high school class would be like that and that's why I loved it."

I, too, valued the lab for its experiential, activity-centered approach to learning. I tried to vary the activities, in part to keep the lab fresh and engaging but also to expand students' experiences, especially in the contemplative mode. One new direction for students' contemplative practice was an increasing focus on brief periods of mindfulness meditation, ranging from about thirty seconds to not more than three minutes. This emphasis on brief practice complemented periods of sitting together that became longer each week. My approach was informed by Arpaia and Rapgay's discussion of "brief centering techniques," an important complement, they believe, to "extended practice sessions" (Arpaia and Rapgay 2008, 30). These meditation teachers point out that if you only engage in extended sitting you won't learn to relax and focus quickly in a variety of settings. One of their brief practices is "rapid recharge," a technique that entails focusing on a thought pattern, such as "calm—relaxed" or "calm—alert," for thirty seconds, following the flow of the breath (31). Students were enthusiastic about the brief techniques. One wrote, "I think the 'mindfulness on the go' focus was great because sometimes we don't have the time to sit for 15 minutes." Another said, "[I] really liked some of the quick centering exercises. I have been using the one where I think one word as I breath in and think a different word as I breath out." Sitting meditation remained at the center of the lab, as a core practice, but I introduced students to other modes and venues for contemplative activity, some of which I've described previously (e.g., mindful eating and walking).

I also arranged a few special activities that introduced students to experiences or structured environments designed to elicit mindfulness—the experience of mindful calligraphy and, a bit later in the course, a visit to a Japanese garden (discussed briefly in the final chapter). For our calligraphy exercise, we spent one lab session drawing some basic characters. No expert myself, my goal was to help students get a feel for moving the brush by engaging the whole body, generating energy from the center, and coordinating it with their breathing.[8]

We usually began by drawing a horizontal line, forming the character *ichi* (the number "one" in Japanese; see figure 3.1). This is a simple character, but I urged students to draw it with intense concentration. They loaded the brush with ink, held it just above the place they intended to begin, and then paused for a moment to focus on their center point, taking a conscious breath. As they exhaled, the brush touched the paper and moved across the page, lifting at the end of the stroke, as though they were making a horizontal cut with a sword. The point of the activity was not to produce great calligraphy but to experience the felt sense of brushing a character with mind-body focus, coordinating movement with breathing. In the following notebook entry, a student captured the essence of the project.

Fig. 3.1. Ichi

It was interesting to explore a new type of meditation unlike what we have tried before (such as our weekly sitting meditation). It was fascinating how important it was to be able to relax your body and control your breathing to get the brush strokes to be just right. When painting normally, breath and body position were never something I would have considered as important. When doing calligraphy brush meditation, I realized how important it really is because my best paintings were the ones where I was most successfully controlling my breath to go with the paint strokes and where my body and brush were positioned just right. On one of the paintings, I was not so focused and right before I began I became distracted by a noise, and the result was that the representation actually reflected this. The strokes did not have the same flow, and the "energy" was lacking. It was surprising how much concentration was actually needed for the paintings to be successful and how much the paintings depicted this. This was one of my favorite labs, because even though I enjoy sitting meditation I also like when we explore other forms.

The final calligraphy exercise—typically the students' favorite—was to draw an *enso* or "circle" (figure 3.2). The goal was to start with an empty mind, as in meditation, clearing the head of hopes and anxieties, expectations and anticipations, comparisons and judgments. Once composed, one breathes out, the brush moves, and the circle is there, whatever it is—a record of one breath, one flowing stroke. A number of students wrote about this experience in their notebooks. One remarked, "[It was] quite fascinating to see a visual representation of how I breathe." Another said, "The part I enjoy the most when we do calligraphy is exhaling before painting the circle. It enables me to gather my thoughts and relax." And in an extended entry, a student captured the experience of painting the circle.

Fig. 3.2. Enso

I am going to hold a paintbrush, breathe out, and create a circle? Okay, I can handle that. Now make that circle without trying to make it—let it "be." Whatever you say. I breathe in, trying not to think about how ridiculous this would look to a bystander, or how everyone is watching as I think I am going to show my artistic talent, or rather my lack thereof. What do I have to lose? Pride—who cares? Here goes! As my brush hits the paper I try to forget everything and just breathe out. I end up with an open-ended circle, starting bold in the beginning and trailing to a firecracker tail with less paint. It could very well be first-timer's luck, but I really liked my circle. I liked how there was no definitive ending, because I don't have an affinity for definitive endings. I don't know where I want to end up in my life, and I don't need my endings to have complete closure. My painting is hanging in my room at home to remind me of one trivial moment in which I was truly present and created my own outcome.

The flow of the brush while drawing the circle also provided a point of connection with the turning sequences we were practicing in our movement work, in which students were circling their bodies around a point of conflict. Just as in painting an *enso*, these turns were performed in a flowing motion, coordinated with the breath, so that executing a *tenkan* maneuver became a kind of moving meditation—an embodiment of the brush in motion—in addition to being an effective martial response.[9] Students were discovering, kinesthetically, that "success in circuit lies."

STEP 3: TURNING TO THE WRITER'S PERSPECTIVE

The next move in the sequence—the transition to the writer's viewpoint on the issue—is perhaps the most challenging step in a conciliatory argument, as it is in a Rogerian essay, in which the writer must make the same kind of turn. In his article "Classical and Rogerian Persuasion," Richard Coe calls attention to the difficulty of this transition: "Though not much discussed in our textbooks, a crucial structure in Rogerian persuasion is the turning point, the transition to the presentation of the writer's position. If this transition is not handled well, the audience will likely decide that all the preceding fairmindedness was just a devious rhetorical trick" (Coe 1992, 93). The turn involved in the third step of the sequence is also the most challenging transition in the aikido exercise we were using as a kinesthetic analogue for conciliatory argument because the receiver has to turn the opponent around to face in the opposite direction. Before the turn, the defender has moved to a location beside the attacker, into a position where the opponent's perspective (or imaginary cue card) is in view. But in the next step both participants must turn to face in the opposite direction, to look at the issue from the writer's original point of view. For the first turn, the opponent could remain stationary, focused on his or her perspective, while the receiver does the moving. For the second turn, however, both participants must change position. And the writer would have to be the one to initiate and direct this turn.

In the aikido sequence, the responder moves her hips and arms slightly forward and then executes a 180-degree turn by pivoting on her left foot while swinging her right leg behind her. By keeping the opponent's wrist and arm in front of her center as she turns, she encourages the other person to turn with her so that both of them end up facing the opposite direction, remaining shoulder to shoulder (see illustration in appendix 1). This reversal must be done noncoercively since too much force (muscle power) at this critical point in the encounter is likely to produce a struggle. In a real attack, such as a punch, much of the force comes from the momentum provided by the opponent's attack. If that momentum can be controlled and directed, the reverse turn takes less additional force than one might imagine: the more forceful the attack, the easier it becomes to turn the attacker around. For a skillful practitioner, very little muscle power is involved because the turn has the same flow of energy students felt when painting an *enso* in a single breath.

The idea of taking advantage of the force of the adversary's attack is one of the fundamental ideas in the Asian martial arts. But what kind of energy is involved at the point of transition in a conciliatory argument when a speaker or writer turns the discussion from a review of the opposing viewpoint to a careful presentation of his or own views? How could the momentum of the opponent's argument energize the transition? I suggested that the process of listening attentively to the opposing viewpoint captures its momentum, giving the writer some leverage—specifically ethical leverage—to use in making the transition gracefully. Tom Rusk uses the phrase "leverage of fairness" to describe the effects of attending to another person's point of view. The term *leverage* indicates that the listening process is tactical, designed to move one's opponent to reciprocate. And the term *fairness* locates the ethical force that provides the leverage: the "right to request and expect a full hearing of your viewpoint later" (Rusk 1993, 69). By first listening to the opposition, the writer (or speaker) creates an expectation—tantamount to an obligation—that reciprocation will ensue. There is an ethical edge to this expectation because most people feel obliged to treat others the same way they have been treated. As Richard Coe has noted, listening first to one's opponent "is an application of the ancient ethical principle, 'Do unto others as you would have others do unto you'; that is, demonstrate that you have considered and understood their position as carefully as you want them to consider yours" (Coe 1992, 95). Although the force behind the transition in the third step of a conciliatory argument comes from listening attentively to the opposition, this crucial transition is facilitated—the turn greased, as it were—if a writer has made an abbreviated disclosure in the opening paragraph. Without a disclosure, the transition can seem abrupt, especially if the reader was convinced that the writer was on his or her side, only to discover, at the turning point, that this is not the case. Everything to that point in the argument will appear to be what Coe aptly calls a "devious rhetorical trick."

Rusk says that listening attentively "brings a tremendous tactical advantage to anyone who initiates it" (Rusk 1993, 86). Yet because the writer has listened carefully to the opposition's views first, he or she has also risked being swayed by opposing arguments.[10] The act of listening carefully to the opposition's views can be a two-edged sword: cutting in one direction, it reduces the listener's sense of threat and induces an adversary to reciprocate, listening attentively to your views; however, it cuts the other way as well, asking the writer to stand in the opposition's shoes, considering the adversary's concerns and arguments. There are risks involved in being fair minded to a view you do not support since by being open to that view you may become more sympathetic to it. Rogers identified this risk in his work on therapeutic communication: "If you really understand another person in this way, if you are willing to enter his private world and see the way life appears to him, without any attempt to make evaluative judgments, you run the risk of being changed yourself. You might see it his way, you might find yourself influenced in your attitudes or your personality. This risk of being changed is one of the most frightening prospects most of us can face" (Rogers 1992, 30).

If you can muster the courage to listen carefully to alternative perspectives, however, more can be gained than tactical advantage: you also have an opportunity to enrich and broaden your views. Perhaps you have been wrong about some things, the opposition right. By giving the opposing viewpoint a fair hearing, you may risk changing your mind; the alternative, however, is to risk living with unexamined beliefs. One of the most interesting examples of a student's opening her mind to a position that seemed threatening, initially, occurred in a project about the controversy over whether to allow a mosque to be built near the site of the 911 attacks. The student made the following notebook entry about her struggle with this topic:

> When writing about the mosque being built by Ground Zero, I had pretty strong convictions against it being built. I was so adamant in my beliefs because I was so moved and affected by what people around me were saying. Being a New Yorker, I knew too many people who tragically lost their lives on September 11th or were severely injured from the attack. I will never forget my friend's facial expression when she had to tell me that her mother had died in the terrorist attack. When I heard about the mosque being built near Ground Zero, my immediate reaction was "Absolutely not! How inconsiderate and despicable!" However, I never took the time to hear the other side to the story. When doing my research for this upcoming conciliatory paper, I read many articles where the author was in favor of the mosque being built. I read their arguments and couldn't believe how much sense their logic made and how many misconceptions there are out there about this mosque. I felt so naïve and uninformed.

Through class discussions, examples, and workshops, students began to identify additional tactics for making the most important transition in a conciliatory argument—the turn from a fair-minded review of the opposition's position to an equally careful presentation of one's own. Students discovered, for example, that they could often use a point of agreement as a fulcrum to move the argument toward their own position. In a paper on surrogate motherhood, for example, a student began her turn by finding common ground with her opponents.

> Because I agree that the well being of the child should be considered a top priority, I feel that surrogacy is ethical only under certain circumstances. I agree that surrogacy is always wrong when done without a medical reason.

In a paper about the advantages of a relatively open policy on immigration, a student did a good job of balancing empathetic and assertive elements: in the following excerpt, she treated concerns respectfully, shifted the focus to judicious policies, and ended with a decisive turn to the pro-immigration position that was developed in the next section of her paper.

> I understand these concerns about the effects of immigration on U.S. citizens. Such concerns are legitimate and deserve to be taken into consideration because we have to be considerate towards those who will be affected by increased immigration. It is true that most of the benefits of immigration go to the immigrants, while U.S. citizens have to pay a high price. However, I think we can carefully and cautiously open up U.S. borders in a way that maximizes the benefits and minimizes the costs for the immigrants and U.S. citizens. A lot is at stake if we choose to open the borders, yet historically there are strong moral arguments for allowing immigrants into the United States that cannot be ignored.

Quite a few students followed this pattern of acknowledging the legitimacy of concerns about unrestricted or unregulated policies while proposing careful and judicious ones that adjust for difficulties. In that way, the writer could make use of the opponents' concerns, using them as a springboard for a different policy. In the following example, a student used this tactic in a paper on legalizing physician-assisted suicide:

> The legalization of physician assisted suicide carries a great potential for abuse; nevertheless, I believe that as long as a strict policy is enforced, allowing for assisted suicide only when appropriate, abuses would be minimized and society would benefit from its legalization.

In other cases, students found it useful to acknowledge the legitimacy of a particular social policy for one situation or historical moment but then to make a transition to a different policy by saying they were addressing a new context or altered circumstances. The writer of a paper on censorship used this tactic, acknowledging that certain kinds of censorship might be applicable for children but questioning whether it was appropriate for young adults: "Censorship may be effective in protecting children, but I think that after a certain age it starts to inhibit adolescents from developing intellectually, that it oppresses students' First Amendment rights, and that it is fundamentally unfair." Another writer claimed that the costs of bilingual education might have exceeded the benefits at one point in time but that circumstances had changed and new options were now available: "Immigration is, after all, at an all time high in America. Although I understand the hesitation that some may feel towards altering the educational system, perhaps the cultural and ethnic shift that America is now experiencing necessitates some changes."

In terms of the movement sequence we were practicing throughout the unit on conciliatory argument, we had completed the third step: a transition after which the two participants are still side by side but face in the opposite direction, the phase in which the writer explains that he or she sees the issue differently for reasons that deserve a fair hearing.

STEP 4: PRESENTING THE WRITER'S POSITION

Once the turn had been made, students were ready to focus on their own positions, a step in the argument that went smoothly for most of them. It's possible to err on the side of over-zealous advocacy at this point, but I had called attention to this possibility so that students consciously tried to avoid it. For example, in a notebook entry about the process of writing the paper, a student thought her way through the steps, noting that she would first summarize the opposing viewpoint so the reader would be able to "see that [she could] understand and empathize with their feelings." After doing that, she wrote:

> I can carefully assert my position. I say carefully because I can't be aggressive when I declare my position; I don't want to be so forceful that the opponents reading my paper will stop reading. I have to show why I feel the way I do, the arguments that back it up. I want to sound assertive but not aggressive. It's kind of a fine line, but I do think I can do it. We'll see though.

The guidelines were to practice reciprocity: the statement of one's own position should be similar to the summary of the opposition's views—more or less the same length and equally clear and even handed, aimed at mutual understanding rather than persuasion. Most of my students needed little assistance when writing this section of the paper, and those who made misjudgments usually received constructive feedback in workshops and conferences before submitting their final drafts.

STEP 5: CONCLUDING

The last step in the movement sequence entails disengagement and a turn back to a position in which the two participants face one another again.[11] To execute this final turn, the receiver releases her grip, pivoting once more on her left foot, swinging the right leg back so that she is facing in the opposite direction, now face to face with the opponent as at the beginning (see appendix 1). In this position, when the two participants are facing one another again, it appears that nothing has changed. In one sense, nothing has: neither party to the dispute has been pressured to change his or her mind; neither participant has been persuaded; positions on key issues probably remain more or less stable. And yet, there is a difference in this final position, one that students could see when they participated in the sequence (or when it was performed in front of them): although the two opponents are facing one another again, they are looking in the opposite direction from the one they faced at the outset. If one person was facing east at the beginning, she was looking west at the end, while the one who started out facing west was now looking to the east. And what each saw in the background was the imaginary cue card that represented the *opposing* perspective rather than their own. Although there is no agreement, what has happened, symbolically, is a state of mutual understanding: the two parties can appreciate the viewpoint of the opposition, as well as their own. Where do they go from there?

As in the deliberative project, conclusions were challenging. Some students decided to foreground empathy, possibility, and hope in the conclusion, especially in the final sentences, in an effort to preserve the conciliatory ethos and end on a note of cooperation. These conclusions emphasized the yin elements in an argument, accenting receptivity and understanding. The student who wrote about stem-cell research concluded her conciliatory paper by calling for ongoing discussion.

> As humans, we only have so much control over our surroundings, and we must make wise decisions about how to use our unique abilities in science and moral reasoning to better our society. My hope is that we can continue to discuss the benefits and implications of stem cell research and work together to develop new insights into this conflict.

A paper on what to do about patients in a persistent vegetative state emphasized ideals of respect.

> Proponents and opponents of life support can agree that, regardless of whether or not it is right to keep patients on life support indefinitely, it is important to treat this issue, and all medical patients, with the dignity and respect they deserve.

And a paper on digital music piracy considered mutual advantage.

> Both fans and music industry professionals are interested in fostering a climate conducive to talented artists, one in which good music is continually produced. This mutual interest in music could potentially help move us toward a mutually beneficial solution to digital music acquisition.

Other students began with a point of agreement or solidarity with the opposition (yin) but then affirmed that they were nonetheless committed to a different view (yang). By starting with an *I understand* or, when possible, an *I agree* statement, the writer draws attention to the fact that he or she has listened with the aim of mutual understanding. The writer who worked with the issue of surrogate motherhood chose to emphasize understanding.

> I understand concerns about the surrogacy contract not being upheld and the surrogate being treated as nothing more than a body for rent. I know that surrogacy is a complex issue, and I respect many of the arguments against it.

Following this restatement of understanding and respect, the writer concluded with a short summary of her own position, noting that whatever might be gained from making surrogacy illegal would not be worth the loss of opportunity for infertile couples to have a blood-related child (an assertive move).

> That is why I feel surrogacy is ethical under certain circumstances and should be an available option for infertile women. I also believe that regulation would be a good choice to improve safety. Considering the technology is available, it should be put to use responsibly.

The writer of the paper "Physician Assisted Suicide" began the final paragraph with agreement.

> I agree with many of the concerns about physician-assisted suicide and do not dismiss them lightly. I try to imagine a situation where a member of my own family were terminally ill and wanted to die. I would want everyone to be very cautious about encouraging them to die.

She concluded with a restatement of her own view that the option should be available.

> Nevertheless, in a situation where all other options had been exhausted, where there was no hope for recovery, where suffering was intense, and where both the dying person and the family agreed, I would want the option of suicide to be available. Death is always sad, but it doesn't have to be tragic.

The challenge was to find a point of balance between yin and yang, between receptivity and assertiveness—a way to be assertive without destroying the conciliatory ethos.

Conciliatory argument is designed for situations in which there are limits to agreement, for occasions when commitments are deep and mutual understanding is the best option. Conflict can be intense and enduring, but it does not have to be destructive. The key appears to lie in attentive listening, a kind of listening that goes beyond hearing but stops short of agreeing.

LISTENING FROM THE CENTER OF ONE'S BEING

In one of the stories in the classic Daoist text ascribed to Chuang Tzu, a character named, ironically, Confucius, consults with one named Yen Hui, who is seeking advice before going on a mission.[12] Yen Hui says he is preparing to intervene in a troubled state, Wei, where the leader has become irresponsible. Yen Hui tells Confucius: "I want to use what I've learned from you to help heal the illness of that land" (Hamill and Seaton 1999, 22).

But Confucius raises objections, saying that the mission is dangerous and suggesting that Yen Hui is simply not ready for it. "Better not preach there at all," Confucius advises, because any effort to intervene, even for noble reasons, is likely to get him in trouble. "The power of your virtue is strong," Confucius tells Yen Hui, "as is your will to goodness. But you don't yet fully understand the true nature of humanity" (23).

Yen Hui proposes other strategies he might use. "I will be principled and selfless, constrained and unified in purpose. Will that do?"

Confucius responds: "It will *not* do."

Next Yen Hui suggests being circumspect, putting his advice into the mouths of authorities by "citing the precedents of the ancients" (24). In that way, although his "words may instruct or reprimand, they are the words of the ancients, not my own. . . . Will that work?" (25)

"It will not," Confucius says. "It will not work. . . . In your heart, you're still too much the preacher."

"May I ask," Yen Hui replies, "what methods you'd employ?"

"Having the method is one thing, carrying it out is another," Confucius notes. But he offers some sage advice nonetheless. After telling Yen Hui to engage in "fasting of heart and mind," Confucius says that to succeed in the kind of dangerous intervention Yen Hui has proposed, the best approach is to listen rather than to preach. But he means more than simply hearing with the ear.

"Don't listen with your ear; listen with your heart and mind. Then stop listening with your heart and mind and listen with your *ch'i*, the very energy of your being. Hearing stops with the ear. Heart and mind stop with words and symbols. The *ch'i* is empty. Being so, it is able to attend to all phenomena. Tao comes to roost in emptiness" (25–26).

The story resonates with the project of conciliatory argument, which assumes that one is involved in a confrontational situation with opponents who are committed to their views. Like Yen Hui, we are conditioned to become the preacher, asserting our views. And even when we listen, we often do so superficially, all the while focused on our own thoughts and points of argument. To listen well to our adversaries, we need a capacity for "emptiness" or receptivity, a capacity cultivated through meditation and mindful awareness. The story from the Chuang Tzu also anticipates the next mode of arguing we would study in the course, one based—like the situation that Yen Hui is considering—on a desire to intervene in a situation where all is not well. In the cases we'd be examining in the next unit, the trouble that's brewing is a conflict between others, an argument not likely to be productive. In the final unit of the course, students would learn to intervene in a dispute with the intention of mediating an argumentative conflict.

Notes

1   As Krista Ratcliffe points out in *Rhetorical Listening*, there has been a "lack of scholarly interest in listening within contemporary rhetoric and composition studies" (Ratcliffe 2005, 18). Although her study moves in a different direction than mine, we share an interest in listening as a "stance of openness that a person may choose to assume in relation to any person, text or culture" (25). "Perhaps through listening," Ratcliffe writes, "people can engage more possibilities for inventing arguments that bring differences together, for hearing differences as harmony or even as discordant notes" (25). Wayne Booth also argues for the value of "listening rhetoric," a mode in which "opponents in any conflict listen to each other" (Booth 2004, 10). What the world needs most, says Booth, "are ways of probing beneath pointless disputes: methods of discovering shared ground beneath surface warfare" (149). My focus is on the act of "attentive listening" to the arguments of one's opponents, a term Makau and Marty use (Makau and Marty 2001, 59–64) and one I ground in the principles of Rogerian rhetoric.

2   I hope it is clear that I was not teaching aikido to students but rather engaging them in movement exercises based on aikido principles, patterns, and body mechanics. The pattern I used in the unit on conciliatory argument is based, loosely, on an aikido sequence called *ai hamni katatedori kotegaeshi tenkan*. I broke this movement into a series of five steps, altering the final one from a throw (in "real aikido") to disengagement and a turn back to face one's opponent.

3   There's another option for this first turn. If the goal is to escape quickly from the grab, the receiver can move so that as the hips pivot, her hand rotates and pops

out of the attacker's grasp. One student tried this escape version during a friendly tussle: "One of my guy friends and I were messing around and fake fighting, and I was able to use aikido. He grabbed my wrist and I did the move we learned in class the other day and he was so confused and thrown off guard that I stopped and laughed. He then proceeded to question me: 'Where the heck did you learn that?' I told him in class on Friday. The look he gave me after that remark was even more satisfying than when I threw him off his fighting game." Although I showed students the escape movement, I emphasized the version in which the receiver stays in contact with the attacker, leading their hands to the receiver's center, where she is in control.

4   Leonard and Murphy describe a similar low-impact turning exercise in which one person "attacks" with a wrist grab while the other executes a turn: "Move slightly toward the attacker and turn to the left, rotating in place as the attacker takes one or two more steps forward, until you are facing in the same direction as the attacker, keeping your arm and hand full of energy. . . . What has happened? You might say that the attack has been diffused or simply that you and your attacker are now lined up in the same direction. But the important point is that you are now seeing the situation from your attacker's viewpoint—*without losing your own*" (Leonard and Murphy 2005, 157; italics in original). The symbolic import of this turning movement (called *tenkan* in Japanese) is a recurrent theme in aikido literature because the maneuver makes visible the ideal of turning confrontation into cooperation, based on empathy and a shared perspective. As Dobson and Miller note in *Aikido in Everyday Life*, after executing *tenkan*, "both the attacker and the responder are facing in the same direction. It is at that point that the responder . . . begins to empathize, begins to walk around in the attacker's skin" (Dobson and Miller 1993, 91). And in *Meditation and the Martial Arts*, Michael Raposa explains that *tenkan* is "symbolically expressive, eloquently describing a new and potentially harmonious relationship between uke ["the defender"] and nage ["the attacker"]. At the moment of attack, they stood opposed to one another, each perceiving a world with a distinctive horizon, but in a sense blinded (at least in that moment) to what the other was able to see. Tenkan represents . . . a literal and symbolic turning away from confrontation with the other in order to experience what the other sees" (Raposa 2003, 23). In *Getting Past No*, William Ury links a *tenkan*-like movement to the tactic of disarming a hostile party during negotiations: "To disarm the other side, you need to do the opposite of what they expect. . . . So don't pressure; don't resist. Do the opposite: Step to their side. It disorients them and opens them up to changing their adversarial posture. Moreover, as practitioners of Japanese martial arts have long recognized, it is hard to attack someone who is suddenly on your side" (Ury 1993, 54).

5   The structure of a Rogerian argument has been described in various ways. In Young, Becker, and Pike's account, the argument has four phases: first, an "introduction to the problem and a demonstration that the opponent's position is understood"; next a "statement of the contexts in which the opponent's position may be valid"; third, a "statement of the writer's position, including the contexts in which it is valid"; and finally, a "statement of how the opponent's position would benefit if he were to adopt elements of the writer's position" (Young, Becker, and Pike 1970, 283). Coe notes that this list actually entails a six-part structure: "(1) an introduction that frames the subject as a problem, (2) a fair and accurate statement of the opposing position, (3) an assertion of the contexts in which that position may be valid, (4) a fair statement of the writer's position, (5) an assertion of the contexts in which the writer's position is valid, and (6) an ending that shows how readers would benefit from adopting at least some elements of the writer's position" (Coe 1992,

85). Maxine Hairston's five-step outline of a Rogerian argument is a bit different: "1. Give a brief, *objective* statement of the issue under discussion. 2. Summarize in impartial language what you perceive the case for the opposition to be . . . . 3. Make an objective statement of your own side of the issue, listing your concerns and interests, but avoiding loaded language or any hint of moral superiority. 4. Outline what common ground or mutual concerns you and the other person or group seem to share . . . . 5. Outline the solution you propose" (Hairston 1976, 375–76). Hairston's presentation is closest to the structure I outline for conciliatory argument.

6   There are, however, technical differences between the two arts. As William Gleason notes, "Throwing in aikido is different from judo. In aikido, you unify with your partner's intention and redirect his or her force to lead your partner off balance. Controlling is also different from other martial arts techniques such as shaolin kung fu (*chin na*) or jujutsu. Rather than controlling through pain or injury to the joints, aikido concentrates the mind in such a way that your partner receives the intensity of your power throughout his body (especially at his center of balance) more than at the place of contact" (Gleason 1994, 24).

7   Even in aikido, the determination to blend with an adversary's aggressive energy is not absolute. As George Leonard notes, this "isn't to say that we should always blend. In some cases, pushing back, standing your ground, and striking out forcefully is necessary or appropriate" (Leonard 1999, 22). In *The Argument Culture*, Tannen says that "sometimes passionate opposition, strong verbal attack, are appropriate and called for" (Tannen 1998, 7). James Crosswhite claims that the "good of universal agreement is just one good, and it must be measured and balanced by other conflicting goods. Sometimes the goods about which we disagree are more important to us than eventually reaching agreement with people who do not share our moral concerns" (Crosswhite 1996, 154).

8   My approach to the calligraphy exercise was informed by H. E. Davey's (1999) book, *Brush Meditation*.

9   There's a visualization exercise that illustrates the connection between the aikido movements and the *enso*. The instructions go like this: "Imagine you are standing on a large piece of white paper, holding a staff that is an oversized calligraphy brush with a long handle, like a mop or broom. Dip the brush in ink, place it on the paper, and execute the *tenkan* movements, keeping the staff-brush vertical and anchored in your center point. As you turn, the brush moves with you, forming a semicircle after the first turn (to stand alongside your adversary) and then completing the circle with the second 180-degree turn." The two turns inscribe an *enso*. For a demonstration of calligraphy with a mop-size brush, I recommend the Chinese film "Hero" (2004), starring Jet Li, a film that also depicts the deep connection between the brush and sword. I often showed the "calligraphy school" scene from this film in class.

10   In a frequently cited essay, Susan Jarratt (1991) has made a "case for conflict," especially for many women students, for whom proficiency in assertive argument offers a source of power. Jarratt points to the limitations of a nurturing, student-centered, expressivist curriculum because it fails to teach women how to engage in productive conflict. Although my approach to teaching argument is rhetorical, not expressivist, Jarratt's concerns are still relevant because it's possible that the open hand disempowers women, making them vulnerable to more adversarial tactics. By drawing on aikido, a nonadversarial but highly effective martial art, I try to show that it's possible to view the open hand as an alternative to both the closed fist and the palm of acquiescence, an alternative that doesn't leave the practitioner exposed or vulnerable, although the risk of seeing the reasonableness of the "other side's" position remains.

11   To repeat the point for clarity, this final step of disengagement and return to a face-to-face position involves an alteration of the traditional aikido movement, which would normally end with a throw and pin.

12   The irony is that Daoism is at odds with Confucianism, philosophically. Thanks to Greg Reihman, Adjunct Professor of Philosophy and Director of Faculty Development at Lehigh, for calling this story to my attention.

4

MEDIATING AND INTEGRATIVE ARGUMENT

Give peace a chance.
John Lennon (1940–1980)

In the third unit of the course, students explored ways to mediate disputes and integrate opposing viewpoints, encouraging adversaries to cooperate on the basis of shared interests or goals. Although the project introduced a new set of circumstances for arguing, it also incorporated skills and tactics familiar from our work on reframing and attentive listening. The main difference from previous assignments was that the writer would be intervening in a dispute between other people, acting as a third party to a disagreement.[1] To illustrate the act of mediating a dispute, I used my red cardboard arrows, positioning them in the familiar point-to-point relationship, facing one another along a linear axis. But this time a blue arrow entered on a right angle near the point of confrontation. The energy of this arrow moved the others out of the line of contact and, as the momentum shifted, all three proceeded along a new trajectory, blue in the middle and the red ones on either side. When I stopped the blue arrow, the other two continued ahead, as though they were trains on parallel tracks. From an initial position in which the arrows met head to head along a single track, pushing against one another, they ended up moving together along coordinated rather than competing paths. The demonstration provided a visual representation of integrative argument, especially the writer's role as a mediator in a dispute.

Integrative argument is similar to what Michael Gilbert calls "coalescent argumentation," a mode of argument that aims "to bring together or *coalesce* diverse positions" (Gilbert 1997, xv). I prefer the term *integrative*, in part because it occurs in some of the literature on conflict resolution I have found most useful. For example, in *When Push Comes to Shove: A Practical Guide for Meditating Disputes*, Karl Slaikeu talks about outcomes that offer "*integrative solutions* to problems, which means that the

DOI: 10.7330_9780874219203.c004

final action plan includes elements that honor the interests of each side" (Slaikeu 1995, 5). Sam Kaner, in *The Facilitator's Guide to Participatory Decision-Making*, discusses methods that "help people synthesize seemingly opposing alternatives into an *integrated* solution" (Kaner 2007, 241; italics added). And in *Toward Better Problems*, perhaps the book that has had the strongest impact on my thinking, Anthony Weston uses the term *integrative* to describe the effort to "weave conflicting and diverse values into a pattern or story . . . that gives us a way to relate them, to connect them, to try to make sense of them together, allowing them to differ without making the tension totally intractable" (Weston 1992, 30–31).

EXPLORING INTEGRATIVE APPROACHES

To give students a preview of what an integrative approach might involve, I asked them to read a newspaper editorial, "A Reconciliation on Gay Marriage" by David Blankenhorn and Jonathan Rauch (*New York Times*, February 22, 2009). The writers announce that they have "very different positions on gay marriage." Yet arguing over these positions has, they say, become unproductive, reaching a point at which further use of adversarial tactics is not going to be useful. To make progress, each side must consider what matters most to themselves and their opponents, agreeing about the core issues. Blankenhorn and Rauch identify the key positions in the following way. On one side, "Most gay and lesbian Americans feel they need and deserve the perquisites and protections that accompany legal marriage." On the other side, "Many Americans of faith and many religious organizations have strong objections to same-sex unions." So where can the argument go from there?

When we talked about the article in class, we focused on the authors' suggestions for how to bring people on the two sides of the issue together around an agreement. Their proposal is that Congress should "bestow the status of federal civil unions on same-sex marriages and civil unions granted at the state level, thereby conferring upon them most or all of the federal benefits and rights of marriage." But there would be a condition: the federal government would "recognize only those unions licensed in states with robust religious-conscience exceptions, which provide that religious organizations need not recognize same-sex unions against their will." There would also be "religious-conscience protections" at the federal level. Neither party gets everything they might want in this proposal, but each achieves important goals. Gay men and lesbians are typically opposed to the idea "that religious organizations could openly treat same-sex couples and opposite-sex couples differently," but in the authors' view "gays can live with such exemptions without much difficulty" because most state laws already include such exemptions and they have been "uncontroversial, even among gays." On the other side, Americans who favor conventional models of marriage "prefer no legal recognition of same-sex unions at either the federal or state level," but the authors believe those Americans "can live with federal unions" as long as religious groups aren't forced to accept them. These opponents may, the authors suggest, come to view civil unions for gay men and lesbians as "a compassionate compromise."

In the concluding paragraphs, the authors appeal for cooperation, noting what stands to be lost if participants continue to pursue the "take-no-prisoners" or "scorched earth" approach of adversarial argument. As they say, in "sharp moral disagreements, maximalism is the constant temptation. People dig in, positions harden and we tend to convince ourselves that our opponents are not only wrong-headed but also malicious and acting in bad faith." The authors believe they have proposed a strategy that will "give each side what it most needs in the short run, while moving the debate onto a healthier, calmer track in the years ahead." Their final appeal is that "when a reasonable accommodation on a tough issue seems possible, both sides should have the courage to explore it."

I began with an editorial that incorporates a number of integrative tactics, even though it is not the single-authored argument that students would be asked to write as a final project for the unit. What "A Reconciliation on Gay Marriage" illustrates well, however, is an important strategy for integrating opposing points of views: proposing a policy that is not quite what either side wants, maximally, but represents what they can "live with," the best they can get—a better alternative, the authors argue, than either giving in to the other side or continuing a debate that has reached a dead end. To consider another example of an integrative approach, students read "The Right to Agree" by Cristina Page and Amanda Peterman, which also appeared in the Op-Ed pages of the *New York Times* (January 22, 2003). This editorial was published on the thirtieth anniversary of Roe v. Wade, and the authors say that like "many of our peers, we, too, are divided: We are activists on opposite sides of the abortion issue." Thus, like the authors of the first editorial, "A Reconciliation on Gay Marriage," Page and Peterman represent committed, but opposing, stances on a divisive social issue. And like the writers of the first editorial, Page and Peterman believe that persisting in adversarial argument is not going to prove productive: "The slogans are old, the battle is tired." Instead of engaging in the old debates, the authors believe they "have a fresh understanding of how to achieve real progress."

But Page and Peterman use a different integrative strategy than the one deployed by Blankenhorn and Rauch, which was based on a "best we can achieve" argument. The tactic illustrated in "The Right to Agree" involves making an end run around the stuck points in the abortion debate by focusing not on the authors' differences but on the "surprising number of important issues on which we agree." Two examples are fundamental agreement about "health insurance coverage for the most effective contraceptive methods" and efforts to make "the workplace more accommodating to the demands of parenthood." Despite such common goals, opportunities for cooperation are "lost in the larger debate." Because women have been divided by their commitments to either pro-life or pro-choice positions, they have missed opportunities to work together on projects of mutual interest—to oppose, for example, the Florida Adoption Act, a law that "is an attack on women and discourages adoption. Collaboration by the two sides of the abortion movement could have benefited all women in Florida," they claim.

Page and Peterman propose that women can—and should—retain their commitments without compromise, accepting the "fundamental disagreements we hold on abortion," but that this need not prevent solidarity and integrative thinking about other issues related to pregnancy and child care. Cooperation is possible, but it means giving up extremism and the "inflammatory terms that serve only to divide us further and create conflict." Around the edges of disagreement, there is a "path to escape this endless cycle of division. We hope," the authors conclude, "the next generation of activists will join us in seeking areas of common ground and merge the power of both movements to serve Americans in a meaningful way."

Although their approaches are different, both sets of authors demonstrate that the strategy of optimizing (considering what is good for both parties) is better than maximizing (seeking everything you want without concession). Blankenhorn and Rauch optimize by finding a compromise that both can live with and therefore cooperate to enact, rather than fighting for everything each wants; Page and Peterman optimize by locating issues that allow for agreement, bracketing unresolvable disagreements so that the fighting doesn't destroy opportunities for cooperation. Nevertheless, this kind of effort is rare, I suggested, because most people who are involved in divisive disputes see no alternative to the familiar strategies of attack and defense, striving to maximize advantage even if they aren't getting anywhere. This is as true of interpersonal disputes as it is of both professional conflicts and public controversies. Because disagreements can be difficult to resolve, there is a role for individuals who are able to intervene in disputes—as arbitrators, negotiators, or mediators. I focused on the work of mediators, individuals who specialize in helping disputants resolve their conflicts in ways consistent with their needs, values, and goals.

For the first several weeks of the unit, students read short articles about conflict resolution and discussed various strategies for mediating disputes. They also examined essays, both professional and student written, that exemplified some of the tactics of integrative argument we were studying.[2] Outside the classroom, they were continuing to keep an eye on patterns of argument around them and to reflect on their own ways of engaging in conflicts with others. In several cases, students reported on their efforts to act as mediators of disagreements, usually between friends or acquaintances. For example, one student noted that she "had a chance to use my mediating skills from class" when a confrontation among friends became heated: "I decided to intervene and dispel some of the tension. I entered the fray with a neutral stance and decided to go with an integrative tactic." Another told the story of a disagreement among students in her residence hall: "After a while of their arguing and not making any progress, I decided to intervene. I got to play the mediator role and try out some of the stuff we've learned in our readings. It's amazing what an unbiased third party can do to an argument." Yet another told the following story:

> Two of my friends got in a fight over the weekend, and the conflict continued to escalate. It got to the point where they stopped speaking and insisted that their friendship was officially over. At that moment, I knew I could help. I was able to recognize that each of the girls had made all the wrong moves—everything they said and did was adversarial, typical of those trapped inside the argument culture. Once I recognized the adversarial situation I applied some of the techniques that we are using to write our papers.

Strategies for mediating disputes were at the center of our work during the initial weeks of the unit. Although I will return to those early lessons, I want to skip ahead to the end of the second week, to an exercise that took place in a lab session, because it put our work on conciliatory argument in a broader framework. For this activity, I asked students to read a story from a compilation of koans, puzzling stories designed to challenge and disrupt discursive thought. Traditionally, Zen Buddhist practitioners are given koans for purposes of contemplation over an extended period of time because they provide opportunities for reflection and realization. Although realization was clearly not my goal in Arguing as an Art of Peace, I did call attention to the idea that not all thought is linear or logical. At the end of the unit, we would return to the koan, drawing some additional lessons about the uses of unconventional and creative approaches when intervening in disputes.

NANSEN CUTS A CAT

The koan that I used for the exercise is "Nansen Cuts a Cat." It appears in several collections in slightly different form each time. I used the version in Gerry Wick's (2005) edition of *The Book of Equanimity*, a collection of koans compiled by the Chinese Master Wanshi Shokaku in the twelfth century. To simplify the exercise, I selected only the main case, where the story is presented for consideration.

> At Nansen's place one day the monks of the east and west halls were arguing about a cat. Seeing this, Nansen held it up before him saying, "If you can say a word, I won't cut it." The assembly made no response. Nansen cut the cat in two. Nansen later told Joshu what happened. Joshu took off his straw sandals and, placing them on his head, went out. Nansen remarked, "If you had been here, you could have saved the cat." (Wick 2005, 31)

I handed out copies of the koan and read it aloud to the students. Next I asked them to think about what significance the story might have in the context of our class, giving them a few minutes to write down what occurred to them. Then I invited discussion.

Students quickly pointed out that this story is about arguing. Although the substance of the dispute over the cat is a matter of conjecture, it's clear that this animal is a desirable object and that the monks from both halls want to claim it. It's also the case that the monks are divided by affiliation into two halls, east and west. As one student pointed out:

> The monks in the two halls should have been unified, but because they identified with east and west halls they got into a dispute and couldn't reach an agreement. These kinds of affiliations can keep people apart, even when they should be on common ground.

Or as another wrote, using terminology from previous discussions, "This type of argument is position based." In other words, the substance of the disagreement has been subsumed by a conflict between two sides. As another student wrote, "The monks are so busy arguing that they don't even care about the cat any more and have lost the focus of the argument."

Because he steps in to help resolve the conflict, Nansen is, students said, a mediator figure. Taking charge of the situation, he challenges the monks to "say a word" in order to spare the cat from being cut in two. This is an unusual intervention, but students interpreted it as something like an attempt to reframe the argument—creating the problem of how to save the cat in order to move away from a disagreement about which hall it belongs to or which side has won the dispute. This effort fails, however, because no one can "say a word." Students weren't certain why this was the case because the monks had just been engaged in verbal argument, but several conjectured that the words the monks had been saying were part of the problem, distracting them from finding the right word, at the right time, to save the cat. One put it this way: "There were a lot of words being said, but none of them could say 'a' word, the right word at the right moment, because they were lost in words." Consequently, Nansen cuts the cat in two. This seems like a fair resolution, according to the logic of equal division of disputed property. As one student said, "If the argument is about which hall the cat belongs to, then the fair solution is to divide the cat between the two groups, like dividing a pie into equal shares. The assembly is mute because they are trapped in either-or thinking, either one side has the cat or the other does."

The phrase about cutting "in two" struck students as significant, perhaps because for a previous class they had read a story about another dispute, this one over an orange. The story is that two cooks were arguing about who got to use the one orange in the kitchen since both said they needed it for a dish they were preparing. To settle the dispute, another chef took the orange, chopped it in two, and gave each cook a half, settling the argument "fairly." But it turns out that one cook needed the juice of one orange while the other wanted only the rind, so both could have had everything they wanted rather than just half of what they needed if the dispute had been handled differently. Cutting in two may seem like a fair solution, but it sometimes fails to optimize the outcome—only half an orange . . . or a dead cat.

After the incident, Nansen tells the story of the argument to Joshu, and his response is the most puzzling event in the tale. Instead of replying, Joshu puts his straw sandals on his head and leaves. Joshu's actions, as the students saw them, involved "a reversal of expectations" (putting shoes on one's head), a comment on the "absurdity of the situation," and a response that was "outside the box." Sometimes it takes this kind of action to break open a conflict and show participants what is at stake. While Nansen also used shock tactics to reframe the argument, his approach was nonetheless conventional, relying on the binary logic of division. Because Joshu isn't limited by conventional thinking, he is the person, Nansen realizes, who could have saved the cat.

I've begun with this exercise because it foregrounds one of the central challenges of mediation and integrative argument: how to find creative ways to lead opponents from conflict to cooperation, especially when they see themselves as adversaries fighting for victory or a larger share of the pie. The literature on conflict resolution offers many promising tactics, and students would explore their uses and apply them when arguing about controversial issues. But Joshu—the one who could think differently—was on the horizon, ready to remind us that more might be needed than those conventional techniques offered.

IDENTIFYING SHARED INTERESTS

During the first weeks of the unit, students considered a variety of approaches to conflict resolution, reading and discussing a series of articles and examples. One of the central ideas in these early readings was the contrast between position-based arguments and interest-based negotiations. The primary source for our exploration of interest-based negotiation was the chapter "Focus on Interests, Not Positions" from *Getting to Yes*, the now-classic book (first published in 1981) by three authors associated with the Harvard Negotiation Project.[3] Roger Fisher, William Ury, and Bruce Patton say that although disagreements may appear to be based on differences between two parties' positions, in many cases the conflict (as well as its resolution) lies at a deeper level, in the "needs, desires, concerns, and fears" (Fisher, Ury, and Patton 2011, 42) each side experiences. One way a mediator can work productively on disagreements, therefore, is to first identify the interests of the disputing parties, bypassing their opposing positions. This works for two reasons, the authors claim. First, for any interest there are likely to be several positions that could satisfy it, so there may be more options to put on the table than the demands that have dominated the argument. Second—and this is the point I emphasized—"behind opposed positions lie shared and compatible interests, as well as conflicting ones" (44).

This idea of shared as well as conflicting interests provides a starting point for integrative argument, encouraging a mediator to look beyond the positions that have shaped the argument and led to an impasse, delving into unexpressed or tacit interests, values, needs, and goals. The work of uncovering interests involves both investigation and sympathetic identification with each party's concerns. Ury, Fisher, and Patton recommend putting yourself in the shoes of the adversaries, asking why they are taking certain positions and what prevents them from agree-ing with the opposing side. The next step is to examine the underlying interests you have excavated, sorting the results into those that seem to be in genuine conflict, those that do not conflict but merely differ, and those that are shared, compatible, or complementary. The authors claim that in most cases there will be "many more interests that are shared or compatible than ones that are opposed" (Fisher, Ury, and Patton 2011, 44). This is good news for writers who hope to engage in integrative argument.

In the editorial on the abortion debate by Page and Peterman, stu-dents had seen an example of how authors could focus on shared inter-ests and concerns (the welfare of women and children) rather than remaining fixated on their positions on the issue (pro-choice vs. pro-life). Although Page and Peterman were able to identify shared inter-ests without outside assistance, writing about their points of agreement, I wanted students to consider how to proceed when the opponents in a debate were not able to find any common ground. I assigned some addi-tional editorials, asking students to identify the places in the argument where a focus on interests (rather than positions) had contributed to mediating a disagreement.

We began with an editorial on terminal sedation (*Washington Post*, October 10, 2000). The author, Abigail Trafford, argues that this pro-cedure appeals to people with different positions in the debate over physician-assisted suicide since both are deeply concerned about doing the right thing for the dying. As she summarizes, the option "works for those who oppose euthanasia but want to ease the suffering of their dying patients. It works for those who believe that helping people die is a part of providing quality and compassionate care." Therefore, termi-nal sedation is "emerging as a middle ground in the debate over end-of-life care." In another example, Tom Kerr (*Morning Call*, November 16, 2000) recognizes that opposing positions pit property owners against critics of uncontrolled growth or sprawl. Claiming that everyone in the community values "clean air, clean water, and the open space for which the beautiful Lehigh Valley is so widely known," Kerr proposes a new model of "smart growth" because its goal is "not to stop growth. It's to discover how to grow in ways that include clean air and water, as well as open space for agricultural and recreational uses." In yet another exam-ple, "Getting to Yes on the Wolf" (*Sports Afield*, July 1989, at the height of the controversy), outdoor writer Ted Kerasote identifies broadly shared concerns about "wildness" and "environmental health" among advo-cates on both sides of the issue—both those who support and those who reject plans for reintroducing wolves in the West—providing a basis for policies that integrate opposing positions.

As I mentioned earlier, students were using these integrative tactics to intervene in disputes among their friends, finding opportunities to play the role of mediators. Housing decisions often generated emotional arguments, and several students found themselves stepping into the middle of them. As one noted, "This has been one of the most heated weeks with my college friends. Housing is right around the corner." She went on to describe the role she played in a dispute among those friends.

> Being a third party, they recruited me and vented all their frustrations. The funny thing was that they didn't realize they all had the same concerns. I sat them all down and they started screaming at each other, accusing others of trying to push them out of rooming and how it wasn't fair to be the odd person out. Then I remembered this class and became the mediator. I tried to see it from all perspectives, talking it out and using phrases like "I understand" or "I sympathize" and then, together, we all came up with ideas on how to solve the rooming issue without leaving anyone behind. We were successful in the end. Could we have done it without the yelling? Not really—we're girls and we are a little irrational when it comes to our friends "betraying" us; however, by refusing to see alternative perspectives, we were hurting each other. As the mediator, I had to work with the common ground they had discussed.

Another student wrote about how she "didn't even have to think twice about applying tactics from class" when she intervened in a fight between friends: "I just naturally thought that way, which was really interesting to me because I came into the class at the completely opposite end of the continuum."

Whether intervening with friends or drafting their papers, students found that appealing to shared goals or common values offered a basis for cooperation, even on divisive issues. In a paper on the death penalty, for example, a student wrote that while "there is no solution to this debate that will leave either side completely satisfied, many people overlook the fact that proponents and opponents of capital punishment share the same underlying values and concerns. They are both ultimately concerned with justice." In a paper on euthanasia, a student noted the fact that "those who support and those who oppose euthanasia embed their opinions in a foundation of compassion for terminally ill patients. Everyone agrees that these patients deserve to die with dignity in a comfortable and safe place. Both groups defend their positions with claims rooted in an ideal of respect for human life." In an essay on the controversial issue of legalizing prostitution, a student wrote that one of the "most important interests of both sides is protecting women against violence." Although this kind of appeal to shared values was rarely sufficient for an integrative argument, it provided a starting point and taught students how to shift their focus from positions to underlying interests. The process opened students' eyes to the fact that beneath people's claims and arguments lay deeper constellations of values and commitments, some at the root of the dispute, some that were shared.

INVENTING OPTIONS FOR MUTUAL GAIN

The first strategy we discussed for integrative argument was to identify shared interests, goals, or values, appealing to common ground as a basis for cooperation. However, there is a second strategy that students found quite useful for making integrative arguments: inventing options for mutual gain. In *Getting to Yes*, Fisher, Ury, and Patton tell the story of the cooks' struggle over the one orange, a case that illustrates a missed opportunity for cooperation and mutual gain. The authors of *Getting to Yes* say that "too many negotiations end up with half an orange for each side instead of the whole fruit for one and the whole peel for the other. Why?" (Fisher, Ury, and Patton 2011, 59). The short answer is that people are often trapped within an either/or, win/lose, all-or-nothing orientation to conflict. The solution is to shift to a different mindset, one that considers both/and, win/win, mutually advantageous options.

To explore how this different mindset works, students read "Beyond the Politics of Blame," an essay in which Jan Beyea urges members of the electrical power industry to cooperate with environmentalists, and vice versa (Beyea was associated with the National Audubon Society). At the outset, Beyea rejects the either/or mindset: "There are those who believe we will ultimately have to choose between economic progress and environmental protection. Unfortunately, that's the sort of adversarial stance—environmentalists on one side, industrialists on the other—that has led to stalemate in the past, to the politics of blame and finger pointing" (Beyea 1993, 14). Instead, he calls for a both/and approach, or what he calls a "politics of vision: a way of setting forth our shared vision of the future and the steps to get there. It's a process that will require more dialogue than argumentation, and it will call for changes not only from industry but from environmentalists as well. However, I'm convinced that at this stage in our history, it's the only way we can achieve both environmental health and economic progress" (14).

Beyea contrasts the "path of resistance" with the "path of cooperation." The second path relies on "a process called negotiated conflict

resolution," a process that involves "getting both sides to sit down together and talk about their real needs and goals, not just their political positions" (Beyea 1993, 16). Beyea admits that this is a new approach, for himself as well as others. He says that a few years earlier, when talking with representatives of the electric utility industry, he "would have been listening intensely for one reason alone: to discover weaknesses in my opponent's arguments so that when it was my turn at the podium, I could demolish the other side's case. . . . Now . . . I listen for another purpose: to see if I can discover common ground" (16). The process of negotiated conflict resolution creates solutions that "give both parties 80% to 90% of what they both need. Not everything, to be sure. But far more, for everyone concerned, than they would achieve by batting their heads against a wall" (16). Beyea's article illustrates the promise of the core strategies recommended in *Getting to Yes*, especially the search for options that provide mutual gain for the parties in conflict.

MAKING INTEGRATIVE ARGUMENTS

The entries in students' notebooks revealed that they were becoming aware of both the possibilities and the challenges of integrative argument. One said he appreciated the integrative approach but added, "I think it may be kind of difficult to master. How does one go about finding ways to get adversaries to agree that they share some common ground or that they can work alongside one another to improve a serious problem?" Another wondered how she would be able distance herself enough from her own views to play the role of a mediator, because "staying unbiased seems nearly impossible."

Despite challenges, most students were able to make integrative arguments on the basis of shared interests and/or mutual gain, moving adversaries in the direction of agreement and cooperation. In their papers, students often talked about points of agreement or shared concern as a basis for mediating differences of view, as in the following example:

> Both those who support and those who oppose euthanasia embed their opinions in a foundation of compassion for terminally ill patients. Everyone agrees that these patients deserve to die with dignity in a comfortable and safe place. Both groups defend their positions with claims rooted in an ideal of respect for human life; they merely differ in ways to go about showing that respect.

Students also made arguments for mutual gain, usually in conjunction with common interests. The writer of a paper about the controversy over standardized testing for college admission identified "fairness" as a value shared by both sides and a common ground on which they could cooperate: "The ultimate goal is to find the most fair college process possible, but this cannot be achieved without cooperation from both sides. . . . As long as both groups see that they share the same goal of achieving fairness, they will become more willing to work together, reaching an optimal resolution." In a paper about the competition between freight and passenger railroads (e.g., for track capacity), the writer noted that a "more unified effort by Amtrak and the freight lines could significantly enhance the fortunes of both and strengthen the whole industry. They both essentially want the same things."

It was important for students to have reasonable expectations about what could be achieved as they wrote their integrative arguments; for that reason, I emphasized the importance of realistic goals. After all, many students had decided to write about long-standing, seemingly intractable disagreements. If they thought their objective was to settle these disputes definitively, they were likely to either become discouraged or claim too much for their efforts. Building on advice in *Getting to Yes*, I urged students to consider agreements of different strengths, such as agreements on procedure, agreements that are provisional or partial, and second-order agreements (agreeing about where you disagree). As Jan Beyea notes, in negotiated conflict resolution "you don't have to agree on everything; you can formally agree to disagree on divisive issues and still cooperate on issues of mutual interest" (Beyea 1993, 17). When they wrote their papers, many students took this advice to heart, proposing next steps in an ongoing process, laying the foundation for resolution, or suggesting the best option available at the present time. For example, in a paper about the complex, seemingly intractable dispute between Israelis and Palestinians, a student proposed that the two sides could take "small steps towards cooperation by first focusing their attention on the effects that the conflict has on their children and working together to foster a positive and peaceful environment in which to raise future leaders of Israel and Palestine. By working together on an issue in which both groups hold a common interest, Israel and Palestine can lay a foundation of cooperation and compromise that can be built upon as they continue together on the long road to a comprehensive, just, and lasting peace in the Middle East."

A MOVEMENT SEQUENCE FOR INTEGRATIVE ARGUMENT

At the same time they were familiarizing themselves with concepts of mediation and strategies for resolving disputes, students were also exploring these topics through movement exercises designed to add an element of kinesthetic learning to their experience. As in previous units, I used the lab session to teach students a movement sequence based on principles of aikido and the interdependence of yin and yang. The activity I developed for integrative argument involves three participants, two in the role of adversaries and a third playing the role of intervener (or mediator). At the beginning of the exercise, two students begin walking toward one another on a direct line, heading for a collision. But when they get close to encountering one another, a third person (an intervener) steps between them, entering on a ninety-degree angle. The intervener's next move is to receive the energy the two opponents are projecting toward one another, absorbing that hostile energy and turning the antagonists in a new direction, along the intervener's vector, orthogonal to the original line of confrontation. After the turn, all three are facing the same direction and moving along a common trajectory. When the three first come into contract, the intervener grasps the others' arms (outstretched in the exercise, one left and one right, as if reaching for one another), bringing their hands (and their aggressive energy) to his or her center in order to move them through the turn. As in other aikido-based movements, the key is to blend with the opposing forces (yin) so the energy of the turn comes from their momentum, rather than forcing the turn by using imposed, muscular force (excessive yang).[4] Next, the intervener links arms with the opponents, embracing them so they are walking together along a different path than the one that brought them to the brink of face-to-face conflict. After several steps, the intervener releases the opponents, guiding them forward to take the next steps on their own (see appendix 1 for an illustration of this movement sequence). Whenever possible, I took the class outside, to a patio area next to the classroom building, so there would be space to do a full version of the exercise.

   This sequence incorporates a number of physical movements students had practiced previously, such as entering a conflict to move it in a new direction, away from the line of confrontation. The concept of absorbing and blending with others' energy was a familiar concept too because students had encountered it from the beginning of the course when doing two-person tai chi as well as aikido-based exercises. The most challenging part of the mediation sequence is to turn the antagonists in a new direction because it must be assertive without becoming aggressive; however, this, too, was a familiar concept because it had occupied our attention when practicing the turning movements associated with conciliatory argument. Because of these familiar elements, it was not difficult to teach students a new sequence near the end of the semester, one that differed mainly in the number of participants involved.

STEPS IN AN INTEGRATIVE ARGUMENT

As in the preceding units, I broke the physical exercise into a series of moves, associating each with a step in an integrative argument: entering, absorbing, turning, leading, and releasing. In the following description, I'll use the term *intervener* when talking about the physical movement and the terms *writer* or *mediator* for the verbal analogue.

In the *entering* phase, the intervener moves into the zone of conflict between the adversaries and makes contact with them. The analogous step for a writer is to introduce the controversy, acknowledging major points of contention and explaining why this is an argument worth mediating. The entry is soft, using the open hand of contact: the intervener receives the adversaries, *absorbing* their energy in order to redirect it. Similarly, the writer-mediator must demonstrate that he or she has taken in the beliefs and goals of the two sides, and this means producing an accurate, sympathetic summary of their arguments. (Students had written these kinds of summaries for their conciliatory argument papers.) The mediator attempts to earn the trust of both sides by showing that he or she has listened to their arguments and understood them. In steps one and two, yin is the dominant response since the mediator strives to yield in order to embrace the contrary views.

Next comes the step of *turning* the adversaries from a position that entails a collision course to one where they are facing in the same direction with the intervener in between, a movement that—like other turning movements we had practiced—involves more yang. In the case of the physical activity, as the intervener steps forward, he or she turns the opponents by redirecting their line of movement. In the written version, the power of the turn comes from the writer's ability to identify common interests and/or options for mutual gain. This move may involve an element of surprise since adversaries often believe they share little or nothing with people on the other side. The key to successful mediation, of course, is not to impose the turn by force but rather to harness the energy of yang in harmony with yin in a turn that feels like leading or guiding—the same kind of move students had used when reframing a controversial issue (in a deliberative argument) and the kind of turn they had employed when leading the reader around to consider the writer's position (in a conciliatory one). For example, in a paper about legalizing marijuana, the writer turned the argument by calling attention to the issue of medical (rather than recreational) uses of marijuana: "Caught between these two sides, a group of people in distress calls for help. These individuals, who come from both sides of the conflict, are people forced to endure serious conditions that could be treated effectively with medical marijuana." And in a paper about the death penalty, a student made the turn this way: "While we are not—and may never be—in agreement on whether or not the death penalty should exists, it does exist and there are problems with the way it is being implemented at present. We can find common ground in these issues."

Once turned, forward movement is necessary, and in the physical sequence this occurs because the intervener has embraced the arms of the two adversaries, *leading* them with him or her. In the written analogue, the mediator develops his or her claims about coalescent interests or mutual gain, providing details that keep the forward momentum going. For example, in a paper about euthanasia, the writer claimed that nearly everyone, regardless of their stance on the issue of legality, hopes that few people get to a place at which they see no alternative to suicide. She developed this point by examining the reasons people seek to be euthanized, identifying fears about suffering and the quality of life in the future. This led to an analysis of palliative care and to her argument that while "the two sides will continue to debate the right to die, they can agree on the importance of palliative and hospice care."

After a few steps together, the adversaries have stopped fighting and are walking side by side. As soon as feasible, the intervener *releases* their arms and lets them go, nudging them to continue in the direction they're heading. Fighting might break out again, of course, but perhaps it won't once the crisis of confrontation has passed, once adversaries are encouraged to "give peace a chance." Similarly, the writer concludes by urging ongoing communication as both sides continue to explore options for cooperation even though they continue to disagree about some important issues. As the writer of the paper on euthanasia said, "By putting aside their differences, proponents and opponents of euthanasia can work together" on ways to reduce the need for euthanasia, while they continue to debate issues of legality. The writer of the paper on legalizing marijuana said that while "all disputes would certainly not be settled, the cooperation of both sides to enact a strict medical marijuana policy would lay the foundations of resolution." In a paper on school violence, the writer called for a unified approach.

> It is time to put aside divisive arguments about which approach to the problem of school violence is better so that we can be united in our efforts to address a problem that everyone agrees is tragic and terrifying. We need to draw on the best, most workable proposals, stressing education,

enhanced student-adult communications, and increased vigilance in identifying potential threats. By integrating these strategies with appropriate
security measures, we can create a unified, comprehensive, and hopefully
effective plan of action for reducing violence in America's schools.

The most challenging cases to meditate are those involving topics
associated with polarized social debates; in such cases, it is can be difficult to identify shared interests or to discover options for mutual gain—
difficult, but not impossible. To demonstrate how mediation might function in tough cases, I asked students to read, in preparation for a class
discussion, a series of short editorials about one of the most polarized
social issues in American society: abortion. That topic served as a kind
of test case for the possibilities—and difficulties—of mediation and integrative argument.

A TOUGH CASE FOR INTEGRATIVE ARGUMENT:
THE ABORTION CONTROVERSY

The editorials about abortion represent three different ways to approach
integrative argument. The first involves identifying common ground in
or around the topic, locating issues on which adversaries can cooperate—despite fundamental differences. Early in the unit, students
had discussed "The Right to Agree," an editorial in which Page and
Peterman—women with opposing positions on abortion—identified
issues of common concern, such as policies on contraception and
child care. Now students considered two additional examples. One, a
short editorial entitled "How Pro-Life, Pro-Choice Can Work Together"
(*Morning Call,* January 30, 2001), highlights efforts by state congressmen
to "see if pro-life and pro-choice advocates can find common ground"
on the issue of abortion. The common ground they identify is a shared
desire to reduce the number of abortions as well as agreement on one
approach to this goal: reducing unwanted pregnancies in teenagers.
"On this," the editorial notes, "both sides agree: The longer teens wait
before becoming sexually active, the better the odds they will avoid AIDS
and prevent pregnancy." Students read another example of the com-
mon-ground approach in a syndicated column by William Raspberry,
"Abortion Foes Can Agree on One Solution" (*Tampa Tribune*, September
16, 1995). In this piece, Raspberry reports that adoption provides the
common ground on which political opponents can begin to cooperate.

The next example illustrates what might be called a *middle-ground*
approach. In "Safe, Legal & Early—a New Way of Thinking About
Abortion" (*Beliefnet*, April 27, 2009), Steven Waldman begins by noting

that many Americans are conflicted about abortion; surveys show that most "think abortion is taking a human life and yet favor the procedure being legal." This conflicted attitude provides the key, Waldman believes, to finding a middle way between extremes: between the pro-life view that "a life is a life, no matter how small" and the pro-choice view that a "woman has a right to choose, whether the pregnancy is in its first day, first month, or ninth month." The alternative, Waldman suggests, is to focus on timing, leading to funding that is "generous for first trimester abortions, minimal for second trimesters, and non-existent for the third." Waldman speculates that his proposal would drain "some of the toxins" from the debate, leading to a situation in which "a few activists might even accept the legitimacy of part of their opponents' argument."

The final article represents another approach, one perhaps best described as *principled ambivalence*—an expression, perhaps, of the conflicted attitudes Waldman says are widespread. In an opinion essay in *Newsweek* (March 25, 1985), Rachel Richardson Smith opens by saying, "I cannot bring myself to say I am in favor of abortion. I don't want anyone to have one." Yet in the next paragraph she writes, "[I] cannot bring myself to say I am against choice." Smith claims to be "uncomfortable in either camp," and she concludes with a series of questions, rather than assertions: "Why can we not view abortion as one of those anguished decisions in which human beings struggle to do the best they can in trying circumstances? Why is abortion viewed so coldly and factually on the one hand and so judgmentally on the other? Why is it not akin to the same painful experience families must sometimes make to allow a loved one to die?" Smith's essay represents a special form of integrative thinking, one in which elements of opposite views are merged in a position that embraces contradictions and accepts tensions, letting them stand rather than trying to resolve them.[5]

These essays demonstrate that even on the polarizing issue of abortion, it's possible to find alternatives to arguing with the fist of contention. Nevertheless, students worried—understandably—that they would not be able to integrate opposing views, especially if they were writing about contentious social issues. I urged them to give mediation their best effort, even in difficult cases, relying on investigation and wide reading as well as searching for precedents, analogies, overlooked strategies, emerging ideas, and so forth. I also encouraged students to consider what speculative and imaginative thinking might contribute to the process of discovering fresh options.

JOSHU AND THE IMAGINATIVE RESPONSE

At this point we revisited the koan in which Nansen cuts the cat in two. Nansen intervenes quite dramatically in the dispute, holding up the cat and then offering to spare it if anyone can "say a word." His actions interrupt an unproductive and contentious argument, opening a space into which he invites a new kind of discourse. His threat is shocking—the kind of surprise tactic that can sometimes break open a dispute. He takes a risk. Nevertheless, his efforts fail to produce a good resolution because when no one says anything, he is apparently left with no option other than to do what he has threatened.[6] It appears that Nansen did not intend to cut the cat in two, that he deployed the threat as a way to reframe the argument among the monks. Yet in the end everyone loses, so the intervention is quite disappointing from a mediator's perspective. One reason, I've suggested, is that at the heart of Nansen's dramatic gesture lies a conventional method of resolving disagreements, which is to split the difference.

The koan includes a coda in which Nansen tells the story of the argument over the cat to Joshu, who responds by removing his sandals, placing them on his head, and walking out, actions that lead Nansen to remark that Joshu could have saved the cat had he been present. Students saw Joshu's actions as a departure from convention, an inversion of norms and expectations—shoes on his head rather than where they belong—so that he is the one who demonstrates the capacity to respond imaginatively. Whether or not that interpretation is valid, I tried to build on the idea that Joshu had demonstrated a capacity to think outside the box, to move laterally, to bypass the limitations of conventional resolution (splitting the difference). I urged students to consider creative options as they searched for ways to integrate opposing positions, even if this was quite challenging work. As one student wrote in her notebook:

> It's challenging to invent options because it's much easier to default to familiar ones: I have come to realize that most of us, when faced with a conflict, are so used to *not* inventing options—rarely are we able to take a step back during a conflict to ask ourselves how we can invent a solution. We overlook the need to think up creative solutions. Why is it so hard to expand our thinking in order to invent new options and think of creative solutions?

To explore further how the creative process might be involved in mediating disputes, students read some excerpts from *The Moral Imagination: The Art and Soul of Building Peace* by John Paul Lederach, an experienced negotiator and expert in conflict resolution. Lederach asks how cycles of violence can be transcended. The answer, he believes, is to "explore the creative process itself, not as a tangential inquiry, but as the wellspring that feeds the building of peace" (Lederach 2005, 5). In the chapter "On Aesthetics: The Art of Social Change," Lederach explains how he learned to rely on poetry writing as a "pathway to peacebuild- ing" (66). Lederach doesn't write poetry for dissemination; he writes to develop his powers of attention and imagination. As he says, "The process of paying attention to poetry, listening to a voice that seems to come from nowhere in the midst of turbulent inner seas, is very much like sorting through the storms of protracted conflicts" (66).

HAIKU MIND

Lederach focuses on haiku, a compressed poetic form that captures the extraordinary quality of ordinary moments of experience. What inter- ests him most is the "haiku moment," which occurs when something "resonates deeply. It connects" (Lederach 2005, 68). It is the experience of the "ah-ha moment," a point when insight occurs—not from analysis but from intuition. As we began our discussion of Lederach's ideas, we talked a little about the form and purpose of haiku, reading a couple of examples of these compressed poems. Then I encouraged students to go outside for a brief walk, looking for something that might be the sub- ject for a short poem. When they returned, I asked them to take a few minutes to write one or two haiku about something they had seen. After the class, a number of them wrote about the activity in their notebooks, reflecting on the way it fostered mindfulness. One noted that "think- ing about writing a haiku helped me to concentrate more on each indi- vidual thing going on around me. Normally, I would just see something pretty or interesting and acknowledge it but then move on. Because I was thinking about things to say about each object, I stayed focused for longer." And another provided an account of the experience along with a short poem about making the notebook entry.

> We went outside and found one element of life to analyze and enjoy fully. Because we looked at it from every angle, it had more meaning. I remem- ber writing haikus in middle school and thinking that it was pointless. However, now that I know the real meaning and purpose of the haiku, I think I will continue to write them:
>
> > Paper. Soft beneath my fingers
> > White and clean you sit there ready
> > to listen to my pen.

But I also wanted students to consider Lederach's claim that "haiku mind" could be a source of fresh ideas for resolving conflicts. The following notebook entry captures this idea well:

> *The Moral Imagination* described haiku in a way that really resonated with me; I was very interested in the way haiku is meant to capture the essence of a complex, multi-dimensional moment in a few words. Given such a small sample of words, it is interesting to see how every minute detail contributes to a deeper meaning that can sometimes only be felt rather than described. By narrowing down a conflict to only a few words, one is almost forced to focus on the situation on a deeper level, far below the superficial clash of positions.

I presented Lederach's account of intuitive insight as an alternative to the more intellectually oriented, analytical strategies most students relied on to gather information for their arguments, presenting the two modes as different but complementary avenues of inquiry and understanding.[7] Lederach claims that "knowing and understanding conflict does not take place exclusively, nor perhaps primarily, through processes of cognitive analysis, the breaking down of complexity into manageable pieces. Knowledge and, perhaps more important, understanding and deep insight are achieved through aesthetics and ways of knowing that see the whole rather than the parts, a capacity and pathway that rely on intuition more than cognition" (Lederach 2005, 69). My students tended to be comfortable with the analytical approaches they had learned from previous schooling; the challenge, for them, was to appreciate the fruits of silence, the contributions of intuition, the relevance of aesthetic knowing. In this respect, they needed to open their hands (and minds) to new ways of knowing.

As Uchiyama says in *Opening the Hand of Thought*, "Thinking means to be grasping or holding on to something with our brain's conceptual 'fist.' But if we open this fist, if we don't conceive the thought, what is in our mental hand falls away" (Uchiyama 2004, 28). Although I've used the image of a closed fist to represent an aggressive approach to conflict, a fist can also suggest a kind of clenching that's associated with rigid patterns of conceptualization, analysis, and argument. Closed fists (and closed minds) often miss opportunities for integrative thinking. By opening the hand of thought—relaxing our grip on the usual modes of analysis and familiar patterns of arguing—we can pay attention to integrative options that are often, as Lederach says, "right there," waiting to be discovered or invented, although it may take a fresh perspective or a certain quality of attention to notice them.

BRINGING PEACE

As they worked on their papers, students realized that finding integrative approaches is often demanding, both intellectually and emotionally, because a mediator must step into a heated dispute and hold opposing views together, proposing a basis for cooperation.[8] To be able to act as peacemakers, mediators need a repertoire of strategies to be sure, but they also need a capacity for insight as well as qualities such as courage, optimism, and an inner sense of peace. Toward the end of the unit, we discussed an excerpt from Daniel Bowling and David Hoffman's essay "Bringing Peace into the Room" (the "room" being a mediation or counseling session), focusing on their claim that the ability to mediate disputes comes "not so much from a particular set of words or behaviors but instead from an array of personal qualities of the mediator that create an atmosphere conducive to resolution" (Bowling and Hoffman 2003, 14). Bowling and Hoffman claim that when mediators are "working with people who are deeply enmeshed in seemingly intractable conflict," those involved in the conflict are most successful when they feel "at peace" with themselves and the world around them (14). This idea resonated with students, as the following notebook entry illustrates:

> I was working on my integrative paper today and suddenly felt that I wasn't being a very good mediator. We were reading one of the articles, "Bringing Peace into the Room," and I started thinking about how difficult it is to be a mediator. I realized that when I was writing my essay, I needed to not just say certain things that a mediator might say, but also really be passionate about what I wanted to accomplish. I have to really step into the role of being a mediator and understand what it is I want to achieve. Writing my paper, I saw how difficult that was. I never understood before just how hard it is to be a mediator.

There is, in short, an inner game to the work of resolving conflicts, one that involves equanimity and focused attention. "Being attentive," say Jennifer Beer and Eileen Stief in *The Mediator's Handbook*, "is essential for mediators; all other skills flow from this ability to be present in the moment" (Beer and Stief 1997, 68).

The open hand is a gesture of peace, a signal of nonaggression. It suggests openness to possibilities, a relaxing of one's conceptual fist. But most important, the open hand provides a way to connect with others and control the flow of an encounter, guiding opponents to common ground or leading them toward shared interests and mutually beneficial goals. When students made their integrative arguments, they were surely practicing the art of peace.

Notes

1   In *The Rhetoric of Reason*, Crosswhite notes that there are times when the arguer assumes a "third party" role in a disagreement: "When differences do come into conflict, and when these conflicts must be resolved, when some choice must be made, argumentation can be called in to play the role of the third party, the mediator. Through the process of responding to challenges by examining, clarifying, qualifying, modifying, and supporting claims, it shapes agreements" (Crosswhite 1996, 202). Mediation has found its way into several college composition textbooks. One of the first (that I'm aware of) was a chapter on "Resolving Conflict: Arguing to Mediate," in Timothy Crusius and Carolyn Channell's (2006) textbook *The Aims of Argument* (first published in 1995). Mediating joined three more traditional aims of argument: inquiry, convincing, and persuading. As the authors note, "Essays can mediate by attempting to argue for middle ground in a conflict" (Crusius and Channell 2006, 268). And in the latest edition of one of the best-selling textbooks in the field, *The St. Martin's Guide to Writing* (9th ed., 2010), Rise Axelrod and Charles Cooper add a chapter on "Finding Common Ground."

2   It may be worth repeating that the focus for most of the regular class sessions—typically three each week—was the topic of *arguing* (or what I've called the *conceptual-procedural* strand), as each unit progressed toward a final assignment in which students wrote papers that used tactics associated with a particular (open-hand) approach. Along the way, students read editorials or opinion essays that exemplified the key tactics as well as excerpts from books and articles that explained principles of mediation and conflict resolution. With the final project always on the horizon, writing was usually the focus, although we also discussed interpersonal disputes, especially at the beginning of the unit. Was Arguing as an Art of Peace a *writing* course? It wasn't designated as one, officially, but it was certainly writing intensive. How did it differ from first-year composition classes at Lehigh? Most of our composition courses are built around a thought-provoking theme and a selection of readings: these materials guide the students' work for the semester and provide a focus for their writing projects. Typically, all of the students are writing about the same issues, using a common set of source materials. In Arguing as an Art of Peace, there was no common theme for writing; instead, students chose a controversial issue they wanted to investigate and write about—a different issue for each student in most cases. In class, therefore, we never discussed the content of students' projects. And instead of discussing readings related to a theme, we talked about articles that presented strategies for handling difficult conversations and adversarial disputes. Thus, the time that, in a theme-based class, would have been spent talking about issues (related to the common topic and readings) was devoted to discussing strategies such as reframing, attentive listening, and mediating. We also spent a lot of time looking at examples; often these were short editorials that illustrated tactics students were learning to use for a project. It's true that students also participated in movement exercises and contemplative activities, but for the most part these were reserved for the lab section each week, a fourth hour in addition to the standard three.

3   I am indebted to Catherine Lamb's (1991) influential article, "Beyond Argument in Feminist Composition," for calling my attention to *Getting to Yes* and the possibility that negotiation and mediation could provide alternative approaches to argument in a composition course. For a thoughtful review and assessment of *Getting to Yes*, on the twenty-fifth anniversary of its publication, see Menkel-Meadow (2006).

4   This movement sequence is based on *futari dori kokyunage (mae ukemi)*. In the aikido exercise, the defender is grabbed from the sides by two attackers, who hold his or

her wrists. The key is to absorb their energy, bringing both attackers' arms into your center and then moving forward, turning them with you and propelling them ahead. In my adaptation of the move, a mediator steps in to redirect the aggressive energy from two people who are on a collision course, leading them to stand at a ninety-degree angle from the line of confrontation. As in other low-impact modifications, the move concludes without a throw. Aikido's core philosophy is consistent with the goals of integrative argument; as Westbrook and Ratti point out, it is "the striving to bring order where there is disorder, *to integrate where there is separation*, to reconcile where there is strife, which marks aikido as a unique and distinctive martial art" (Westbrook and Ratti 1970, 361; italics added).

5   James Crosswhite considers situations in which arguments do not have to lead to choice or closure, in which case "contradictions may simply stand. That is, we may admit equally compelling arguments. . . . For example, we can make a claim that there are equally compelling arguments for incompatible claims and so subsume the apparent contradiction under a more general claim—one for which we have noncontradictory evidence. Or we could let contradictions stand provisionally, to see where such tolerance would lead, to see what the contradiction would enable in the way of understanding. . . . Further, we could let contradictions stand because that is simply as far as we can get with our reasoning" (Crosswhite 1996, 263).

6   In an intriguing commentary on this case, Norman Fischer (2006) compares the situation to the one that Solomon must adjudicate: "The present case is probably the best-known—and most disturbing—case in all of Zen. We could compare it to a similar story that appears in the Bible, involving the wise king Solomon and a baby. As the tale goes, two women are arguing over a baby, both claiming to be the mother. Like Nanchuan [an alternate form of Nansen], Solomon proposes to solve the dispute by cutting the baby in two. He intends to give half to each of the women, an eminently fair solution. One of the women speaks up immediately and says, 'No, don't do it. I am not the mother. Give the child to her!' And so Solomon discovers that she is the real mother, the one who cares most for the child's welfare." In the Biblical story, the threat of cutting works out well; not so in the Zen koan.

7   I sometimes described the search for creative solutions as a process with yin and yang components, yin representing the intuitive and imaginative elements, yang the intellectual and analytical. Although dated, Young, Becker, and Pike's model of the "four stages of inquiry"—preparation, incubation, illumination, and verification—has served me well over the years. Two stages, preparation and verification, involve problem posing and analysis of evidence (yang), whereas the other two stages, incubation and illumination, provide a role for subconscious, intuitive, and imaginative processes (yin). Young, Becker, and Pike point out that people tend to ignore the importance of subconscious activity in discovery because it is "somewhat mysterious and hard to discuss explicitly" (Young, Becker, and Pike 1970, 73). This leads many to place an "undue emphasis on the conscious analytical procedures as if these alone were sufficient for solving problems. But each of us has a subconscious intelligence, a strong and vital force in our mental life that seems to have a greater capacity than reason for dealing with the complex and unfamiliar. . . . In the incubation period this subconscious intelligence is brought to bear on the problem" (73–74). Inquiry flows between yin and yang in a process the authors describe as "undulatory" (75), with "the human intellect working as a kind of dialogue between reason and intuition" (76).

8   When groups of people with differing views are trying to find common ground, they often go through a period Kaner calls the "Groan Zone," an apt label for the struggle involved in finding a basis for cooperation. Kaner notes that this part of the process can be "unpleasant," "difficult to tolerate," and "a struggle"; nonetheless,

the "effort to understand one another's perspectives and build a shared framework of understanding—this *struggle in the service of integration*—is the defining work of the *Groan Zone*" (Kaner 2007, 223; italics in original). While a writer's task is different, it's still the case that the work of discovering or creating grounds for cooperation is the most challenging aspect of integrative argument.

5
BOWING OUT

In the beginner's mind there are many possibilities.
Shunryu Suzuki (1904–1971)

Over the five semesters that I taught the course, Arguing as an Art of Peace was an ongoing experiment, an effort to find better ways to incorporate three modalities of learning—contemplative, kinesthetic, and conceptual-procedural—into a course structured around a series of projects, each affiliated with a different tactic for arguing with an open hand. In the preceding chapters, I've focused on those projects— deliberative, conciliatory, and integrative—and the associated tactics of reframing, attentive listening, and mediating. Although I've considered the learning modalities throughout my discussion, in this final chapter I want to structure my review around them, highlighting their centrality to the course.

I have described the course as a series of conventional classes punctuated by weekly lab sessions devoted to contemplative as well as kinesthetic learning. Most of those sessions took place in a regular classroom, transformed into a lab only by moving the chairs to the walls to clear a space for activities in the center—sometimes sitting in meditation, sometimes performing movements associated with tai chi or aikido. In one special session, described in the previous chapter, I set up a calligraphy station to give students the experience of brush meditation. When conditions permitted, we went outside to practice some of our movement patterns on a patio next to the classroom building. And once, typically toward the end of the semester, we left campus for a short field trip, a fifteen-minute walk across the Lehigh River into the city of Bethlehem, to visit a Japanese garden, the "Garden of Serenity."[1] Our purpose was to visit a site designed to foster contemplation through its arrangement of boulders, plants, structures, waterway, and raked gravel path. When we reached our destination, the class gathered on a circle of benches outside the garden area, where we talked about the fact that we were not merely visitors because we had brought with us a capacity for meditative

DOI: 10.7330_9780874219203.c005

awareness and a recognition that this garden was meant to support mindfulness. At the same time, we were not quite prepared to be inside participants either, reinforced by the fact we had to view the garden from outside a low fence, which restricted access but did not interfere with a full view of the enclosed area. For me, these visits were a reminder that all of us were in a liminal space between outside and inside perspectives, between observer and participant roles, separated by a physical and cultural fence from getting inside, yet with a greater proximity than we would have had without the experience of contemplative practice.[2]

I asked students to find a place to stand along the fence and, from that perspective, to focus on a feature that caught the eye, holding it in attention for a sustained period. I rang the meditation bell to begin the activity and rang it again, ten minutes later, to signal the conclusion. After the second bell, we gathered again on the benches. Because the field trip usually took place in late fall, there was often a chill in the air, so we couldn't linger long. I brought cookies and thermos bottles of hot tea, and while students warmed up, I asked them to write for a few minutes, recording reflections they posted later in their notebooks. Many wrote that the trip provided an opportunity to be "centered and present in the moment," allowing one student to state she felt "more mindful than [she had] been in several weeks" and another to say she had attained a degree of "mindfulness unlike what [she had] experienced so far during this course."

THE CONTEMPLATIVE MODALITY

Most of the students in Arguing as an Art of Peace responded positively to meditation, mindfulness, and activities such as slowly eating a raisin, painting a circle in a single breath, and visiting a Japanese garden. Nevertheless, the contemplative component was the most unconventional aspect of the course and the one with the least straightforward connections to argument. I was not too surprised, therefore, to find that some students were uncertain, sometimes even skeptical, about the relevance of the contemplative practices for arguing. One reason for their uncertainty, I suspect, is that the connections are subtle and indirect— and in that respect different from the clearer and more straightforward applications of the kinesthetic sequences we were learning. When students commented on the relevance of the movement activities (a topic I'll discuss in the next section), they were able to talk about mapping various steps directly onto rhetorical patterns, explaining how an aikido sequence provided a kinesthetic analog for a certain kind of written argument. But there isn't the same analogical relationship between breath-centered meditation and the steps in an argument. Mindfulness is not a *model* for arguing differently but a *practice* that supports arguing with an open hand. The connections are therefore nested in a sequence something like this: contemplative practices foster awareness and equanimity; awareness enables one to notice what's happening, internally and externally, as an argument arises; equanimity provides a calm space within which to respond thoughtfully rather than impulsively; and thoughtfulness generates options other than an aggressive or passive response.[3] Some students struggled to articulate these relationships explicitly, even if they understood them implicitly. As one student wrote in his notebook:

> Although it is difficult to explain the connection between mindfulness and argument in this course (I have attempted to explain it to my mom and some of my friends, probably in vain), anyone in our class can most likely recognize the connection, even if it is in a deep, more abstract way that cannot be translated into words.

The connections to *written* argument are particularly subtle. Because writers are removed in time and space from readers, the problem of impulsive response would seem to be less serious, the need for equanimity and mindful awareness less important. Paradoxically, however, distance from readers can exacerbate mindlessness because it's easy to rely on familiar scripts and conventions for arguing—typically, for my students, assertive and confrontational ones—without assessing the situation, the available options, and the impact of one's words. Because readers are not present for us, it can be difficult to recognize and control impulses to engage in combative argumentation—the tendency to close the fist. I sometimes saw this tendency in the students' early drafts.

I didn't expect every student to embrace the connections between mindfulness and arguing, and I understood why there might be uncertainty about them. But these skeptical students also said that the mindfulness practices had been quite meaningful for them, often identifying the contemplative mode of learning as the most memorable and significant aspect of the course. I was struck by the comments I received from some of the students in the first course I offered, in 2007. When I read their final course evaluations, I found several remarks like these:

- I feel very affected by the mindfulness parts of the course, although to be quite honest I felt that the connections to arguing were not as relevant as I hoped.
- The contemplative strand of the course particularly resonated with me. I think I was rather awful at meditating, but I still enjoyed it. I'm

not sure that these practices helped in writing the papers; in fact, they probably didn't.

- I understand how the contemplative works into the class, but I don't really connect it to argument. It is very useful though and will definitely stick with me.

These kinds of comments challenged me to find better ways to explain the relevance of contemplative practice for arguing, although I was careful not to be overly didactic, believing that students needed to experience the connections and express them for themselves, even if this took time.[4] Nevertheless, I made some adjustments each semester, attempting to make the connections clearer.

For example, I put more emphasis on difficult conversations early in the course, in part because it was easier for students to see the relevance of mindfulness in these emotionally charged encounters. Judging from their notebook entries, many students realized that if they took a deep breath, maintained awareness, and let the urge to react aggressively (or submissively) pass, they would be more likely to respond with an open hand. One student told the story of a conflict that arose when his mother visited him on campus. While they were together in the car, he found that tensions were rising and the language was becoming adversarial and accusatory. "I quickly realized that I was in an argument," he wrote, "and I was completely ignoring what I'd learned over the past few weeks." To reorient, he "took a second to center" himself.

> I took a few deep belly breaths and viewed the argument from a more detached, mindful perspective. I asked myself, "Why am I in this argument?" I was angry because I thought it was too soon for her to visit me— plus I had work to do. Then I asked myself, "Why is my mom responding so defensively?" I realized that she must see my behavior as selfish. Now mindful of both dynamics of the argument, I had a clearer and more "present" conception of the situation. I stopped attacking and apologized, thanking my mom for taking the time to see me. After mulling over this situation for a few days, I've come to grasp the power of mindfulness.

Another student wrote about a phone conversation with her father, an exchange that made her quite annoyed.

> I felt that familiar feeling of extreme annoyance, and all I wanted to do was hang up the phone and avoid the situation. But this time I tried a different approach: I took a deep breath. I took a big, deep breath, and it really calmed me down. It dissolved the immediate rush of feelings I got in the beginning of the argument and allowed me to see the argument clearer. This breathing was a sort of meditation; it settled my emotions and relaxed my mind. I also tried to listen. Normally, I don't pay much attention to what my mom and dad have to say in these arguments; I simply

try to end the conversation. This time, I listened. It actually calmed me down and gave me time to assess the situation instead of just reacting on first impulses.

Yet another notebook entry reveals a student making connections between the qualities of attention that she was cultivating during meditation and her ability to stay focused on what another person was saying, under distracting circumstances. "It was not," she wrote, "until after a conversation with one of my friends that I realized how important the meditative aspects were."

> The conversation took place in a busy stairwell with people jostling to get by, and I was a little dazed from my previous class. My mind was so scattered that I was unable to listen and pay attention to what the other person was saying. I realized that if I had been able to control my thoughts, like we do during meditation, and had been mindful of what the other person was saying, the conversation would have been a lot easier. In fact, I can now understand why these techniques are so important during an argument. If both sides are flustered by a barrage of attacks, neither side will stop long enough to center their thoughts and move calmly towards a resolution.

Over the semesters that I taught Arguing as an Art of Peace, I found accumulating evidence—in notebook entries and final evaluative comments—that students recognized the benefits of contemplative practices for arguing, especially in interpersonal situations. Some said they were getting better at considering others' perspectives, particularly when they needed to demonstrate that they had listened attentively to opposing points of view. As one student wrote, "I definitely used mindfulness as a model for listening to my opponents in an argument and generally being more attentive in life." Another commented in her notebook:

> Being engaged in the present moment has helped me start to see how to approach arguing from a different perspective. The same breathing practices that make me more mindful of my everyday activities can help me become more mindful during conflicts. Being more mindful during conflicts will help me be more open and understanding of opposing viewpoints.

Others felt that meditation and mindfulness supported fresh thinking and creative ideas, especially when reconstructing problems and inventing solutions. One student wrote, "[The contemplative strand] was my favorite component of the class. I believe this is important for creating fresh, inventive strategies in argument."

Across all six semesters, students were enthusiastic about the contemplative practices and claimed they had had an impact on their lives with benefits beyond the goal of arguing with an open hand. Mindfulness had given them a way to cope with the pressures of college life during periods of intensive study or when taking exams. Several students mentioned the value of contemplative practices when writing papers for other courses. For example, one woman wrote about the "terrible writer's block" she experienced while trying to complete a paper for her first-year composition course: "I couldn't stop my mind from wandering," she says. So she cleaned her room as a distraction and, in the process, came across the kitchen timer I offer to students who want to use one for meditating on their own.

> *Hmmm*, I thought to myself. *Maybe this will help.* I sat on my newly cleaned floor, set the time to five minutes, and closed my eyes. I heard only the blowing of the fan and my breathing. I pictured a brick wall (this is weird but it worked for me). When distracting thoughts would involuntarily try to come into my mind, I pictured them bouncing off the wall and disappearing. Once the distracting thoughts were gone, the brick wall disappeared and my mind was clear. I focused on my breathing, appreciated the moments of bliss, and then heard the beeping of the timer. I opened my eyes, sat back down at my desk, and thought about my topic. It was much easier to focus now that I had a clear mind. I continued with my essay, only to discover that my writer's block was gone! Ideas were flowing out of my mind continuously; I was no longer distracted by the chatter of my own thoughts. It's really cool to me how useful meditation and being purposefully aware is both inside and outside of the classroom. I like how what we do isn't just germane to the class only, but it's more of strategies and tactics that can be applied to everyday life.

At the end of the course, quite a few students identified the contemplative strand as the one most likely to have a lasting impact on their lives.[5] As one wrote:

> Being that this is my last notebook entry, I thought I'd talk about what I've concluded is the most important thing I'm going to take with me as the class comes to an end. I thoroughly feel that the focus on mindfulness and being in the present has allowed me to grasp a new appreciation for life. By cultivating the habit of consciously appreciating these moments I am confident that I will continue to feel more fulfilled, content, and aware.

Another said she thought about being mindful every day, in a variety of circumstances.

> One of the most important things I've improved about myself over this semester is being mindful. I think about it every day as I walk to class. There are so many aspects to which this concept applies, not only to appreciation of nature and significant moments in life, but to sensitivity

to other people's feelings and opinions, and finding ways to make things better instead of only winning.

Yet another student claimed that contemplative practices were what would stay with her, now that the class had ended.

> In all honesty, I probably gained the most from the contemplative strand of the course. I think that what struck me most was the realization that contemplation has relevance in almost every aspect of daily life. I think that this idea will stick with me for a long time.

One reason for this impact, I've suggested, is that practices such as silent meditation and focused breathing provided a respite from the stresses of being a first-year college student. It's also the case that mindful awareness makes one feel alert and alive, wide awake in a world where one's experience of ordinary objects, familiar places, and everyday events is enhanced through attention and appreciation[6]—a state of mind expressed in the following notebook entry:

> After class I spent the remainder of the afternoon relishing in what I would call the most important thing I've learned thus far in the course. We had just finished our twelve-minute meditation, and I was feeling more awake than usual. I felt on a level beyond the all-too-common, mind-racing, jittery state of awareness that follows my routine caffeine jolts. I felt different that afternoon: clear-headed, fully conscious, and purely awake. This experience has undoubtedly been one of the most important things I have learned thus far.

Looking back on the course, I have few doubts about the value of the mindfulness activities for first-year college students, especially in the context of a seminar designed to facilitate their transition to college. While students often associated contemplative practices with stress management or the quest for awareness—connections I certainly didn't discourage—I emphasized the significance of mindfulness for arguing with an open hand. According to Leonard Riskin, a professor of law, mindfulness should be a "foundational" component in the training law students receive in dispute resolution because mindfulness "provides methods for calming the mind, concentrating, experiencing compassion and empathy, and achieving an awareness of, and 'distance' from, thoughts, emotions, and habitual impulses that can interfere with making good judgments and with building rapport and motivating others" (Riskin 2004, 86). And for those same reasons, I'm persuaded that mindfulness is important, perhaps even "foundational," for first-year students who are learning to reframe controversies, listen attentively to their adversaries, and mediate divisive disputes.

THE KINESTHETIC STRAND

The martial movement strand, like the contemplative one, was also an unconventional element in a college course. For many people—students, their parents, as well as many educators—the idea that one can learn something about arguing by moving one's body probably seems far fetched. If argumentation is understood as a process of written reasoning, primarily, then it makes sense to view it as an intellectual capacity, best developed through rational modes of instruction. My emphasis, however, was on argument as a way of engaging in conflict, encompassing interpersonal disagreements as well as debates about public issues. If, as James Crosswhite suggests, "argument and war are processes of human conflict that share many features" (Crosswhite 1996, 127–28), then it makes sense to draw on the wisdom of martial traditions, bodily arts in which conflict figures so prominently. That wisdom is somatic, coded in forms of physical movement and hence best understood kinesthetically.

One way students talked about the movement exercises was to say they provided a "feel" (or bodily felt sense) for what was involved in the tactics they were studying. As one student wrote, "This week in class we practiced a physical way of dealing with verbal attacks known as 'blending.' As we practiced the physical movements, we tried to get a 'feel' for how this physical experience could translate into a verbal response." However, many students used terms associated with *seeing* or *visualizing* when they explained the significance of the movement activities. One wrote that "seeing blending as an action helped root the idea of verbal blending," and, as another noted, "Being a very visual person, it was interesting to *see* argument through body movements." Quite a few students talked about visualization as a mental operation, an imaginative reconstruction of the movement sequence. Several said the movements offered a mental "model," and one talked about having a "movie reel of the 'turning' aikido move playing on a loop" subconsciously when writing one of the papers. The movement sequences seem to have provided a bodily mnemonic, an internalized representation of the movement sequence that was available to guide students through the steps in the associated pattern—especially when making a *written* argument. These connections are clear in comments such as the following:

- When trying to remember the different types of argument and how they work, it was helpful to visualize the motions we practiced during class.
- The movement part of the class was really cool because it provided a kind of visual for what we were learning about argument. It was really

interesting to see the similarities between movement and different forms of argument. As I wrote the papers, I visualized different parts of them in terms of the associated movements.

- Movement work helped *so* much. When writing my papers I constantly envisioned the aikido movements we practiced to help myself make the proper moves in my writing.

- I am a very visual person, so seeing the techniques helped me understand the concepts more fully and be able to use them in my papers. It was a completely new experience for me, and something I have never considered before. I've seen tai chi and even taken classes, but I've never linked the movements with rhetorical devices, and it is a connection that I am not likely to forget.

- Doing the movements repeatedly made the moves stick in my head, and when I would write my papers I would visualize these moves. In a way they would help me remember to make my "turns" and know how aggressive/nonaggressive to be.

These kinds of comments solidified my conviction that kinesthetic learning warranted a place in the syllabus, perhaps deserving even more attention than I was able to give it. In reviewing the impact of the contemplative activities, I noted that even though some students were uncertain about the relevance of the activities for arguing, virtually all of them identified mindfulness as the practice with the greatest immediate and, potentially, long-term impact on them. In certain respects the situation was reversed for the kinesthetic component: students almost universally affirmed the relevance of the martial movements for learning new ways to argue, but none of them appeared to have been personally affected by the practices or claimed that they would pursue them further after the course ended. Perhaps this should be no surprise because their exposure to aikido was brief and limited. In my modified exercises, students did not have an opportunity to take falls, for example; yet the ability to be thrown and then recover rapidly is an important part of aikido training, with implications, symbolically and psychologically, for responding to adversity and defeat. Nor did students have a chance to experience the full power of the open hand because they didn't get to respond to an assertive attack.

In retrospect, I've wondered whether a more intensive experience in martial movement might have enhanced students' learning and created a deeper commitment to these arts.[7] Nevertheless, I continued to use a low-impact (no throws or falls) version of aikido because it meant students were able to practice movement sequences in a regular classroom, without risk of injuries.[8] I did what I could with the resources at my disposal, realizing that my aim was not to train students in the basics of aikido or recruit them to the martial arts (as much as I value the practice personally); rather, my goal was to provide a kinesthetic mode of learning in a course about arguing with an open hand—a goal that the martial movement activities clearly achieved for many students.

THE CONCEPTUAL-PROCEDURAL STRAND

The component at the heart of Arguing as an Art of Peace was the one I've called *conceptual-procedural*, a compound term that foregrounds the relationship between theory and practice: between the conceptual (the *why* of arguing differently, e.g., why it can be advantageous to listen to your opponent first) and the procedural (the *how* of using tactics, e.g., how to apply the principles of attentive listening when producing a written argument). By the time I offered Arguing as an Art of Peace for the first time, in 2007, I had been exploring these conceptual-procedural issues for a number of years, first in classes that included a unit on Rogerian argument and then in a series of courses, Arguing Differently, structured around deliberative, conciliatory, and integrative projects. The new element in Arguing as an Art of Peace was an increased attention to tactics: connecting deliberative argument to the tactic of reframing, conciliatory argument to the process of attentive listening, and integrative argument to methods of mediation.

What students learned from their work on the three writing projects was not only how to deploy new tactics for arguing, however, but also—and in my view most importantly—how to think rhetorically. The key was to put students in situations in which they could *not* simply argue by rote, in which they couldn't rely on familiar strategies such as making an arguable claim (often one that invites controversy) or deploying a support-refutation mode of development. These are standard tools in the writer's repertoire, to be sure, and if students need basic instruction and practice, it makes sense to focus on them in a course on college writing. But if the goal is to expand the rhetorical repertoire in order to give writers options and choices, then students need to set aside, at least temporarily, the approaches they know reasonably well from previous training in order to try some unfamiliar ones. This quality of mind is captured by the Japanese word *shoshin*, roughly translated as "beginner's mind."

In a widely quoted statement from *Zen Mind, Beginner's Mind*, Shunryu Suzuki says, "In the beginner's mind there are many possibilities, but in the expert's there are few" (Suzuki 1999, 21). The expert has mastered one or two ways to accomplish a task, acquiring a few well-learned approaches that have proven successful in many situations. But precisely because of this success, an expert can get stuck in a rut, relying on a limited repertoire and resisting new patterns. The beginner, by contrast, is flexible and open to possibilities. The students I taught had been trained to write traditional arguments, and if they weren't quite "experts," perhaps, they relied heavily on their expertise with conventional approaches. The challenge was to let go of some successful strategies in order to practice new ones, as beginners. This was not easy for them because most of my first-year students didn't want to be beginners; they wanted to get better at what they could already do reasonably well so they could build on their strengths and previous successes.

It's not surprising, therefore, that students were unsettled by the unconventional assignments they encountered in Arguing as an Art of Peace. I've cited examples of their frustration in previous chapters.

- As the deliberative argument paper draws near, I find that I'm having a hard time imagining how my paper is going to work. . . . In the end I think it's going to take a lot of thinking and creativity to master this assignment.

- I think that writing a conciliatory argument is harder than it seems. . . . For years, all essays have followed a formula: introduction with thesis, supporting body paragraphs, and conclusion. This style has been ingrained in our heads . . . . I had no idea writing an argument without presenting a clear side would be so difficult.

- The goal of integrative arguments is to reach into both sides of an argument to find some of the same things that both sides are concerned about and use those shared interests as a basis for an agreement . . . . Now although integrative arguing seems like a great way to argue, I think it may be kind of difficult to master.

The point of challenging students with these new tasks and tactics was to enable them to make choices about how to proceed when they engaged in argumentative conflicts. Without a repertoire of options, there can be no choice—just formulaic response. And without choice, there can no consideration of the "available means" (as Aristotle puts it) that a writer can use to accomplish various purposes. By teaching students to use tactics of an open hand, I tried to expand their options and instill a fundamental principle of rhetorical thinking: that we can make thoughtful *choices* about how to argue with others, especially those who oppose or disagree with us.

CLOSED FIST, OPEN HAND

The images of the closed fist and, especially, the open hand were at the heart of Arguing as an Art of Peace, and while I tried not to oversimplify them, I drew on their figurative power. Early in the semester, I asked students to take a careful look at what occurs in the disputes, disagreements, debates, and difficult conversations they were observing in their daily lives. When they looked around—at televised "debates" and talk shows, at conflicts in their residence halls, at their own interactions with family and friends—students were struck by the pervasiveness of the contentious atmosphere Deborah Tannen calls an "argument culture." Some identified the spirit of adversarialism on certain news channels: "I can specifically recall one time this summer when the host of the program was debating with two guests, both of whom had very extreme views. I was both shocked and somewhat entertained by the fact that three adults were almost yelling at each other."[9] And when they examined everyday arguments, students saw patterns of interaction that failed, in many cases, to provide successful resolutions or harmonious closure. As one student wrote, "It feels like people are always looking for a fight." Or as another noted, "It seems to me that the argument culture obviously exists in our culture, yet it is so ingrained in us that we don't even realize how much and how often we argue."

Moreover, when they reflected on their own propensities, many students recognized a tendency to use a closed fist when they engaged in disagreements and argumentative conflicts: "Every time I argue with someone, whether it is a sibling, parent, or friend, my main concern is winning and crushing my opponent." A number of students admitted to argumentative tendencies.

> I have always been a very argumentative person. I would not take no for an answer in any situation and would never stop until the other person admits defeat. Even if I realized I was wrong halfway through the argument, I still would not give up my position.

Others noted that they thought about arguments as win-lose contests.

> My usual approach to argument is aggressive, fierce, and some may say relentless. I really don't like to lose arguments and even more than that, I thoroughly enjoy winning.

Conventional—even confrontational—argument has a place in one's repertoire because there are occasions for principled advocacy, responsible assertion, spirited defense, and strenuous opposition. But these are not the only or always the best ways to argue with adversaries. As Young, Becker, and Pike note in *Rhetoric: Discovery and Change*, traditional forms of argument are usually "ineffective in those dyadic situations that involve strong values and beliefs," whenever, that is, "commitments to values are powerful and emotions run high" (Young, Becker, and Pike 1970, 274).

In those situations, people are likely to construe even logical, reasonable, and evidence-based arguments as threatening because the claims suggest they are wrong and should change their views. As Young, Becker and Pike put it, "A strong sense of threat may render the reader immune to even the most carefully reasoned and well-supported argument" (274).

Some composition instructors believe contentious topics should be avoided in college composition, so they point students away from controversial, value-laden, threat-producing issues, encouraging them to choose less divisive topics so their arguments are more thoughtful and better reasoned.[10] In my classes, however, I *encouraged* students to write about controversial and contested issues, inviting them to choose topics that had the same ethical and emotional intensity found in everyday disputes, disagreements, and difficult conversations. My goal was to teach students how to enter those conflicts differently: with the open hand of connection rather than the fist of contention. Therefore, I focused on tactics designed to lead arguments in the direction of productive discussion, attentive listening, and cooperative problem solving. These tactics aren't always going to succeed, but they are nearly always worth considering and usually worth trying.[11] By urging students to consider tactics of the open hand as a first response to argumentative conflict, I hoped to counterbalance the emphasis on confrontational argument in their previous training and experience.

Initially, I thought these alternative tactics would be of greatest importance for students who closed their fists reflexively. But I discovered that tactics of the open hand were equally pertinent for those who were conflict adverse, students who tended to avoid confrontations.[12] There were a number of them in every class I taught.

> I've realized something surprising about my personal arguments. I'm so afraid of confrontations and contradicting others that I try desperately to avoid argument.

Some felt that arguing made tense situations worse:

> I tend to avoid confrontations, conflict, and sensitive issues because of my nervousness that the situation will only get worse.

Others believed that arguing damages relationships.

> Conflict has always been a delicate matter for me. I detest quarrels that arise with my friends; I feel that if I fight back, I could accidentally damage a friendship. To solve this problem, I tend to avoid arguing entirely.

And some students admitted that they avoided arguments whenever possible.

Throughout my life, I have always tended to be extremely non-confrontational. The moment an argument breaks out between my father and sister, I quickly run up to my room to avoid the situation.

The tactics of reframing, attentive listening, and mediating gave conflict avoiders a way to enter arguments—not as brokers of contention and coercion, but as agents of connection and control. Because open-hand tactics incorporated elements of both assertiveness and receptivity, they were equally relevant for conflict-prone and conflict-adverse students.

YIN AND YANG IN ARGUMENTS

Throughout the course, I used the concepts of yin and yang to give students a fresh vocabulary for talking about receptivity and assertiveness in arguments. We used these terms to characterize the tenor of different types of arguments: in some of the examples we examined, there was a preponderance of assertiveness (yang), while in others, receptivity (yin) was dominant. Although there are times to fight and occasions when it makes sense to submit,[13] our focus was on options that lay between the poles of the continuum, where the interplay of assertiveness and receptivity provided options for arguing as an art of peace.[14] The first project, Reframing and Deliberative Argument, had a yang component since it involved using the force of entering on a slant to move the opposition away from confrontation and toward discussion of less contentious issues. Yet the movement began with blending (yin) rather than blocking (yang), and it entailed guiding the energy of the argument with an open hand, rather than shoving one's opponent in a new direction. Yin was, therefore, an essential element in a successful deliberative argument. Is deliberative argument assertive or receptive, yang or yin? Compared with confrontational arguing, it would appear to be mostly yin; next to more compliant approaches, however, it would seem to be yang.

The second project, Attentive Listening and Conciliatory Argument, was predominantly yin, since the first response to conflict was to turn away from confrontation in order to listen sympathetically to the opponent's views, and the goal was mutual understanding rather than persuasion. Nevertheless, conciliatory argument includes a yang component, particularly during the transition from a review of the opponent's views to a presentation of one's own, a transition in which the opponent must be turned 180 degrees. The third project, Mediation and Integrative Argument, also contained elements of both yin (articulating both parties' views sympathetically) and yang (moving them off the path of confrontation to consider common ground and options for mutual gain). In sum, the forces of yin and yang—receptivity and assertiveness—are rarely absolute but rather coexist in a relationship of correlativity and complementarity: a statement is yin or yang in relationship to other forces at play in an argument, and effective rhetorical action will include elements of both receptivity and assertiveness, operating together.

HITTING THE TARGET

The culminating project for each unit was a paper about a controversial issue—the same issue for all three papers. The decision to ask students to choose a controversial issue, conduct their own research, and then write three papers about it—using deliberative, conciliatory, and integrative approaches—was successful, I believe, at keeping the focus on rhetorical strategies. Most students appreciated the opportunity to write about self-chosen topics and to focus on tactics of argument, as the following comments from the final course evaluations attest:

- I definitely see the upside of keeping the topic consistent across papers, so students aren't bogged down by research. Also, definitely keep choice of topic up to the students—nobody enjoys writing about something they have no interest in.
- I liked that we chose our own topic and wrote three papers about it. By the end of the course, I felt like I knew and understood all the factors involved in my topic. With each paper, I felt that I gained some new degree of insight.
- For the papers, I thought it was really good that we kept the topics constant for all three papers and that we chose our own. I think choosing our own ensures we will be interested, and personally I feel I worked harder because I was interested in my topic. Also, I think having the same topic for all three papers was important so that we could really distinguish the three papers and the strategies we used.

I've described the three writing projects in some detail in the preceding chapters, examining the challenges they posed for students as well as the strategies that helped students negotiate difficulties, especially when composing introductions, transitions, and conclusions. Because they were accustomed to relying on conventional strategies as templates for successful writing, students were anxious about untested alternatives. So we talked about how hard it can be to unlearn familiar tactics, to experiment with new alternatives, to achieve "beginner's mind." I tried to assure them that I understood their situation, saying that I realized an unfamiliar task could take a toll on their writing competencies, and that I was more interested in seeing a determined effort to argue differently, even if a paper had some flaws, than a polished argument relying on traditional structures and strategies. To elaborate on these points, I asked students to read an excerpt from Eugen Herrigel's *Zen in the Art of Archery*, an account of the author's study of archery under a Japanese master.

Herrigel tells a story of mounting frustration because he can't seem to get any better at Zen archery, mostly because he isn't able to release the arrow in a way that meets his Master's standards. What's difficult for Herrigel to grasp is that, for the Master, it is the manner of shooting that matters, not whether the shot hits the target. Here is an excerpt from one of the Master's explanations:

> "Your arrows do not carry," observed the Master, "because they do not reach far enough spiritually. . . . In order to unleash the full force of this spiritual awareness, you must perform the ceremony [of shooting] differently: rather as a good dancer dances. If you do this, your movements will spring from the center, from the seat of right breathing. . . . If you hit the target with nearly every shot you are nothing more than a trick archer who likes to show off. . . . Put the thought of hitting right out of your mind! You can be a Master even if every shot does not hit" (Herrigel 1981, 54–56).

We discussed this passage when the students' final drafts of the deliberative argument were nearing completion. How could we apply the Master's thinking to their papers? What, I asked, did it mean that the highest goal wasn't to hit the target with every shot? And what was the target they were aiming at? A particular grade? A positive comment? Even if the paper reached that target, could the writer be the "trick archer" that the Master talks about? Like Herrigel, students had to revise their goals and explore new ways to participate in the art of arguing. If they didn't always score a direct hit, nearly all of them began to make better shots—shots that sprang from the intention to use arguing as an art of peace, blending the forces of receptivity and assertiveness. I have included examples of three complete papers (all "good shots"), one for each project, in appendix 2.

Although the culminating project for each unit was a written argument, I viewed the first-year seminar more broadly as a course in rhetoric and communication.[15] So while I was gratified to find good shots in students' papers, I was equally pleased when I saw evidence of the open hand in their everyday conflicts and disagreements with others. When I reviewed the notebook entries at the end of the semester, I found some striking examples of changes in students' approaches to conflict—some that involved minor disagreements but others that entailed serious disputes. One student, for example, found herself in parallel situations during the first and last weeks of the course when she encountered fellow students who were disturbing her concentration while she was studying in the library. In her first notebook entry, the student documented the incident as it was occurring: "I am considering telling them that I cannot concentrate and requesting them to stop talking, but I wonder whether it will make a difference. I am secretly also scared my 'polite request' will elicit an unfavorable response." The student got increasingly annoyed. "I wonder why I'm being tolerant. I know I am right. It makes perfect sense for me to tell them. If this goes on for five more minutes, I will say something." But in the end, "luckily, one of them left. I heaved a sigh of relief." Fear of conflict silenced this student, preventing her from confronting others about a legitimate concern. Had the situation continued, she might have gotten up and moved to a different location, avoiding confrontation. Or perhaps her smoldering anger would have reached a point of combustion, leading her to react aggressively. She's relieved that she doesn't have to take any action.

Then in her final entry of the semester, the student wrote about an experience that was similar to the one she had documented in her first entry. Once again, the student found herself in the library, trying to concentrate but being disturbed by others who were talking and laughing. But this time her response was different.

> I looked up at them, with the sweetest smile I could muster under the circumstances, and said: "Would you mind lowering your voices, I'm finding it hard to concentrate." They apologized and looked like they meant it. And that was it. That was all it took. Now that I think of it, it seems like that was the most natural thing to do. But as I re-read my first notebook entry, I realized how far I have come from there, and just how instrumental this journey has been in my growth as a human being.

The incident in the library was trivial, perhaps, but for the student—who was adverse to confrontation—it signified a breakthrough in facing a disagreeable conflict courageously. And the key was her awareness that assertiveness (yang) can be accomplished with an open hand and sweet smile (yin).

Other students wrote about more serious conflicts. One who stands out in this regard is a woman whose first notebook entry revealed her longing for a more productive way to talk with her father, with whom she had had a long-standing adversarial relationship.

> My main reason for taking "Arguing as an Art of Peace" is quite straightforward: I need to learn how to better communicate with my father. Our relationship began deteriorating when I was in high school. I was

developing new perspectives, many of which did not align with his. For the majority of high school, I found myself confronting him about a variety of issues—from politics to who was going to do the dishes. We were both stubborn and opinionated. As time went on, I gave up trying to talk to him and we grew further apart. I simply stopped talking because I felt that he would unconditionally oppose me. I was tired of arguing. This is the phase in which our relationship is now. Whenever he says something I strongly disagree with or find offensive, I simply hold my tongue. This has prevented us from arguing in the traditional sense, but it has often left me to seethe for hours. Clearly I need to learn how to fix our inability to communicate. Can a different type of argument help me heal my relationship with my father?

At the beginning of the course, this student, like many others, knew of only two options when faced with a disagreement: fight or flight, the closed fist of confrontation or the passive hand of avoidance. When the fight strategy ceased to be successful, she withdrew from further confrontation. Although this put an end to argumentative conflict, it halted communication.

About a month later, this student wrote about a conflict with her father over issues related to paying for college. As she said, "Financial aid and money have always been a conflict point in my family." As they worked on the family's contribution to college costs, the student grew concerned about what was about to transpire: "Judging from the look on his face, I knew that all he was thinking about was whether or not we would be able to pay for college next year. His facial expression was indeed reflected in the things he said next. He suggested that I should transfer to a different, less expensive university, and that I should move back home." The next comments in the notebook were especially interesting.

In the past, my reaction to this statement would have been completely defensive. I might have started getting angry and I might have said mean things. I might have even burst out crying. This time, I stopped and took a very slow, calming breath. I knew that arguing with him as we always have would get me nowhere. Then, choosing my words carefully, I said: "I understand your concern about paying for college, and if I were you, I would ask myself to transfer also. However, I am working very hard at Lehigh and I am extremely happy there. But I also don't want to put you and mom in a bad situation. If worse comes to worse, I will consider transferring to a different university. But as of now, it seems that I will be able to get a good financial aid package and I am filling out scholarship applications all the time. Also, I understand that you worry a lot about me and that is why you really want me to come back home instead of living at college. But you should also know that giving me the opportunity to live on my own has really helped me get an education in every sense of the word, and I am truly grateful for that."

Her father's response was "completely unusual;" rather than arguing back, he told her, "[I'm] counting on you to work hard. Just please
be careful and mom and I will try our best to pay for college." The
student commented, "He then exited the room and I was left in awe."
The positive atmosphere continued for the rest of the day. The student
concluded:

> I guess my learning to be mindful and reading all about the different
> ways to argue made it easier for me to converse with my father. I reframed
> anything remotely negative my father would say into something positive,
> and I tried really hard to put myself in his shoes. I said the phrase "I
> understand" more times than I could count. Doing all this was really dif-
> ficult at times, and there were many moments when I thought I could not
> handle being calm and diplomatic for one more second. I guess breaking
> out of the argumentative mindset takes a lot more effort than I thought,
> but it is definitely worth it. It helped me take the first step to changing my
> relationship with my father.

Two months later, near the end of the semester, the student wrote
again about her goal of communicating with her father, commenting
that "this class has fundamentally changed the way I approach potentially argumentative situations. I see this change coming through in my
conflicts with my father—what would have been conflicts a few months
ago are now adult conversations." She mentioned a specific situation as
an example, a conversation in which she needed to confront and challenge her father's views. As she said, this situation was difficult, given
a long history of adversarial conflict: "Although I was scared to bring
the topic up, I knew I had to confront my father about the problem.
I approached the issue head on." But the student used an open hand
rather than a closed fist: "Instead of saying that he was terrible and possi-
bly leading to a fight, I went in another direction. I voiced my concerns.
I got a silent reply and took this as my sign to go on. Once again, instead
of attacking my father, I voiced concerns. Before I knew it, my father was
agreeing with me. He even admitted that he was wrong." The student
concluded her notebook entry with the following comment:

> Several months ago, this conversation would have taken all the wrong
> turns. I would have gotten emotional and my father would have gotten
> angry that I was complaining about something after all he has done for
> me. However, I am now able to use different techniques to get what I
> want, without resorting to counterproductive argument. Taking this
> course really did help me achieve the goal of being able to talk to my
> father. It still takes conscious effort, but I can now sustain a reasonable
> conversation with my father without having to give up my values or having
> to disrespect his.

For this student, the lessons about balancing assertiveness and receptivity during arguments had significant personal benefits.

BOWING OUT

After an intense semester, I always felt nostalgic on the final day when the students walked out the classroom door for the last time.[16] Fifteen weeks earlier, the doorway to our classroom had provided a portal to a different kind of course, a space where we would clap in, sit together mindfully, participate in movement activities, and learn new tactics for engaging in argumentative conflicts. On the last day there were administrative details to take care of, such as university course evaluations, and I usually offered a recap of the semester. But for the final minutes we moved the chairs back, put the meditation cushions in a circle, and sat together one last time. I told students to leave when they were ready, silently, taking a small bow of gratitude before walking contemplatively through the doorway. If some students lingered, I rang the meditation bell to signal the end of the session. I was the last to leave.

In the silence of the empty classroom, I took a few minutes to reflect on the events of the past semester. And in the weeks, months, and now years following, I have attempted to take stock of Arguing as an Art of Peace. In these pages, I've done my best to explain what I did and what I learned, hoping this account will encourage others to explore the possibilities of arguing with an open hand. I also hope my efforts will stimulate interest in a pedagogy that includes multiple modalities of learning—teaching that engages the head, the hand, and the heart.[17] So I take my own bow of gratitude, to patient readers as well as the young men and women who participated in my first-year seminars over the years. To all I offer my heartfelt thanks: as we say at the end of every aikido session, *domo arigato gozaimashita.*

Notes

1   The garden is listed in Dorothy McFadden's *Oriental Gardens in America*, pp. 204–205.

2   Robert Carter makes some wise comments about realizing the limitations of one's understanding of another culture while also recognizing the value of expanding one's perspective beyond the familiar. Carter notes that whenever "one looks at ideas and concepts translated from another culture, the seemingly familiar language may contain implications that are quite different from one's own tradition." And yet, "difficult as it may be to 'read' another culture, the struggle to clarify can move us closer to grasping cultural differences, as well as similarities. An open-minded approach yields something of a fusion of horizons, at the very least, whereby one is forever changed by differences in approach, meaning, and life stance" (Carter 2008, 7).

3   Astin, Astin, and Lindholm describe a similar pattern, based on their study of the spiritual and religious concerns of more than 14,000 first-year students at 136 colleges and universities, conducted by UCLA's Higher Education Research Institute. In *Cultivating the Spirit*, the authors describe the links in the chain that connects contemplative practice with awareness and control of emotional responses: "One of the central goals of . . . contemplative practices is to enhance self-awareness . . . . Enhanced self-awareness, in turn, would likely contribute to the development of equanimity, since it enables the individual to devise alternatives to the reflexive 'fight or flight' reaction that typically arises in response to adversity. . . . The self-aware individual is able to (1) recognize an intense emotional response to a negative life event, (2) pause and reframe the situation, and (3) channel the emotional energy in constructive ways. Self-awareness, of course, is the critical prerequisite condition for such a reframing process, since it enables one to recognize powerful emotional states as they arise, rather than simply act on them" (Astin, Astin, and Lindholm 2011, 57).

4   In retrospect, I've wondered whether I should have offered a clearer explanation of the mechanisms by which mindfulness can help people control their emotional responses, especially during heated exchanges. In *Communicating Mindfully*, for example, Dan Huston draws on the work of psychologist Paul Ekman to explain the role that the "refractory period" plays in high-intensity encounters, noting that once a person interprets a situation as threatening (or otherwise emotionally intense), he or she enters a refractory period during which it is nearly impossible to change one's interpretation of the situation. One option is to let the refractory period pass before reacting. But Huston emphasizes the importance of responding *before* the refractory period begins, by being mindful that an argument is arising and that certain responses are being generated. As he says: "It is possible to develop our attentional abilities to the point that we can become increasingly aware of the initial impulse to react—the very first indication that a refractory period is about to begin. If we observe that impulse, we still have time to reconsider. We are no longer doomed to act out our habitual reactions; instead, we are able to choose a response based on a more careful observation of the situation at hand" (Huston 2010, 32).

5   As Holly Rogers and Margaret Maytan—psychiatrists who teach mindfulness to "emerging adults"—point out, students are often enthusiastic initially but tend not to stick with meditation: "In our experience, traditional methods of teaching mindfulness and meditation don't engage students long enough for them to experience the benefits" (Rogers and Maytan 2012, 21). In my course, students practiced meditation in the lab session about once a week, and they also did a series of mindfulness exercises in and out of class, often on their own initiative. Thus I tried to encourage habits of mindfulness over the entire semester. But I realized that students would find it difficult to sustain contemplative practice once the course ended. I simply do not know for sure how many of them continued to engage in mindfulness. What stands out are the unsolicited comments from those students who told me, often several years later, that they were still using the practices of mindfulness (and methods of arguing) they'd learned in Arguing as an Art of Peace. I hoped I was planting seeds of mindfulness that might lie dormant for a while but would sprout when conditions were right.

6   Some students in my classes were drawn to the existential or spiritual dimensions of meditation, although I did not emphasize those aspects. According to the UCLA study of college students' spiritual and religious concerns, these matters are important to first-year students, and they expect to explore them in college. Contemplative practices can play a role in this process of exploration and discovery; as the authors of the study note, one of the "central goals of meditation, self-

reflection, and other contemplative practices is to enhance self-awareness, that is, to 'know thyself' at a deeper level" (Astin, Astin, and Lindholm 2011, 57). Students sometimes associated meditation with their own spiritual quest or religious quest, a connection I didn't discourage. As one religiously committed woman wrote in her notebook: "I recently realized that I have been practicing a form of mindfulness and meditation since the age of 11, through a religious practice. One of the five pillars of Islam is the offering of prayers at five specific times of the day. During the prayer, we are supposed to remain focused and alert—something that is also an integral part of meditation."

7   Each time I taught the course, I pondered the benefits (and difficulties) of finding a space where students could do some "real" aikido. I was envious of college teachers who had the resources and facilities to include traditional aikido training in a course. Several years ago, I visited Professor Donald Levine's class Conflict Theory and Aikido, a sociology course at the University of Chicago. As explained in his book, *Powers of the Mind*, Levine's course "directs students to connect what they learn with their bodies"—through three hours of traditional aikido training each week—"to concepts and ideas they read and talk about in a conventional academic setting" (Levine 2006, 252). Although my goals are similar, I realized after my visit to Chicago that I could not duplicate Levine's approach because of limitations and restrictions—time, space, and expertise (see also Levine, 1990). But because of my more limited approach, students did not have an opportunity to experience the transformative potential of aikido. In his survey of several Japanese arts of "self-cultivation," Carter notes the difficulty of explaining, to someone who has not experienced aikido, "how remarkably transformative it is." Carter says that "*aikido* eliminates most competitiveness, teaches the importance of positive rather than negative thinking, creates a cheerful outlook, and turns physical contact into an act of friendship and the expression of goodwill. Whether or not one comes from a religious background, the flavor of genuine spirituality is here abundant: it does not replace religion but deepens it and renders the spiritual an actual, living, and direct experience. Ethically, one is taught how to show genuine respect for others and to make their learning and development one's own responsibility" (Carter 2008, 21).

8   Another advantage of simplified, low-impact exercises is that even teachers who don't practice aikido or a related martial art should be able to use the movement sequences I have described and illustrated in appendix 1. Although training is certainly valuable, I believe simplified, low-impact exercises can be implemented with thoughtful preparation and perhaps a bit of consultation with a practitioner.

9   Wayne Booth calls this kind of talk-show performance "Crossfirism." As he reports, "In the past month I have spent eight and a half painfully wasted hours watching some of these shows, and I can honestly, scrupulously, objectively report that not once has *any* participant said anything like, 'Oh, I see now that you're right; I've been wrong. I hadn't known about . . . or thought about . . . or seen X, Y, or Z. Listening to you has changed my mind.' And every program has ended with their shouting at each other all at once, with no viewer able to make out more than an angry word or two" (Booth 2004, 146).

10   In *The Rhetoric of Reason*, for example, James Crosswhite recommends that students should be dissuaded from writing about topics on which they have strong commitments, or about controversies for which there are already polarized positions, or about issues that are familiar because they've been discussed frequently in the popular press, or about conflicts from students' personal lives. Crosswhite's warnings make sense, given his goal of teaching college students a form of "written reasoning." Instead of controversial issues, he prefers topics like "the causes and

treatment of schizophrenia," a topic that, he admits, will be "a distant issue for most students," (Crosswhite 1996, 286) but one that can, precisely because of its distance, stimulate inquiry and reasoned argument, in his view.

11   The question in any argumentative conflict is whether to fight, submit, or attempt to transform the situation. If fighting back is sometimes warranted, how would one know when to use the closed fist and when to depend on the open hand? In a thoughtful discussion of this issue, Robert Mnookin (2010) asks "Should you bargain with the Devil?" By "bargain," Mnookin means attempting to "resolve the conflict through negotiation—rather than fighting it out" (Mnookin 2010, 1). His answer is that there is no easy answer: sometimes it's wise to negotiate; at other times it's important to resist and fight. So he asks, "If there is no easy, categorical answer—if sometimes you should bargain with the Devil and other times you should refuse—how in particular circumstances should you decide?" (3-4) Mnookin offers several useful guidelines. One is to systematically compare costs and benefits, not because rational analysis always produces a clear answer but because it prevents one "from relying *solely* on intuition or unarticulated moral claims" (263). But the guideline I find most compelling is to "have a presumption in favor of negotiation, but make it rebuttable." Mnookin asks, "Why tip the scales in *favor* of bargaining with the Devil?" One reason is "to provide an additional safeguard against the negative traps," including the automatic impulse to fight back or flee. But the presumption also puts the "burden of persuasion" on "those who don't want to negotiate" as well as "on that part of *yourself* that wants to fight." Mnookin says that his presumption to bargain "is not a flat rule. It is simply a guideline—and it is rebuttable" (264–65). My advice to students is to approach conflicts with a presumption that the conflicts can be transformed into productive and cooperative exchanges, rather than with the more typical assumption that any conflict is an invitation to fight. Of course this is a guideline or rule of thumb, one that, as Mnookin says, must be "rebuttable" or revisable in the face of contrary evidence.

12   I'm grateful to Susan Burggraf, of Naropa University, for alerting me to the significance of tactics of the open hand for students who are adverse to conflict.

13   Although the arguments students practiced in the course lay between the extremes on the yang-yin continuum, integrating elements of both, it was useful to consider some approaches closer to the poles. To represent a highly adversarial approach, I often used excerpts from a chapter in Robert Greene's *The 48 Laws of Power*. In "Law 15: Crush Your Enemy Totally," Greene says that more "is lost through stopping halfway than through total annihilation: The enemy will recover, and will seek revenge. Crush him, not only in body but in spirit" (Greene 1998, 107). This action is necessary because a terrible fate awaits us "when we sympathize with our enemies, when pity, or the hope of reconciliation, makes us pull back from doing away with them. We only strengthen their fear and hatred of us. . . . Reconciliation is out of the question. Only one side can win, and it must win totally" (109). Greene notes that this law "has applications far beyond the battlefield. Negotiation is the insidious viper that will eat away at your victory, so give your enemies nothing to negotiate, no hope, no room to maneuver. They are crushed and that is that" (112). For a counterpoint to Greene's theory of power, see Keltner (2008). Located at the other end of the continuum are submission, acquiescence, surrender, avoidance, and retreat—and perhaps also a principled nonviolence that precludes use of force to persuade others. Sally Miller Gearhart expresses the reasoning behind this principled position when she says that "any intent to persuade is an act of violence" (Gearhart 1979, 195). In Gearhart's view, "Where the intent is to change another, the difference between a persuasive metaphor and a violent artillery attack is obscure and certainly one of degree rather than of kind" (197).

14   In a chapter entitled "Closed Fist, Open Palm," Adam Kahane tells a story that provides a useful image of the complementarity of yin and yang. At the end of a tai chi lesson, Kahane's teacher bowed while holding his hands in a gesture that Kahane had not noticed before—right hand in a fist, left hand open and cupping the right. The teacher explained that this was an ancient "mudra or sacred hand gesture" in which the "right hand, in a loosely clenched fist, represents the yang . . . . [while] the left hand, which softly holds the right, represents the yin" (Kahane 2004, 112). I encouraged students to practice this gesture as way to represent and remember the yin and yang elements in arguing as an art of peace, pointing out that the open hand (which Kahane associates with empathetic listening) contains and controls the assertiveness of the closed fist.

15   Students also completed a fourth graded project—an oral report, not an argument—near the end of the semester. The presentations were based on a mindfulness experiment that students conducted independently. One student documented her effort to eat mindfully when she was at a casino in Las Vegas for Thanksgiving break, a setting that, as she put it, "actively discourages mindful awareness." Other students investigated the degree to which electronic devices work against focus and presence: several spent twenty-four hours with cell phones turned off, an experience that felt like withdrawal from an addiction. Others tried to be mindful in challenging circumstances, such as shopping malls or on the crowded and noisy streets of a city such as New York or Philadelphia. And a scientifically minded student measured decibel readings at about a dozen locations on campus, at various times of the day, to determine which provided the quietest place for meditation and reflection. I asked students to take an unusual approach to their oral presentations, adhering to a Japanese format called *Pecha Kucha*, a presentation style in which the speaker builds a talk around twenty slides. During the talk, the slides change automatically, every twenty seconds, so a presentation must be timed for six minutes and twenty seconds and coordinated with the changing slides.

16   I did my best to keep in touch with the students from my seminars over the four years they were in college. Several transferred to other institutions. Some didn't respond to emails and invitations. But something like half of the students from each class stayed in touch in at least a limited way. About once a year I held an event at my house that provided a kind of reunion for students who had taken Arguing as an Art of Peace. To provide a focus for this gathering, I invited students to participate in an Asian-inspired craft activity that embodied an element of mindfulness. One spring, a small group made *mala* (meditation) bracelets. That fall, a larger number came for a cookout and opportunity to print Tibetan-style prayer flags from hand-carved blocks. Another fall we made clay *Daruma* dolls, coloring in one eye to express a hope or wish. And for the seniors who graduated in spring 2012, I organized an activity in which we made miniature kites decorated with words and symbols that reminded students of the class.

17   I hope my account of Arguing as an Art of Peace demonstrates that arguing can be conceived and taught differently than it usually is, with positive benefits for first-year students. I developed my course in a particular institutional context, as part of a first-year seminar program, so I don't present it as a "package" that would work the same way in other situations. That's why I've refrained from including a syllabus, preferring to emphasize activities and projects. But several aspects of the course may be worth adapting to fit other contexts. I believe, for example, that many college students—not just those in first-year courses—would benefit from learning how to use nonadversarial approaches to address disagreements and argumentative conflicts. In fact, the course might work well as an advanced writing class for students who want to expand their repertoire of rhetorical strategies, although

I haven't tried it at more advanced levels. I had an opportunity to build an entire first-year course around alternative strategies of arguing, but I realize others may not have that flexibility. In a composition program that has a series of prescribed objectives, it may be more feasible to supplement a conventional focus on academic argument by including a unit or module on tactics of the open hand (as I noted previously, the most recent edition of a best-selling composition textbook, *The St. Martin's Guide to Writing*, now includes the chapter "Finding Common Ground"). I also believe my experiments with the kinesthetic modality suggest the promise of learning about argument through bodily movement. I have focused on aikido (and a simplified version of two-person tai chi) because it is the movement discipline I know best from experience, but other writing teachers might draw on different movement arts to teach principles of composing and arguing. The contemplative component of my course may be the one with the most untapped potential. In the field of composition-rhetoric, discussions of the contemplative domain are likely to be identified, almost automatically, with an "expressivist" approach that prioritizes creative expression and personal growth. By contrast, my approach was fundamentally rhetorical because I emphasized the relevance of contemplative practices for engaging in argumentative conflict. Although mindfulness helped many students become more aware, more focused, and at greater peace with themselves and others—benefits I fully supported—they were nonetheless added benefits in a course that emphasized arguing with an open hand.

Appendix 1

PHOTOGRAPHIC ILLUSTRATIONS OF MOVEMENT SEQUENCES

The photographs below supplement the verbal explanations of the movement sequences described in chapters 2, 3, and 4. The individuals who appear in these photographs were (at the time the photos were taken) first-year students at Lehigh who had recently completed Arguing as an Art of Peace. Although the photographs were shot in a studio on campus, the students did the movements just as they had practiced them in class.

1. PUSH HANDS AND BLENDING (discussed in chapter 2)

Step 1

The first movement sequence students practiced in the lab was a basic version of tai chi push hands, designed to give them a feel for blending with an opposing force, for sensing the interplay of yin (yielding) and yang (resisting). In the following photographs, the student on the right is the pusher and the one on the left is the receiver. They begin by connecting with their hands.

DOI: 10.7330_9780874219203.c006

Step 2

The pusher exerts some pressure and the receiver yields and blends, keeping enough resistance to guide the push away from her center and extending the pusher.

Step 3

Then the roles reverse as the receiver pushes back and her partner yields and blends.

After students had some experience with the basic movement sequence, I often altered it by showing the receiver how to step into the pusher's extended arm so their bodies turned and they faced away from one another on an angle to the vector of confrontation. This modified pattern set up the reframing exercise we did next.

2. ENTERING AND REFRAMING (discussed in chapter 2)

The exercise begins with a cross-hand grab. In the photograph, the student on the right is the attacker: he has reached out and grasped, with his right hand, the receiver's right wrist.

Step 1

The receiver responds by yielding a bit (as in push hands), then pivots on her left foot and brings her right leg back so she is no longer facing the attacker but positioned to his side, on a slant to the original vector of confrontation. She brings the attacker's hand to the center of her body, where she is in control.

Step 2

Linking arms with her opponent, the receiver steps forward, turning her attacker and leading him in a new direction. From an initial position of confrontation, the encounter has been reframed as a side-by-side effort to understand a problem and its possible solutions. Although the two students have linked arms in a gesture of cooperation, the receiver maintains control and directs the movement.

Step 3

3. TURNING AND ATTENTIVE LISTENING (discussed in chapter 3)

This turning maneuver is the most complicated sequence students practiced. It begins, however, with the familiar cross-hand grab, attacker on the right, receiver on the left.

Step 1

Step 2

The receiver yields and swings her right leg around so she is standing orthogonally to the original line of confrontation. Her hands move to control the attack, centering the energy at her midpoint.

Step 3

Next, the receiver pivots on her left foot and swings the right behind her, standing beside the attacker and facing in the same direction: the receiver has turned so she is looking at things from her adversary's position. At this point, a face-to-face encounter has been transformed into a side-by-side stance that represents attentive listening. Note, however, that the receiver is still in control of the encounter.

Step 4

In the most challenging step in the sequence, the receiver leads her opponent in a 180-degree turn to face the opposite direction.

Step 5

Once turned, the two opponents remain side by side, looking at the issue from the receiver's perspective.

Step 6

The receiver executes one more turn, moving back to face her opponent. They are still connected.

Step 7

Having viewed the conflict from each other's perspective, the opponents are ready to disengage. Neither has capitulated; their final position reflects the fact that differences remain. But they are now facing in the *opposite* direction from the one they assumed at the beginning: they may not agree, but they have reached a new level of understanding.

4. CONNECTING AND MEDIATING (discussed in chapter 4)

Step 1

The final movement activity differs from the others in that it includes three participants: two opponents and a mediator. In the first step, the two opponents approach one another on a vector of confrontation, arms outstretched, reaching out in a gesture of antagonism.

Step 2

Then a mediator appears, coming between the antagonists to intercept them before they make contact. The mediator steps into the conflict, grasping the opponents' arms at the wrist.

Step 3

The mediator steps forward, controlling the antagonists and turning them with her, away from the vector of confrontation.

Step 4

The mediator steps ahead, leading the opponents so they are walking side by side, with the mediator embracing their arms and controlling the movement.

Step 5

After a step or two, the mediator releases the opponents, nudging them forward to walk by themselves. Once opponents realize they share common interests or that there are opportunities to realize mutual gains, they may be willing to walk along parallel paths without the mediator's assistance.

I want to thank the students who volunteered to participate in the photo session and agreed to have their pictures appear in this appendix— Ryan, Kendall, Jasmine, Taylor, Sunny, Tamara, and Sonja—shown here with the author.

Appendix 2
THREE STUDENT PAPERS

You can be a Master even if every shot does not hit.
Eugen Herrigel, Zen in the Art of Archery

In this appendix, I include the three assignments and, for each of them, an example of a complete student paper, accompanied by a brief commentary. I chose good shots, examples of strong student writing. I edited these papers lightly, correcting some errors and infelicities, but in every important respect they are the students' original work. I include these examples because they illustrate some of the best deliberative, conciliatory, and integrative arguments my first-year students produced. In the main chapters of the book, I include excerpts from student writing to illustrate various tactics, but those short excerpts fail to provide a view of the whole compositions from which they are drawn. I hope these examples and commentaries give readers a better sense of the three projects and the papers that they generated.

EXAMPLE OF A DELIBERATIVE ARGUMENT
Assignment for the Deliberative Argument Paper:
Your assignment is to write a paper about a controversial issue. But rather than asserting a view or refuting the opposition, you should argue in a way that reframes the issue as a deliberative discussion of a problem and its solutions, rather than a two-sided debate.

Comments on "A Cure for Alzheimer's?"
To write a deliberative argument, students explored reframing, a tactic designed to redirect attention—away from a debate about intensely disputed points and toward a discussion of problems, options, and creative solutions. The idea wasn't to avoid all points of disagreement but to embed them in a broader discussion so there could be careful consideration before decision.

DOI: 10.7330_9780874219203.c007

The writer of the following paper was interested in the controversy over the use of stem cells in medical research, a hot-button issue. To reframe this debate, she decided to direct attention to a larger problematic situation: the incidence of Alzheimer's disease, an incurable condition that afflicts many elderly people in our society. She chose this disease in part because she believed many of her readers would be concerned about it and also because of the evidence that stem-cell research may hold the key to effective treatment.

In the opening paragraphs, the writer puts Alzheimer's disease in the foreground, establishing it as a serious illness without a cure. These paragraphs draw in (or connect with) readers who have an interest in the disease, explaining the current options for dealing with Alzheimer's (medicating and managing) and directing their attention to a "third option," one that involves stem cell research. The writer notes the potential of this research but also acknowledges obstacles, chief of which are moral objections to obtaining stem cells from human embryos. At this point, the writer blends with concerns about "legal and ethical issues," attempting to understand them rather than refuting their legitimacy. She uses the open hand of contact and control, rather than the closed fist of refutation and counter argument.

The writer makes another reframing move in paragraph six ("The political turmoil . . . ") when she rejects the two-sided framework that has dominated public discussion of the issue, noting that both moral issues and medical solutions need to be considered. At this point, the writer introduces a new possibility, private funding, and while it isn't sufficient to address the need, the idea nonetheless moves the discussion toward creative thinking and fresh alternatives. This sets the stage for the writer's final appeal. Accepting the legitimacy of ethical concerns, she adopts a moral point of view by asking why it is right to discard invalid embryos from fertilization clinics when they could be used for good purposes. Thus she reframes the question: Which is more ethical, to waste embryos that could be used in promising medical research or to use them to find cures for diseases like Alzheimer's? The writer asserts her position in the final paragraph, arguing for a policy that permits use of certain kinds of stem cells in the search for cures for diseases such as Alzheimer's.

A Cure for Alzheimer's?

An estimated 4.5 million Americans suffer from Alzheimer's disease, found mainly in the older generations ages 65 and up. One in ten people over the age of 65 are diagnosed with it, and an astounding 50% of

Americans over the age of 85 are currently living with the disease. The risk of getting Alzheimer's for those over the age of 65 is increasing, as the number of people it affects doubles every five years. Women are more frequently affected than men, and almost all cases are inherited, meaning there is no real way of preventing the disease. Alzheimer's disease is suspected to be a genetic disorder that causes dementia through the loss of memory and control over emotions and inhibitions. As lesions in the brain cause brain cells to disintegrate, patients lose their ability to interact in everyday life and their ability to recognize their friends and family (WebMD).

So what can we do about this destructive disease? There is currently no cure for Alzheimer's disease, however typical treatments include undergoing medication to help patients manage some of its symptoms such as depression, behavioral problems, and insomnia. Another option is to provide home or facility care for those in later stages of the disease, primarily focusing on nutrition, exercise, and social interaction. Though these methods may help prolong a person's ability to continue their daily routines, they are not proven to slow the progression of the disease or reverse any of the damage it causes.

There is, however, a third option that could lead to promising results in the treatment of Alzheimer's disease. The much debated stem cell research has led to findings that stem cells could be used to create neurons that are destroyed in the brain as a result of Alzheimer's disease. Though the research and implementation of this treatment will take time and may have complications, researchers say it may lead to new insights about the genetic aspect of the disease and to understanding how new drugs can be used to treat it. Scientists can use stem cells to "help identify the molecular errors that underlie Alzheimer's, which in turn would help chemists design new drugs to slow or even reverse the disease" (Weiss). Scientists are aware of the difficulty in reconstructing the complex structure of the neurons and synapses that make up the brain, but also emphasize the auspicious potential of stem cell research in finding a cure for Alzheimer's. As promising as stem cell experimentation is to those suffering from the disease and those likely to develop it later in life, it faces a formidable challenge in gaining enough support to be used in medical science.

The debate has been going on since November 5, 1998, when the first stem cells were isolated at Johns Hopkins University and the University of Wisconsin (Washingtonpost). It was discovered that stem cells can be reproduced to form any type of body tissue, with the ultimate potential to aid in the cure of various diseases, such as bone marrow for cancer patients, neurons for patients with Alzheimer's disease, and pancreatic cells for those suffering from diabetes. But this milestone achievement comes with concerns regarding the legal and ethical issues that arise in the creation of stem cells. In order to obtain stem cells, human embryos must be destroyed. President Bush has limited the amount of federal funding for stem cell research since 2001, and some say this hinders the lifesaving capabilities of the research (Weiss). However, the ethical implications of stem cell research are vast, falling along the lines of other hot topics such as the abortion debate, cloning, and "designer babies." All of these concerns rotate around the ethics of medical science and how far we are willing to go to advance the human species. We have within our grasp the key to unlocking the cures to diseases that have ailed humanity for decades, and the possibility of protecting ourselves and those we love from suffering. At the same time, we face a slough of moral choices that require careful consideration and discussion as we move forward with scientific research. At this point, the focus must be on figuring out a framework for a solution that will encompass a multitude of interests surrounding the issue of stem cells and allow for the progression of this promising study.

The current policy regarding stem cell research limits the use of embryos to designated cell lines left over at fertility clinics, and allows states to allocate funds to either support or restrict the research. As a result, California passed Proposition 71 in November 2004, making it the first state to vote to spend $3 billion over a 10-year period on stem cell research. Closely following California, New Jersey, Connecticut, and Illinois passed similar bills in 2005 allocating more funding for research; however, President Bush remained firm in his position to veto any bills that loosened his restrictions on federal funding. President Bush's first veto occurred in July 2006, when the Senate approved the bill H.R. 810 that allowed for the use of stem cells that were discarded by fertility clinics. A ceremony was held at the White House where the president introduced children that were produced by "adopted" embryos, or unused embryos at in vitro fertilization clinics. He said the bill would "'support the taking of innocent human life in the hope of finding medical benefits for others'" and emphasized his moral standpoint by saying that "these boys and girls are not spare parts" (Babington).

The political turmoil in the White House over stem cell research illustrates the difficulty in approaching this issue as a two-sided debate. The scientific and moral ambiguity of the issue calls for a more complex answer than simply "yes" or "no." It is clear that the medical benefits of such research are astounding, and as displayed by many states' willingness to fund the research, much needed. At the same time it is also clear that this research will not be federally funded in the near future because of the moral dilemmas that surround it. The political division over the issue draws attention away from the fact that this discovery has an amazing potential to revolutionize medical science and save millions of lives from the grips of Alzheimer's disease in the future.

In an effort to find some sort of compromise solution to this issue, we must encourage open discussion of differing views on the subject. There is no right or wrong answer, as the gray areas surrounding the issue indicate that any progress towards resolution will be an integration of multiple ideas and viewpoints. Aside from the obvious options to either allow stem cell research or prohibit it, there are different routes we can take that might answer some of the questions involving how to go about this research in a way that incorporates people's varying beliefs.

One possible option for gaining support for stem cell research with regard to Alzheimer's disease is private funding. Private research companies, universities, hospitals, and laboratories could take on the monetary burden of furthering the research, therefore alleviating the problem of attaining national agreement on the issue and allowing scientists to begin working on new treatments for Alzheimer's disease. This approach also takes the burden off taxpayers so that people with mixed views on the ethics of the research will not feel forced to make payments. The only drawbacks to this route are the limited supply of funding and the many liabilities companies will be subjected to in the process. By not having federal backing, researchers could face a severe lack of financial resources and numerous legal battles that may in turn further delay their progress in stem cell research and in finding a cure for Alzheimer's.

Perhaps there is a better way to go about finding the support needed for stem cell research as a possible answer to the problem of Alzheimer's disease. One major point that is often overlooked in regard to the ethics of stem cell research is the fact that thousands of embryos are discarded everyday at in vitro fertilization clinics for being unusable in pregnancy. Because invalid embryos cannot create a successful pregnancy and will never grow to human existence, they appear to be the perfect option for the study of stem cells. If we have fertilized embryos that are deemed incapable of producing human life, but are able to be used for the greater purpose of finding cures not only to Alzheimer's disease but many other degenerative diseases, then isn't the ethical decision to use them for this purpose? I would say yes. When the choice is to throw them away or to use them positively, the answer seems clear; we must use invalid embryos for stem cell research in order to continue the fight against diseases like Alzheimer's.

An unfortunate consequence of the political debate over stem cell research is the loss of time that could be devoted to developing treatments and saving the lives of those afflicted with Alzheimer's disease. As we move forward in finding a solution to this problem, we must keep in mind the costs we incur as a result of delayed action and argument. I believe the key to progress in stem cell research and the battle against Alzheimer's is to fundamentally redefine the moral issue of stem cell research, focusing on the fact that embryos not destined for pregnancy are actually still useful for research and have the potential to help those with critical illnesses. By looking at this issue in a new light, we can see that the moral choice here is to use these invalid embryos for a greater purpose, to better the lives of those we love.

Works Cited

"Alzheimer's Disease Health Center." WebMD. WebMD Inc. 24 April 2007 http://www.webmd.com/alzheimers/default.htm.

Babington, Charles. "Stem Cell Bill Gets Bush's First Veto." Washington Post. Ed. Jim Brady. 20 July 2006. The Washington Post Company. 16 April 2007 http://www.washingtonpost.com/wp-dyn/content/article/2006/07/19/AR2006071900524.html.

"Timeline of Stem Cell Debate." Washington Post. Ed. Jim Brady. 18 July 2006. The Washington Post Company. 16 April 2007 http://www.washingtonpost.com/wp-dyn/content/article/2006/07/18/AR2006071800722.html.

Weiss, Rick. "A Crucial Human Cell Isolated, Multiplied." Washington Post. Ed. Jim Brady. 6 Nov. 1998. The Washington Post Company. 16 April 2007 http://www.washingtonpost.com/wp-srv/national/cell110698.htm.

Weiss, Rick. "Stem Cells: An Unlikely Therapy for Alzheimer's." Washington Post. Ed. Jim Brady. 10 July 2004. The Washington Post Company. 24 April 2007 http://www.washingtonpost.com/wp-dyn/articles/A29561–2004June9.html.

EXAMPLE OF A CONCILIATORY ARGUMENT

Assignment for the Conciliatory Argument Paper

Your assignment is to write a paper in which you take a conciliatory stance toward readers who hold a different position on an issue than you do. You should write about a divisive public issue, one associated with the broad topic you're exploring for the course. For purposes of this assignment, you should position yourself on one side of the dispute, addressing your essay to readers who identify with the other side. Instead of deploying traditional, adversarial tactics (such as asserting your position or attacking your opponents' views), you should use the alternative, conciliatory tactics we've been studying.

Comments on "Standardized Testing"

The writer of the paper "Standardized Testing" was opposed to the policy of using a test as a requirement for high-school graduation, the policy being implemented in her home state through the Massachusetts Comprehensive Assessment System. Although it is not an intensive social issue, the topic of testing is one that first-year college students often debate. To write a conciliatory argument on this topic, the student needed to use the tactic of attentive listening, demonstrating that she understood the rationale for the test before enumerating the reasons to oppose it.

In the first paragraph, the writer gives some information about the local and state requirements for high-school graduation in Massachusetts, noting that requirements are reasonable but asking whether it is fair to use a test as a basis for graduation. There are two perspectives on this issue: one questions the fairness of testing while another argues for the importance of standards. In the final sentence, the writer discloses her view but asserts that the test can be "helpful" and shouldn't be eliminated completely. This leads into a presentation of the case for testing.

To make the transition (the turn to the opposing viewpoint), the writer says that supporters of testing have "valid reasoning" for their position, and she proceeds to enumerate them. The test establishes standards, and standards are a step toward ensuring that graduates have skills that will allow them to succeed. Testing also provides schools with data about student performance, and this objective information can be used to improve education. These arguments for testing are, the student affirms, "valid and reasonable," and she commends the state for making education a high priority.

But then the writer must make the turn to the opposing position, presenting her concerns about a testing requirement for graduation. She accomplishes this transition with a question: "But if the test stops some students from graduating at all, doesn't that hurt the students more?" She follows by saying there must be an alternative that accomplishes the goal of setting standards without making a single test the basis for graduation.

In the next two paragraphs, she considers her concerns about testing. One basis for her concern is the fact that the MCAS appears to discriminate against students from certain groups; another is that teachers are likely to teach to the test, limiting education; and a third is that when students fail or drop out, nothing good is accomplished. In the final turn, the writer returns to the debate about a testing requirement and proposes a compromise: continue to use standardized testing for purposes of improving education but stop using it to determine eligibility for graduation.

Standardized Testing

High school graduation is one of the most important and memorable moments in a teenager's life. After twelve years of schooling and countless hours of work, it signifies that a student is finally ready to move on to the next part of their life. In Massachusetts, every student must meet their school's graduation requirements and pass MCAS, the state's standardized test, in order to graduate. Both requirements are in place in order to ensure that every student who receives a diploma is ready and able to move on to higher education. A student's education is very important and requirements need to be put in place to ensure that every student is at a certain academic level that will allow them to be successful. However, should one standardized test be the basis for a student's graduation? There are strong arguments that MCAS cannot be truly fair for every student in the state and therefore should not be used as a graduation requirement. Yet, from the state's view, the test ensures that students are at a certain level that will allow them to be successful once they graduate. Although I tend to question the use of MCAS as a graduation requirement, I feel that the test is helpful in its own ways and should not be removed altogether.

Those who support the use of MCAS as a graduation requirement express valid reasoning for their views. Most importantly, the test guarantees that every student is at a certain academic level that will help ensure his or her success. By setting certain standards on the English, math and science portions of the test, the state is able to ensure that every student who receives a diploma is educated up to the level the state chooses. The standards are also put in place to make certain that students are at a level that will allow them to be successful in pursuing higher education. One of the concerns of the state, and a reason for putting the test requirements in place, was that Massachusetts students do not do as well in college as students from other states: "The board adopted the rule two years ago in an attempt to reduce the likelihood that Massachusetts high school graduates would have to take remedial courses in college" (Vaznis 1). This concern is one that prompted the legislature to put the requirements into place. Although students may not see it this way, the state devised the standards to benefit the students and help them in the long run.

Standardized testing is also used to help the school district as a whole. The data collected from the tests show the strengths and weaknesses of the schools and can be used to improve the education the students receive. If the graduation requirement was taken away, the test would no longer be high-pressured and the students would not take it as seriously. In this case, the data received might not be accurate and would hurt public education in the state, since there would be no way to see what needs improvement and what does not.

The reasoning behind making MCAS a graduation requirement is valid and reasonable. A student's education should always be the top priority and the test requirements were put into place to help the students. But if the test stops some students from graduating at all, doesn't that hurt the students more? There should be another way to ensure that students are at a certain academic level without making one test the basis for their high school graduation.

To administer the same test to every student throughout the state makes it hard to ensure the test is fair for all the students. For the graduating class of 2010, 36 percent of the class has not met the graduation requirements. However, 90 percent of white students have met the requirements while only 75 percent of African-American students, 67 percent of those with learning disabilities, 49 percent of those who speak English as a second language, and 79 percent who live in a low income household have met the same requirement (Chester). If the MCAS is going to be a graduation requirement, it needs to be a test that is fair for every student, regardless of his or her race, learning abilities, and social and economic backgrounds.

Using the test as a graduation requirement puts more pressure on both the teachers and students. For the teachers, they are expected to teach in a way that will ensure their students' success on the MCAS. Those against the requirement argue that the test takes away from valuable classroom time: "We are placing an additional requirement on kids that will get in the way of a richer curriculum" (Vaznis 2). The teachers are not given as much freedom with their curriculum and cannot teach what is best for the student and their education but must instead focus on what will allow them to pass the MCAS. Although the test is used to help ensure students' success in college, it can also hurt them by limiting their education. By restricting curriculums in efforts to improve MCAS scores, a student's education is narrowed and they will not be as ready to take on courses outside of the three MCAS subjects tested. The test also puts more pressure on the students because they know that even if they pass their school's requirements, they still have to get through the MCAS in order to reach graduation. For some students, the experience of repeated failure is worse than not receiving a diploma, so they choose to just give up instead of taking the test again. "Good students we interviewed understand that the lack of a diploma is a disaster. Still, many who have already failed MCAS once do not view the 'opportunity' to repeat that failure as a strong motivator for working harder" ("MCAS"). The test should be used to help these students instead of deterring them from reaching the goal of graduation. The test and its graduation requirement were put into place to help the students and to ensure their success after they left high school. However, it is preventing some kids from graduating who without the test would have moved on to college. Watching kids fail is not something anyone wants, and we can all agree that that was not the purpose of the test when it was put into place as a graduation requirement.

The state needs to ensure that the students in its schools are being educated at a certain level that will enable them to perform well after high school. Making MCAS a graduation requirement achieves that goal but it also has potential drawbacks that can hurt the student. The test should not be removed altogether because there are benefits that would be hard to replace. But I believe that we should rethink the use of the test as a graduation requirement. If we focus on using the test to improve the student's education, then success after graduation will come automatically. Education is important for every student, so we should be focusing on improving that, instead of whether a student can successfully pass a test or not.

Works Cited

Chester, Mitchell. *Spring 2009 MCAS Tests: Summary of State Results.* Massachusetts Department of Elementary and Secondary Education. September 2009. 10 September 2009. http://www.doe.mass.edu/mcas/results.html.

"MCAS: Making the Massachusetts Dropout Crisis Worse." Fair Test: The National Center For Fair and Open Testing. 22 August 2007. Fair Test. 10 September 2009. http://www.fairtest.org/mcas-making-massachusetts-dropout-crisis-worse.

Vaznis, James. "New Rule Casts Cloud on MCAS Results." *The Boston Globe.* 29 September 2008. 10 September 2009. http://boston.com/news/local/articles/2008/09/29/new_rule_casts_cloud_on_mcas_results/.

EXAMPLE OF AN INTEGRATIVE ARGUMENT
Assignment for the Integrative Argument Paper

Your assignment is to write a paper in which you take an integrative stance toward readers who hold divergent positions on an issue. As in your other papers, you should write about a divisive public issue. For this assignment, however, you should position yourself between the two parties in the dispute, in the role of a mediator, demonstrating to both sides that, despite opposing positions, they share important interests, concerns, or values and that they can achieve something important by coming to agreement—or, if agreement isn't possible, by setting aside certain differences into order to achieve goals both parties value and can best achieve through cooperation (mutual gain).

Comments on "Feminism and Pornography"

The student who worked with the topic of feminism and pornography was fascinated by the idea that critics who call themselves feminists would nonetheless disagree about some key issues and policies. As someone interested in women's studies and feminist issues, she wanted to mediate a dispute, internal to that field, about whether pornography is harmful or liberating. In her paper, she keeps the focus on shared interests and mutual gain as the basis for an integrative approach.

In the opening sentences, the writer focuses on the fact that feminists have *worked together* to make strides for women in society, including sexual freedom. But on the topic of pornography, the movement has divided into two camps. This division concerns the student because she believes the two sides have not tried to understand one another. Hence, her initial act of meditation entails articulating the opposing perspectives so people on the two sides will understand the other's point of view. She spends a paragraph explaining the antipornography view, based on the idea that pornography objectifies women, turning them into sexual commodities. Saying that these feminists make "important points," the writer turns to the propornography arguments. In this paragraph, she notes that domestic violence is high in countries where pornography is rare (and vice versa), that pornography works against oppressive ideals of feminine beauty, and that it also provides a valid expression of women's sexuality.

Having expressed the two positions, the student foregrounds the commitment that both sides have to increasing "respect for women." The disagreement over pornography is more a misunderstanding than a divisive dispute, in her view. It's easy to misconstrue the antipornography view as an argument for censorship. But on the issue of censorship, feminists from both sides are largely in agreement, and once this is clear there are new possibilities for cooperation. Both camps agree that violence against women is a primary issue, and it's important not to let disagreements about less critical issues mitigate action for the common good. The student concludes by urging cooperation, despite disagreements. She has intervened not to argue for a view on pornography but rather to bring the two sides together around shared values and mutual goals.

Feminism and Pornography

Over the past century, feminists have worked together in order to gain equal rights for women in a male-dominated society, resulting in significant strides in areas such as suffrage, work, and marriage and divorce. Another goal of the feminist movement has been to eliminate the image of the repressed woman from Victorian times by fighting for women's sexual freedom. However, the expression of such freedom in the form of pornography has divided the women's movement. The anti-pornography feminists feel that pornography encourages violence and gender inequalities while the pro-pornography feminists say that pornography is a liberating expression of female sexuality. Such a division does nothing but slow, if not completely stop, the progress of the feminist movement. What is more harmful than the disagreement itself is the misunderstanding between feminists of the true intentions of each side. While each side has a different opinion on the effects of pornography, all feminists are working towards the common goal of the advancement of women's rights.

Anti-pornography feminists argue that pornography degrades and objectifies women. To these feminists, pornography is essentially the sale of a woman's body. Since women can be so easily purchased, pornography teaches men that they are "entitled to frequent, unconditional use of women's bodies" without any emotional attachment or responsibility (Flowers 19). It would seem that pornography enforces the idea that sex is a female service and a male right, which not only perpetuates gender inequalities, but also teaches women to reduce their self-worth to their appearance (Fear Us). By making a woman's body a commodity, pornography compares all women to an impossible standard of beauty. Another problem with pornography is that it reduces the value of sex. Since the elements that make sex important involve a deep understanding and relationship with the other person, so the sex portrayed in pornography does not support a woman's right to explore her sexuality (Cleveland). Instead, it merely exploits a woman's body, portraying women as "sexual objects who exist primarily to be manipulated by men in order to satisfy male desires" (McCabe 136). Finally, anti-pornography feminists are concerned that pornography may increase violence against women by glamorizing women in pain (Flowers). The anti-pornography position on pornography, as described by Laura Lerderer, is that it is produced by "the ideology of a culture which promotes and condones rape, woman battering, and other crimes against women" (Flowers 20).

While the anti-pornography feminists provide important points, it is important to consider the pro-pornography argument as well. First, pro-pornography feminists suggest that pornography may actually reduce violence, citing Saudi Arabia and Germany as comparative examples. In areas where pornography levels are extremely low, such as Saudi Arabia, domestic violence is incredibly high and the culture in these areas focuses exclusively on male dominance. However, in countries where pornography is readily accessible, such as Germany, violence is at a minimum and gender equality is exceptionally high (Gever). A second argument is that pornography supports feminism's struggle against unrealistic, and therefore harmful, ideals of feminine beauty. Unlike advertising that enforces the idea of the perfect woman, pornography helps destroy this image. Consider models and actresses: these women are all portrayed as tall and thin with flawless skin and impeccable features. Contrary to this idea of perfection, a wide variety of women are portrayed in pornography, thereby offering "a more realistic view of women's diversity—and desirability—than can be found in any other genre" because different people find different features attractive (Carol 174). This makes the pornography industry less likely to stereotype women into one general representation of beauty. Finally, pro-pornography feminists argue that pornography is a valid expression of a woman's sexuality. As opposed to showing women as objects, pornography portrays women as "sexual beings" and provides a means for experimentation by removing "the emotional confusion that so often surrounds real world sex" (McElroy 162). Pornography offers a wider outlook of the sexual possibilities and alternatives in a safe environment.

While each side has takes a different position on the argument, they both share the same interest—destroying this image of the repressed Victorian lady while continuing to raise respect for women. Perhaps the biggest division of feminists comes from a misinterpretation of the anti-pornography argument. Anti-pornography feminists are often accused of being pawns of the moral-right. However, by paying attention to their real interests, it becomes clear that anti-pornography feminists are not against sex, only the misrepresentation of sex in pornography.

In fact, many anti-pornography feminists understand that censorship of pornography is more harmful than the pornography itself. While anti-pornography feminist David McCabe says that it is fair for anti-pornography feminists to dislike pornography because they believe it "expresses a morally repellent attitude," he also understands the logic that "[this] is not by itself a reason to ban it. Our First Amendment, after all, guarantees the liberty to express even abhorrent views" (McCabe 137). This corresponds with the pro-pornography argument that "legislation restricting sexual content always became a weapon against feminist speech as well as other material meant to create ... a challenge to the status quo" (Carol 171). Since both sides are working towards the common goal of women's rights, cooperation is necessary for the advancement of the women's movement. If miscommunication continues to impede the dialogue, then progress will end and other aspects of the women's movement will suffer.

Not only are both sides fighting for a fair representation of women's sexuality, but they are also working towards decreasing violence against women. Arguing over pornography takes energy away from the more important issue of violence. Both sides could work together to learn more about the causes of violence and new approaches to preventing it. In fact, working together on violence may lead to other forms of constructive cooperation between the two camps. All feminists can agree that "work against violence must be directed at actual instances of violence . . . rather than at images in sex magazines and videos" (Dority 85).

As women continue to strive for equality, it is important that the feminist movement remain unified against the injustices that still stand against women because only through solidarity has the women's movement been able to make important changes. However, the controversial topic of pornography and feminism has divided the movement. While one side argues that pornography is a progressive force in removing the stigma of the pristine and sexually repressed woman, others believe it enforces objectification of women and violence. But such a division hurts the overall goal of gaining rights for women. Rather than focusing on the fine points of whether pornography is an expressive or oppressive force, feminists need to focus on the larger view of women's rights.

Works Cited

Carol, Avedon. "Anti-Pornography Feminists Harm the Women's Movement." *Pornography.* Opposing Viewpoints Series. Ed. Carol Wekesser. San Diego: Greenhaven Press, 1997. 170–76. Rpt. of "Free Speech and the Porn Wars." *The Phi Kappa Phi Journal* 75 (Spring 1995).

Cleveland, Stephanie. "Pornography Is Harmful to Women." *Feminism.* Opposing Viewpoints Series. Ed. Christina Fisanick. Detroit: Greenhaven Press, 2008. 67–76. Print. Rpt. of "Hot Cherry Pies: Pornography and Justice for Women." www.adonismirror.com, January 16, 2006.

Dority, Barbara. "Pornography Is Not Harmful to Women." *Feminism.* Opposing Viewpoints Series. Ed. Christina Fisanick. Detroit: Greenhaven Press, 2008. 77–87. Rpt. of "Feminist Moralism, Pornography, and Censorship." http://privat.ub.uib.no/bubsy/dority.htm.

Fear Us. "Pornography Causes Sexual Violence." *Sexual Violence.* Opposing Viewpoints Series. Ed. Helen Cothran. San Diego: Greenhaven Press, 2003. 32–35. Rpt. of "Pornography." www.fearus.org. 2001.

Flowers, R. Barri. "Pornography Causes Sexual Violence." *Sexual Violence.* Opposing Viewpoints Series. Ed. Mary Ed Williams and Tamara L. Roleff. San Diego: Greenhaven Press, 1997. 17–23. Rpt. from *The Victimization and Exploitation of Women and Children: A Study of Physical, Mental and Sexual Maltreatment in the United States.* Ed. Ronald B. Flowers. Jefferson, NC: McFarland, 1994.

Gever, Mathew. "Pornography Does Not Cause Violence." *Pornography.* Opposing Viewpoints Series. Ed. Helen Cothran. San Diego: Greenhaven Press, 2002. 52–56. Rpt. of "Pornography Helps Women, Society." *Daily Bruin,* December 3, 1998.

McCabe, David. "Censorship of Pornography May Benefit Women." *Censorship.* Opposing Viewpoints Series. Ed. Byron L. Stay. San Diego: Greenhaven Press, 1997. 134–37. Rpt. of "The Politics of Porn: Not-So-Strange Bedfellows." *In These Times,* March 7, 1994.

McElroy, Wendy. "Feminists Should Work to Protect Pornography." *Feminism.* Opposing Viewpoints Series. Ed. Jennifer A. Hurley. San Diego: Greenhaven Press, 2001. 159–65. Excerpted from "A Feminist Overview of Pornography, Ending in a Defense Thereof." *Free Inquiry.* http://www.wendymcelroy.com/freeinqu.htm.

REFERENCES

Arpaia, Joseph, and Lobsang Rapgay. 2008. *Real Meditation in Minutes a Day: Optimizing Your Performance, Relationships, Spirituality, and Health.* Boston: Wisdom.

Astin, Alexander W., Helen S. Astin, and Jennifer A. Lindholm. 2011. *Cultivating the Spirit: How College Can Enhance Students' Inner Lives.* San Francisco: Jossey-Bass.

Axelrod, Rise B., and Charles R. Cooper. 2010. *The St. Martin's Guide to Writing.* 9th ed. Boston: Bedford/St. Martin's.

Beer, Jennifer E., and Eileen Stief. 1997. *The Mediator's Handbook.* 3rd ed. Gabriola Island, BC: New Society.

Beyea, Jan. 1993. "Beyond the Politics of Blame." *EPRI Journal* (July/August): 14–7.

Blakeslee, Sandra, and Matthew Blakeslee. 2007. *The Body Has a Mind of Its Own: New Discoveries about How the Mind-Body Connection Helps Us Master the World.* New York: Random House.

Booth, Wayne C. 2004. *The Rhetoric of Rhetoric: The Quest for Effective Communication.* Malden, MA: Blackwell.

Bowling, Daniel, and David A. Hoffman. 2003. *Bringing Peace into the Room: How the Personal Qualities of the Mediator Impact the Process of Conflict Resolution.* San Francisco: Jossey-Bass.

Brent, Doug. 1991. "Young, Becker and Pike's 'Rogerian' Rhetoric: A Twenty-Year Reassessment." *College English* 53 (4): 452–66.

Browne, Robert M. 1970. "Response to Edward P. J. Corbett, 'The Rhetoric of the Open Hand and the Rhetoric of the Closed Fist.'" *College Composition and Communication* 21 (2): 187–90. http://dx.doi.org/10.2307/356560.

Bush, Mirabai. 2011. "Contemplative Higher Education in Contemporary Life." In *Contemplation Nation: How Ancient Practices Are Changing the Way We Live,* edited by Mirabai Bush, 221–236. Kalamazoo, MI: Fetzer Institute.

Carter, Robert Edgar. 2008. *The Japanese Arts and Self-Cultivation.* Albany: State University of New York Press.

Cheville, Julie. 2001. *Minding the Body: What Student Athletes Know about Learning.* Portsmouth, NH: Boynton/Cook-Heinemann.

Coe, Richard. 1992. "Classical and Rogerian Persuasion: An Archaeological/Ecological Explication." In *Rogerian Perspectives: Collaborative Rhetoric for Oral and Written Communication,* edited by Nathaniel Teich, 83–108. Norwood, NJ: Ablex.

Corbett, Edward P. J. 1969. "The Rhetoric of the Open Hand and the Rhetoric of the Closed Fist." *College Composition and Communication* 20 (5): 288–96. http://dx.doi.org/10.2307/355032.

Crompton, Paul H. 1989. *T'ai Chi for Two: The Practice of Push Hands.* Boston: Shambhala.

Crosswhite, James. 1996. *The Rhetoric of Reason: Writing and the Attractions of Argument.* Madison: University of Wisconsin Press.

Crum, Thomas F. 1987. *The Magic of Conflict: Turning a Life of Work into a Work of Art.* New York: Simon and Schuster.

Crusius, Timothy W., and Carolyn E. Channell. 2006. *The Aims of Argument: A Brief Guide.* 5th ed. New York: McGraw Hill.

Dang, Phong Thong, and Lynn Seiser. 2003. *Aikido Basics.* Rutland, VT: Tuttle.

Dang, Phong Thong, and Lynn Seiser. 2006. *Advanced Aikido.* Rutland, VT: Tuttle.

Dang, Tri Thong. 1994. *Beginning T'ai Chi.* Rutland, VT: Tuttle.

Dang, Tri Thong. 1997. *Toward the Unknown.* Rutland, VT: Tuttle.

Dang, Tri Thong. 2001. *Beyond the Known: The Ultimate Goal of the Martial Arts*. Rutland, VT: Tuttle.

Davey, H. E. 1999. *Brush Meditation: A Japanese Way to Mind and Body Harmony*. Berkeley: Stone Bridge.

Diepersloot, Jan. 1995. *Warriors of Stillness: Meditative Traditions in the Chinese Martial Arts*. Vol. 1. Walnut Creek, CA: Center for Healing and the Arts.

Dobson, Terry, and Victor Miller. 1993. *Aikido in Everyday Life: Giving in to Get Your Way*. 2nd ed. Berkeley: North Atlantic Books.

Elbow, Peter. 1998. *Writing without Teachers*. 2nd ed. New York: Oxford University Press.

Elbow, Peter. 2005. "Bringing the Rhetoric of Assent and the Believing Game Together—and into the Classroom." *College English* 67 (4): 388–99. http://dx.doi.org/10.2307/30044680.

Fischer, Norman. 2006. "Quick! Who Can Save This Cat?" *Buddhadharma: The Practitioner's Quarterly*. http://archive.thebuddhadharma.com/issues/2003/spring/zoketsu_norman_fischer_save_cat.html.

Fisher, Roger, William Ury, and Bruce Patton. (1981) 2011. *Getting to Yes: Negotiating Agreement without Giving In*. 3rd rev. ed. New York: Penguin.

Fleckenstein, Kristie. 1999. "Writing Bodies: Somatic Mind in Composition Studies." *College English* 61 (3): 281–307. http://dx.doi.org/10.2307/379070.

Foss, Sonja K., and Karen A. Foss. 2012. *Inviting Transformation: Presentational Speaking for a Changing World*. 3rd ed. Long Grove, IL: Waveland.

Foss, Sonja K., and Cindy L. Griffin. 1995. "Beyond Persuasion: A Proposal for an Invitational Rhetoric." *Communication Monographs* 62 (1): 2–18. http://dx.doi.org/10.1080/03637759509376345.

Frey, Olivia. 1990. "Beyond Literary Darwinism: Women's Voices and Critical Discourse." *College English* 52 (5): 507–26. http://dx.doi.org/10.2307/377539.

Gage, John T. 2006. *The Shape of Reason: Argumentative Writing in College*. 4th ed. New York: Pearson/Longman.

Gallagher, Shaun. 2005. *How the Body Shapes the Mind*. New York: Clarendon. http://dx.doi.org/10.1093/0199271941.001.0001.

Gardner, Howard. 2011. *Frames of Mind: The Theory of Multiple Intelligences*. New York: Basic Books.

Gearhart, Sally Miller. 1979. "The Womanization of Rhetoric." *Women's Studies International Quarterly* 2 (2): 195–201. http://dx.doi.org/10.1016/S0148-0685(79)91809-8.

Gilbert, Michael A. 1997. *Coalescent Argumentation*. Mahwah, NJ: L. Erlbaum Associates.

Gleason, William. 1994. *The Spiritual Foundations of Aikido*. Rochester, VT: Destiny Books.

Greene, Robert. 1998. *The 48 Laws of Power*. New York: Viking.

Hairston, Maxine. 1976. "Carl Rogers's Alternative to Traditional Rhetoric." *College Composition and Communication* 27 (4): 373–7. http://dx.doi.org/10.2307/356300.

Hakuin, Ekaku. 2006. "The Voice of the Sound of One Hand." In *Sitting with Koans: Essential Writings on the Practice of Zen Koan Introspection*, edited by John Daido Loori, 211–28. Boston: Wisdom.

Hamill, Sam, and J. P. Seaton. 1999. *The Essential Chuang Tzu*. Boston: Shambhala.

Hawhee, Debra. 2004. *Bodily Arts: Rhetoric and Athletics in Ancient Greece*. Austin: University of Texas Press.

Herrigel, Eugen. 1981. *Zen in the Art of Archery* [Zen in der kunst des bogenschiessens]. New York: Vintage Books.

Hirsch, Gretchen. 2007. *The Complete Idiot's Guide to Difficult Conversations*. New York: Alpha Books.

Homma, Gaku. 1990. *Aikido for Life*. Berkeley: North Atlantic Books.

Huston, Dan. 2010. *Communicating Mindfully: Mindfulness-Based Communication and Emotional Intelligence*. 5th ed. Mason, OH: Cengage Learning.

Hutcheon, Linda. 2003. "Rhetoric and Competition: Academic Agonistics." *Common Knowledge* 9 (1): 42–9. http://dx.doi.org/10.1215/0961754X-9-1-42.

Isaacs, William. 1999. *Dialogue and the Art of Thinking Together: A Pioneering Approach to Communicating in Business and in Life*. New York: Currency.

Jarratt, Susan C. 1991. "Feminism and Composition: The Case for Conflict." In *Contending with Words: Composition and Rhetoric in a Postmodern Age*, edited by Patricia Harkin and John Schilb, 105–23. New York: Modern Language Association.

Johnson, Mark. 1987. *The Body in the Mind: The Bodily Basis of Meaning, Imagination, and Reason*. Chicago: University of Chicago Press.

Kabat-Zinn, Jon. 1990. *Full Catastrophe Living: Using the Wisdom of Your Body and Mind to Face Stress, Pain, and Illness*. New York: Delacorte.

Kabat-Zinn, Jon. 1994. *Wherever You Go There You Are: Mindfulness Meditation in Everyday Life*. New York: Hyperion.

Kahane, Adam. 2004. *Solving Tough Problems: An Open Way of Talking, Listening, and Creating New Realities*. San Francisco: Berrett-Koehler.

Kaner, Sam. 2007. *Facilitator's Guide to Participatory Decision-Making*. 2nd ed. San Francisco: Jossey-Bass.

Kasulis, Thomas P. 2004. *Shinto: The Way Home*. Honolulu: University of Hawaii Press.

Kauz, Herman. 1997. *Push-Hands: The Handbook for Noncompetitive Tai Chi Practice with a Partner*. Woodstock, NY: Overlook.

Kazan, Tina S. 2005. "Dancing Bodies in the Classroom: Moving Toward an Embodied Pedagogy." *Pedagogy: Critical Approaches to Teaching Literature, Language, Composition, and Culture* 5 (3): 379–408. http://dx.doi.org/10.1215/15314200-5-3-379.

Keltner, Dacher. 2008. "The Power of Kindness." *Utne Reader* (May–June): 10–11.

Knoblauch, A. Abby. 2011. "A Textbook Argument: Definitions of Argument in Leading Composition Textbooks." *College Composition and Communication* 63 (2): 244–68.

Kohn, Tamara. 2010. "Iaido, Aikido, and the Other." In *Martial Arts and Philosophy*, edited by Graham Priest and Damon Young, 117–28. Chicago: Open Court.

Krein, Kevin. 2010. "Sparing with Emptiness." In *Martial Arts and Philosophy*, edited by Graham Priest and Damon Young, 81–91. Chicago: Open Court.

Kroll, Barry M. 2000. "Broadening the Repertoire: Alternatives to the Argumentative Edge." *Composition Studies* 28 (1): 11–27.

Kroll, Barry M. 2005. "Arguing Differently." *Pedagogy: Critical Approaches to Teaching Literature, Language, Composition, and Culture* 5 (1): 37–60. http://dx.doi.org/10.1215/15314200-5-1-37.

Kroll, Barry M. 2008. "Arguing with Adversaries: Aikido, Rhetoric, and the Art of Peace." *College Composition and Communication* 59 (3): 451–72.

Kroll, Keith, ed. 2010. *Contemplative Teaching and Learning*. New Directions for Community Colleges, vol. 151. San Francisco: Jossey-Bass.

Lamb, Catherine E. 1991. "Beyond Argument in Feminist Composition." *College Composition and Communication* 42 (1): 11–24. http://dx.doi.org/10.2307/357535.

Lederach, John Paul. 2005. *The Moral Imagination: The Art and Soul of Building Peace*. New York: Oxford University Press. http://dx.doi.org/10.1093/0195174542.001.0001.

Leonard, George. 1999. *The Way of Aikido: Life Lessons from an American Sensei*. New York: Dutton.

Leonard, George, and Michael Murphy. 2005. *The Life We Are Given: A Long-Term Program for Realizing the Potential of Body, Mind, Heart, and Soul*. New York: Jeremy P. Tarcher/Penguin.

Levine, Donald N. 1990. "Martial Arts as a Resource for Liberal Education—the Case of Aikido." In *Japanese Martial Arts and American Sports: Cross-Cultural Perspectives on Means to Personal Growth*, edited by Minoru Kiyota and Hideaki Kinoshita, 173–87. Tokyo: Nihon University.

Levine, Donald N. 2006. *Powers of the Mind: The Reinvention of Liberal Learning in America*. Chicago: University of Chicago Press. http://dx.doi.org/10.7208/chicago/9780226475783.001.0001.

Lynch, Dennis A., Diana George, and Marilyn Cooper. 1997. "Moments of Argument: Agonistic Inquiry and Confrontational Cooperation." *College Composition and Communication* 48 (1): 61–85. http://dx.doi.org/10.2307/358771.

Makau, Josina M., and Debian L. Marty. 2001. *Cooperative Argumentation: A Model for Deliberative Community.* Prospect Heights, IL: Waveland.

Mancuso, Carolina. 2006–2007. "Bodies in the Classroom: Integrating Physical Literacy." *Journal of the Assembly for Expanded Perspectives on Learning* 12 (Winter): 25–35.

Mann, Jeffrey K. 2012. *When Buddhists Attack: The Curious Relationship between Zen and the Martial Arts.* Rutland, VT: Tuttle.

Mao, LuMing. 2009. "Returning to Yin and Yang: From Terms of Opposites to Interdependence-in-Difference." *College Composition and Communication* 60 (4): W45–W56. http://www.ncte.org/cccc/ccc/issues/V60-4.

Marback, Richard. 1996. "Corbett's Hand: A Rhetorical Figure for Composition Studies." *College Composition and Communication* 47 (2): 180–98. http://dx.doi.org/10.2307/358792.

Marino, Gordon. 2010. "The Glove of Wisdom." In *Martial Arts and Philosophy*, edited by Graham Priest and Damon Young, 189–93. Chicago: Open Court.

McFadden, Dorothy Loa. 1976. *Oriental Gardens in America: A Visitor's Guide.* Los Angeles: Douglas-West.

Menkel-Meadow, Carrie. 2006. "Why Hasn't the World Gotten to Yes? An Appreciation and Some Reflections." *Negotiation Journal* 22 (4): 485–503. http://dx.doi.org/10.1111/j.1571-9979.2006.00119.x.

Miller, Andrea. 2008. "The Mindful Society." *Shambhala Sun* (September 2008): 56–63, 106.

Minnema, Lourens. 2002. "The Paradox of Koan." *Contemporary Buddhism* 3 (1): 21–9. http://dx.doi.org/10.1080/1463994022000026057.

Mnookin, Robert H. 2010. *Bargaining with the Devil: When to Negotiate, When to Fight.* New York: Simon & Schuster.

Mnookin, Robert H., Scott R. Peppet, and Andrew S. Tulumello. 2000. *Beyond Winning: Negotiating to Create Value in Deals and Disputes.* Cambridge, MA: Harvard University Press.

Mortensen, Chris. 2010. "Budo for Buddhists." In *Martial Arts and Philosophy*, edited by Graham Priest and Damon Young, 157–69. Chicago: Open Court.

Nakano, Hiroko. 2004. "Shinto Shrine: The Heart of an Ancient Religion." *Kateigaho: Japan's Art and Culture Magazine* (Autumn): 166–67.

Olson, Stuart. 1999. *T'ai Chi Sensing-Hands.* Burbank, CA: Multi-Media Books.

Raposa, Michael L. 2003. *Meditation and the Martial Arts.* Charlottesville: University of Virginia Press.

Ratcliffe, Krista. 2005. *Rhetorical Listening: Identification, Gender, Whiteness.* Carbondale: Southern Illinois University Press.

Riskin, Leonard L. 2004. "Mindfulness: Foundational Training for Dispute Resolution." *Journal of Legal Education* 54 (1): 79–90.

Rogers, Carl R. [1951] 1992. "Communication: Its Blocking and Its Facilitation." In *Rogerian Perspectives: Collaborative Rhetoric for Oral and Written Communication*, edited by Nathaniel Teich, 27–33. Norwood, NJ: Ablex.

Rogers, Holly, and Margaret Maytan. 2012. *Mindfulness for the Next Generation: Helping Emerging Adults Manage Stress and Lead Healthier Lives.* New York: Oxford University Press.

Rusk, Tom. 1993. *The Power of Ethical Persuasion: From Conflict to Partnership at Work and in Private Life.* New York: Viking.

Schoeberlein, Deborah R. 2009. *Mindful Teaching and Teaching Mindfulness: A Guide for Anyone Who Teaches Anything.* Somerville, MA: Wisdom.

Shifflett, C. M. 2009. *Aikido: Exercises for Teaching and Training.* Rev. ed. Sewickley, PA: Round Earth.

Shusterman, Richard. 2008. *Body Consciousness: A Philosophy of Mindfulness and Somaesthetics*. New York: Cambridge University Press. http://dx.doi.org/10.1017/CBO9780511802829.

Slaikeu, Karl A. 1995. *When Push Comes to Shove: A Practical Guide to Mediating Disputes*. San Francisco: Jossey-Bass.

Smalley, Susan L., and Diana Winston. 2010. *Fully Present: The Science, Art, and Practice of Mindfulness*. Cambridge, MA: Da Capo.

Stahl, Bob, and Elisha Goldstein. 2010. *A Mindfulness-Based Stress Reduction Workbook*. Oakland, CA: New Harbinger.

Stone, Douglas, Bruce Patton, and Sheila Heen. 1999. *Difficult Conversations: How to Discuss What Matters Most*. New York: Viking.

Strozzi Heckler, Richard. 1993. *The Anatomy of Change: A Way to Move through Life's Transitions*. Berkeley: North Atlantic Books.

Susskind, Lawrence, and Jeffrey L. Cruikshank. 2006. *Breaking Robert's Rules: The New Way to Run Your Meeting, Build Consensus, and Get Results*. New York: Oxford University Press.

Suzuki, Shunryū. 1999. *Zen Mind, Beginner's Mind*. Rev. ed. New York: Weatherhill.

Tannen, Deborah. 1998. *The Argument Culture: Moving from Debate to Dialogue*. New York: Random House.

Teich, Nathaniel, ed. 1992. *Rogerian Perspectives: Collaborative Rhetoric for Oral and Written Communication*. Norwood, NJ: Ablex.

Thompson, George J., and Jerry B. Jenkins. 1993. *Verbal Judo: The Gentle Art of Persuasion*. New York: Morrow.

Tompkins, Jane. 1988. "Fighting Words: Unlearning to Write the Critical Essay." *Georgia Review* 42 (3): 585–90.

Uchiyama, Kōshō. 2004. *Opening the Hand of Thought: Foundations of Zen Buddhist Practice*. Translated by Thomas Wright, Jishō Cary Warner, and Shohaku Okumura. Boston: Wisdom.

Ueshiba, Kisshōmaru. 1984. *The Spirit of Aikidō* [Aikidō no kokoro]. New York: Kodansha International.

Ueshiba, Morihei. 2002. *The Art of Peace*. Edited and translated by John Stevens. Boston: Shambhala.

Ury, William. 1993. *Getting Past No: Negotiating Your Way from Confrontation to Cooperation*. New York: Bantam.

Weiss, Andrew. 2004. *Beginning Mindfulness: Learning the Way of Awareness*. Novato, CA: New World Library.

Wenger, Christy. 2012–2013. "Writing Yogis: Breathing Our Way to Mindfulness and Balance in Embodied Writing Pedagogies." *Journal of the Assembly for Expanded Perspectives on Learning* 18 (Winter): 24–39.

Westbrook, Adele, and Oscar Ratti. 1970. *Aikido and the Dynamic Sphere*. Rutland, VT: Tuttle.

Weston, Anthony. 1992. *Toward Better Problems: New Perspectives on Abortion, Animal Rights, the Environment, and Justice*. Philadelphia: Temple University Press.

Wick, Gerry Shishin. 2005. *The Book of Equanimity: Illuminating Classic Zen Koans*. Boston: Wisdom.

Williams, Mark, and Danny Penman. 2011. *Mindfulness: An Eight-Week Plan for Finding Peace in a Frantic World*. New York: Rodale.

Windcaller, Alexandra A. 2010. *Leading Chaos: An Essential Guide to Conflict Management*. Rev ed. Wendell, MA: ZoomOpzoom Productions.

Young, Richard E., Alton L. Becker, and Kenneth L. Pike. 1970. *Rhetoric: Discovery and Change*. New York: Harcourt, Brace & World.

Zajonc, Arthur. 2009. *Meditation as Contemplative Inquiry: When Knowing Becomes Love*. Great Barrington, MA: Lindisfarne Books.

ABOUT THE AUTHOR

BARRY M. KROLL is the Robert D. Rodale Professor in Writing at Lehigh University, a position he has held since January 1995. Prior to joining the faculty at Lehigh, he taught at Iowa State University (1977–1982) and Indiana University (1982–1994), where he was professor of English and administered several facets of the composition program. At Lehigh, Kroll has been director of first-year writing and chair of the Department of English. His research interests have included children's writing development, the psychology of audience awareness, and approaches to teaching the literature of the Vietnam War. In 1992, he published *Teaching Hearts and Minds: College Students Reflect on the Vietnam War in Literature* (Southern Illinois University Press). He has also collaborated on editing two anthologies of essays, *Perspectives in Literacy* (with Eugene Kintgen and Mike Rose) and *Literacy: A Critical Sourcebook* (with Ellen Cushman, Eugene Kintgen, and Mike Rose). Most recently, he has been exploring alternative ways to conceptualize and teach argument. In addition to composition, Kroll teaches courses on prose style, nonfiction writing, and popular literature and film. He is an avid fly fisherman who yearns for more time on the water.

INDEX

Writing Without Teachers (Elbow),
26–27(n15)

Yen Hui, 84–85
yin and yang, 7, 10–11, 33, 52, 59(n10),
112(n7), 127–28, 136–37(nn13, 14); in
conciliatory arguments, 82–84; in integrative argument, 103–4; in movement
exercises, 35, 68

Young, Richard, *Rhetoric: Discovery and
Change,* 4, 8, 65, 73, 126–27

zazen, 13, 14–15
zen, 13, 112(n6); koans in, 23, 93–96, 107
Zen in the Art of Archery (Herrigel), 129
Zen Mind, Beginner's Mind (Suzuki), 123–24